THE OXFORD HISTORY
OF ENGLISH ART

Edited by T. S. R. BOASE

THE OXFORD HISTORY OF ENGLISH ART

Edited by T. S. R. Boase
President of Magdalen College, Oxford

Plan of Volumes

I. ENGLISH ART TO 871 A.D.

II. ENGLISH ART   871-1100

III. ENGLISH ART   1100-1216

IV. ENGLISH ART   1216-1307

V. ENGLISH ART   1307-1461

VI. ENGLISH ART   1461-1553

VII. ENGLISH ART   1553-1625

VIII. ENGLISH ART   1625-1714

IX. ENGLISH ART   1714-1800

X. ENGLISH ART   1800-1870

XI. ENGLISH ART FROM 1870

THE ADORATION OF THE MAGI
Late 11th century

ENGLISH ART

871–1100

———

D. TALBOT RICE

OXFORD

AT THE CLARENDON PRESS

1952

Oxford University Press, Amen House, London E.C.4

GLASGOW NEW YORK TORONTO MELBOURNE WELLINGTON
BOMBAY CALCUTTA MADRAS CAPE TOWN

Geoffrey Cumberlege, Publisher to the University

PRINTED IN GREAT BRITAIN
AT THE UNIVERSITY PRESS, OXFORD
BY CHARLES BATEY, PRINTER TO THE UNIVERSITY

EDITOR'S PREFACE

THE aims of the Oxford History of English Art were stated in some detail in the preface to Volume V, the first of the series to appear. Briefly recapitulated, these aims are to set out chronologically the development of the visual arts as part of the general history of England; to define the English achievement in terms of the main European styles; to try to show the various branches, architecture, painting, sculpture, in their relationships to one another and to those so-called minor arts, which with a peculiar fascination become from time to time dominant themes; Anglo-Saxon jewellery, thirteenth-century embroidery, eighteenth-century furniture.

Different periods will entail somewhat different methods of approach. Dr. Evans in the fourteenth and fifteenth centuries emphasized the rise of various forms of patronage. Professor Talbot Rice, dealing with a period where the works of art are far less clearly datable, sets out the general background and then traces the development of the arts under their particular headings. He is fortunate in having in manuscript-illustration of the so-called Winchester school a central feature which stands comparison with anything that we consider great in the English contribution to European art.

T. S. R. B.

MAGDALEN COLLEGE
OXFORD 1951

PREFACE

IN the first volume of this series to be published (Vol. V), its author was confronted with the problem of choosing what monuments and works of art should be included from a very wide and rich selection of material. Here it has been a case of presenting practically all the known works to the reader in order to restore as far as possible a very damaged and fragmentary picture. There the literature was wide and generally familiar; here it is far more restricted, and much of it is known only to specialists. As a result the method of treatment has been rather different, and inevitably the story is more incomplete. At the same time it tends to embrace a rather wider sphere, for it is my belief that later Anglo-Saxon art is only properly to be understood if the close relations that bound the material culture of England to the continent are taken fully into account.

In writing the text I have tried to make the sections complementary to one another, but at the same time to make each one as far as possible complete in itself, so that a reader whose primary interest is in one branch of art only will be able to omit the chapters on other branches without missing any of the more essential points of more general significance. This has involved a certain amount of repetition which I must ask any reader who is ready to peruse the work as a whole to condone. But the first three chapters, namely the Introduction, the chapter on Art and History, and that on England and the Continent, are of wider import, and will, it is hoped, prove of interest to all.

In selecting the material for the plates, I have aimed at illustrating both those works that help to give a perspective of Anglo-Saxon art at its best and most characteristic, and those that are not very generally familiar. But works of local character or of little artistic merit have in general not been included, even if they are of great importance from the archaeological point of view, for the book is one about art and not about archaeology. But it is hoped that no very serious gaps in the story have been left entirely unfilled.

All the books and articles dealing with later Anglo-Saxon art that are known to me have been included in the main bibliography. This is preceded by a short list of more general works which the reader who approaches the subject for the first time will be glad to know. References in the text or footnotes to books and articles on Anglo-Saxon art have in most cases been abbreviated, but the reader will be able to find the full titles in the bibliography. Books on kindred subjects, which are not directly concerned with Anglo-Saxon art, are not included in the bibliography; in this case, however, the full title, together with date and place of publication, is included in the footnote.

The text-figures are mostly the work of Mrs. Scott of Glasgow, and I take this opportunity of thanking her for the care taken on this work. I should also like to thank all others who have helped in the preparation of the book, especially the editor of the series, Mr. Boase, for reading and commenting on the text at various stages, and the late Sir Alfred Clapham and Professor Francis Wormald for a number of learned and most helpful notes. I also owe a sincere debt of gratitude to those who have helped me to procure photographs, notably Miss Enriqueta Harris of the Warburg Institute, Mr. Cecil Fathing of the National Buildings Record, Dr. Zarnecki of the Courtauld Institute, the Librarians of Trinity College and Corpus Christi College, Cambridge, the Dean of Wadham College, Oxford, M. Porcher of the Bibliothèque Nationale, the Rev. Chancellor Dimont of Salisbury, and the late Sir Eric Maclagan. Finally, may I also add a word of thanks to the curators of all libraries in which Anglo-Saxon manuscripts are preserved for affording me ready access to the volumes and for granting me permission to reproduce photographs of them? The constant help and courtesy of the officials in the manuscript room of the British Museum have throughout rendered my work additionally pleasant and attractive.

D. T. R.

EDINBURGH
1951

CONTENTS

CONTENTS

LIST OF PLATES

LIST OF FIGURES

LIST OF ABBREVIATIONS

Arch. Journ.	*Archaeological Journal.*
Archaeol.	*Archaeologia.*
Bull. Mon.	*Bulletin Monumentale.*
Burl. Mag.	*Burlington Magazine.*
E.H.R.	*English Historical Review.*
Journ. Brit. Arch. Ass.	*Journal of the British Archaeological Association.*
R.C.H.M.	*Royal Commission on Historical Monuments.*
Soc. Ant. Journ.	*Society of Antiquaries Journal.*
V.C.H.	*Victoria County History.*

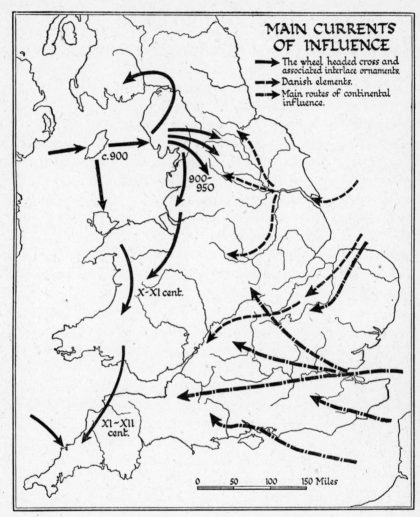

MAIN CURRENTS
OF INFLUENCE

→ The wheel headed cross and
associated interlace ornaments.
--→ Danish elements.
-·-→ Main routes of continental
influence.

c.900

900-
950

X-XI cent.

XI-XII
cent.

0   50   100   150 Miles

FIG. 1. *Art currents in England in the tenth and eleventh centuries*

INTRODUCTION

THE period of English art from 871 to 1100 is marked by a number of particular problems which do not arise for the historians of later and earlier ages. On the one hand, in later periods, there is in general a wealth of material, and a comparatively rich written documentation on which to base conclusions and theories. On the other, at earlier times, the science of archaeology comes to the aid of the historian of art and of events alike, and where documents are deficient, provides, through the evidence of stratification, a basis of reliably dated material on which to establish conclusions. Sometimes, indeed, such researches also present a clear picture of the cultural life, even perhaps of the events, of a particular age. Thus in pagan Britain pots, personal ornaments in metal, enamel, or precious stones, vessels of bronze, and so forth, were as a natural rule buried with the dead, whereas in Christian times this practice ceased wellnigh entirely, and such things became conspicuous by their absence. In the earlier period, therefore, what we now usually call the domestic crafts furnish a very important part of the evidence on which we base our ideas of the art of the age, whereas in Christian times these things until very recently hardly concerned us, and it is towards richer products such as ivories, textiles, ecclesiastical treasures, and, above all, books, that our eyes are directed. The art with which we shall be concerned is, in fact, essentially church art, and the secular world, its doings, and its products fade very much into the background.

Though the historical records are far less ample than from the time of the Norman conquest onwards, they do, nevertheless, afford some help in a study of Anglo-Saxon art. Thus some of the manuscripts can be dated on the evidence of written record, the texts now and again inform us when and where certain things were made, and other accounts tell of the glories that once existed, though they have now, for the most part, perished. Indeed, the work of reconstructing in the mind's eye the nature of the treasures that are mentioned in the records is one of the more hazardous and at the same time exciting tasks that confront the student of this age. So much has perished that, if one set out to present a full and complete picture, the surviving monuments would only furnish in respect of ivories hardly as much as a quarter, of metal-work and textiles less than a twentieth, and of pottery hardly one per cent. of what once existed: the rest would have to be supplied by the imagination.

In a passage of great significance, for example, William of Poitiers, chaplain to the Conqueror, records that William took immense spoils from English churches and abbeys, melted some of them down, and handed the rest over to similiar foundations on the continent.[1] To the pope he gave vast amounts of gold and silver and ecclesiastical ornaments, and to numerous churches all over France dispatched great crosses of gold adorned with precious stones, metal vessels, embroidered vestments and other treasures. Most of these appear to have been of English workmanship; it was perhaps the textiles that were the most valued.

Nevertheless, the little that has survived serves to attest the very great importance and quality of the art of England, and, especially, of Wessex, in the years between the rise to power of Alfred and the Norman conquest. Germany undoubtedly took the lead in the ninth century, and France in the later eleventh and twelfth in the creation of Romanesque, but in the intervening period, the tenth and early eleventh centuries, it was in England that the most subtle and truly artistic works were produced, even though they have not survived in such abundance as from Ottonian Germany or Capetian France.

In the realms of metal-work and textiles England's reputation far surpassed that of any other country in contemporary Europe. In the time of Edward the Confessor and Canute there are numerous references to the quality of English embroideries; William of Poitiers had something to say of the skill of the English women with the needle at gold embroidery; rather later we find that this country gave its name as a general term to describe textile work

---

[1] 'Gesta Willelmi Ducis Normannorum', ed. I. A. Giles, in *Scriptores Rerum Gestarum Willelmi Conquestoris*, London (1845), 144. See also E. A. Freeman, *History of the Norman Conquest* (1871), iv. 61 f.

of a superfine character, namely, Opus Anglicanum. Luckily two pieces which are now generally accepted as English survive to attest the truth of these records, one from Saxon and one from early Norman times; they are the stole and maniple from St. Cuthbert's tomb at Durham (c. 910), and the Bayeux tapestry (c. 1080).

In painting a rather greater proportion of the work survives than is the case with metal-work or textiles, but still our study cannot be completed, for no large-scale pictures on wall or panel have been preserved. But by a lucky chance a considerable number of tenth- and eleventh-century Anglo-Saxon manuscripts have come down to us, and the quality of the illuminations that adorn them, whether it be the full-page plates or the initial letters at the openings of the chapters, is outstanding. These manuscripts will be fully discussed in their place; here we need do no more than call attention to the penetrating humanism, the charm, the delicacy, and the elegance that mark the Anglo-Saxon school.

In the matter of sculpture, though monuments from certain regions are fairly plentiful, other areas have proved well-nigh completely barren. This does not necessarily mean that nothing existed in those regions, but rather, in all probability, that sculpture in those areas was executed in some other and more easily perishable material than stone, such as stucco or wood. Bréhier, in his delightful book Le Style Roman (1941), has stressed the importance of stucco in the Carolingian world, and England, which learnt much from the empire of Charles the Great, may well have followed Germany in making use of this material for sculpture. And Strzygowski, in practically all his works, has repeatedly emphasized the importance of wood as a material both for construction and for sculpture all over northern Europe. A distribution map of the surviving buildings is especially suggestive in this respect, for the areas where forests were numerous and where wood was no doubt the normal building material are, generally speaking, barren of churches, though they were so far as we know by no means barren of inhabitants in Saxon times. On the map at the end of this volume the surviving churches are indicated by a dot, the forest areas are shaded, and the regions where good building stone is easily available are hatched. It is clear that over the whole country the distribution of the surviving buildings coincides almost exactly with the extent of those areas where a good natural building material was ready to hand; thus, the limestone belt running from Somerset to Lincolnshire and the similar outcrops in Yorkshire are marked by the largest number of sites of Saxon churches. As we know that other areas were as, if not more, fully populated in Saxon times, it is only reasonable to conclude that churches existed in these areas, built in the materials proper to them, that is, wood, wattle, or half-timber, just as houses in wood or half-timber characterize certain regions of England to this day.

It is equally reasonable to conclude that not only decorative work of wood but also wooden sculptures existed inside many of the churches, though no such things have, unfortunately, survived. Much of this wood-carving may have been of Norse inspiration; the magnificent carved doorways, lintels, and other details that we know in Norway, for instance at Urnes,[1] serve as an example of what may well have existed in parts at least of Britain, and the presence of a few pieces of stone sculpture in a similar style, for instance at Kilpeck in Herefordshire in the twelfth century, or at Bibury in the early eleventh on stones now in the British Museum, shows beyond doubt that it had penetrated deeply into England. In addition to such decorative work, however, we would expect to find free-standing figure sculptures, either of wood alone, or as we see frequently on the continent, of wood covered over with some precious material, such as gold or silver; the well-known figure of St. Foy at Conques in France may serve as an example.[2] There is indeed evidence to show that such sculptures existed, and Abbot Brithnoth of Ely (c. 981) is recorded to have made four wooden statues of the Virgin which were enriched with gold, silver, and precious stones.

Even if this lack of material must be stressed at the outset of any study on the subject, far more has been done to remedy it than would have been suspected a generation or so ago. Archaeological exploration has to some extent been responsible for increasing what we have, both by excavation and by rescuing from neglect objects

[1] J. Strzygowski, *Early Church Art in Northern Europe*, London (1928), ch. iv.
[2] Joan Evans, *Art in Medieval France*, Oxford (1948), Pl. 5.

hitherto disregarded. But the collecting together of the material has also come about to a great extent as a result of the changes in taste and outlook that have characterized the progress of this century. In the eighteen hundreds the arts of the ninth, tenth, and eleventh centuries were usually considered to be barbarous and uncouth. Carolingian manuscripts, when recognized at all, were studied only for the script; such Ottonian art as was known was considered little more than grotesque; Romanesque architecture aroused interest only because it constituted a prelude to Gothic; Romanesque sculpture was ignored; and if Byzantine art was studied, it was because of its technical proficiency and its craftsmanship rather than because of its aesthetic significance. And of all the arts, that of later Anglo-Saxon times probably awoke the least interest. Because of the paucity of metal-work, it could only compare unfavourably with the earlier pagan age, the concern of the archaeologists; the books were mostly unknown, and somehow failed to impress except because of their affinities with work done on the continent; the carving seemed to be crude and incompetent, and when it was not frankly retrospective in character, it was either regarded as of the twelfth century or, if in a material such as ivory, was at once assigned to Germany, France, or even Spain. Indeed, the curious habit of attributing all good work to the continent and denigrating the role of England was a governing factor of taste.

Today, however, criteria of judgement have changed. The high artistic quality of much Carolingian work has been accepted; the products of the Ottonian artists are extolled as of great significance, especially by modern German scholars; Romanesque sculptures, and, more recently, Romanesque wall-paintings, are accepted as things of outstanding beauty, and the fact that good work was already being produced in France as early as the end of the eleventh century has now also been admitted, albeit in face of opposition. The researches of a number of scholars, again, have disclosed the remarkable quality of Byzantine painting at this period, whether in books, upon walls, or on panels,[1] and

---

[1] For preliminary illustrations and further references see P. Muratov, La Peinture Byzantine, Paris (1928), or D. Talbot Rice, Byzantine Art, Oxford (1935).

the charm of contemporary Italian sculpture and the importance
of 'First Romanesque' architecture have now been acknowledged.[1]
Yet in no instance has the necessity for this change of vision been
more strikingly substantiated than with regard to Britain. It may
perhaps have been in Germany that the most important buildings
of western Europe were erected in the ninth century, in Italy that
the best decorative carving was executed in the tenth and eleventh
centuries, and in France that the most impressive, and at the same
time the most expressive, figure-sculpture was done in the twelfth.
But nowhere in Europe, even in Byzantium itself, was there a more
advanced conception of manuscript illustration and decoration
than in Britain. Nowhere, even in Persia, were finer textiles
embroidered; nowhere was finer sculpture in stone executed—
witness, for example, such a work as the Romsey Rood; nowhere
were finer ivories carved; and even if the Alfred jewel must take
a secondary place beside some of the best works of the Byzantine
enameller, it is a work of a quality equalled nowhere else in the
west of Europe at the time.

It is perhaps with regard to the excellence of sculpture in stone
that the most striking revelations have been made as a result of the
researches of the last fifty years or so, and it is safe to say that
this country led the world in late Saxon times in sculpture, just
as it had in the Northumbrian age. Yet even so, the manuscript
illustrations perhaps show a greater subtlety and accomplishment, and they are, on the whole, more important, if only because
in this art examples of the best work are more numerous. The most
striking innovations for which the Anglo-Saxon artists were
responsible are indeed to be found in the manuscripts, and that
particular light, agitated style of drawing usually associated with
the name of Winchester, but which was really something intrinsically English, was first developed by them. An extremely delicate
and light touch became, as the result of their work, a national
idiom, and it is to their pioneer activities that must be attributed
not only the English style of the Gothic age and the work of such a
master as Matthew Paris, but perhaps also the delicate line that
became characteristic of this country in subsequent times and

[1] See Puig i Cadafalch, *Le Premier Art Roman*, Paris (1928).

which we notice as late as the nineteenth century in the drawings of a Charles Keen or a Cruikshank.

Of the major problems that confront the art historian at this period, the most important is probably that of dating. The manuscripts are, it is true, often to be dated fairly exactly on the basis of external evidence, while a few of the examples of minor arts that have come down to us are also accurately fixed, thanks to inscriptions or records. But with regard to the sculptures in stone and to most of those in ivory such guiding factors are absent, and nearly all the more accomplished work that is in the following pages termed Saxon has at one time or another been regarded as twelfth century. Isolated stylistic features are often far from reliable as guides to dating, but so large a volume of evidence for the early dating of such works as the Bristol Christ, the Romsey Rood, or even the York Madonna has now been assembled that the scales seem, to the author at least, to be heavily weighted in favour of the Saxon age.

In respect of architecture, fortunately, things are more definite, for as is well known, a completely new style came in with the conquest, and there is little possibility of confusing Norman buildings with those of the earlier age. Even so, certain interesting conclusions can be reached if the Saxon buildings that we know are examined in the light of historical events, and as time goes on study along these lines may well furnish more details about them than are at present available. More especially, if further excavations like those undertaken in the twenties at St. Augustine's at Canterbury can be embarked upon, a great deal of unexpected and important information may well be forthcoming.

One final point may be made before we embark on the study of the actual monuments, namely, the religious character of most of the art. Not only was practically all of it produced for the church and not for the secular patron, but also most of it was executed by artisans who were sustained by sincere religious beliefs and often inspired by profound religious emotions. In a sermon of the early twelfth century which is bound up in one of the Durham manuscripts (B. IV. 12, No. 59), the outlook that the illuminator of manuscripts should acquire is set down at some length, and although the illuminators were normally monks, whereas the sculptors, ivory-carvers, or metal-workers were probably more often laymen, something of the same feeling would seem to have dominated their approach. The passage reads:

'Let us consider how we may become scribes of the Lord. The parchment on which we write for him is a pure conscience, whereon all our good works are noted by the pen of memory, and make us acceptable to God. The knife wherewith it is scraped is the fear of God, which removes from our conscience by repentance all the roughness and unevenness of sin and vice. The pumice wherewith it is made smooth is the discipline of heavenly desires. . . . The chalk with whose fine particles it is whitened indicates the unbroken meditation of holy thoughts. . . . The ruler by which the line is drawn that we may write straight is the will of God. . . . The tool that is drawn along the ruler to make the line is our devotion to our holy task. . . . The pen, divided in two that it may be fit for writing, is the love of God and our neighbour. . . . The ink with which we write is humility itself. . . . The diverse colours with which the book is illuminated not unworthily represent the multiple grace of heavenly Wisdom. . . . The desk whereon we write is tranquillity of heart. . . . The copy by which we write is the life of our Redeemer. . . . The place where we write is contempt of worldly things.'[1]

Such ideas and emotions were at the back of most medieval art, but it is, from our point of view, interesting to find that the outlook was actually recommended to a craftsman of the eleventh century. And when such men as St. Dunstan and St. Æthelwold were renowned not only as patrons of art, but also as actual artisans, we may assume that the same profound faith dominated throughout the whole of the period with which we are concerned. It was this faith that gave Anglo-Saxon art its character, and if secular paintings, sculptures, or minor works are rare, it is not only because they have suffered especially seriously at the hand of time, but rather because art as a whole was in essence primarily religious.

[1] R. A. B. Mynors, *Durham Cathedral Manuscripts*, p. 9.

I

ART AND HISTORY

THE foundation of the Carolingian Empire by Charlemagne in the last quarter of the ninth century marked a vital stage in the history of western Europe, and it was to prove as important in the sphere of art as it was in that of politics. The very essence of Charlemagne's empire was eclecticism; the Germanic world of the day possessed little of what he most ardently desired, and it was to the vestiges of classicism and to the contemporary products of Italy, to contemporary Byzantium, and even to contemporary Islam that he turned for the raw material that was to be welded into Carolingian culture rather than to pre-Carolingian Germany and Merovingian France. Before his day the area which his empire was to cover had been ruled by a series of minor princes; its inhabitants, even the most cultured of them, were still little more than barbarians; its monasteries boasted little that was indigenous as regards the more cultured side of the life that was led within their walls. Art was confined to a few principal centres and was very limited in scope, taking the form either of the jewellery and metal-work that had long been popular in the old barbaric world of the north, or of rather primitive carving and perhaps also painting in the manner that we know as Merovingian, a mixed style, made up of barbaric and debased classical elements. But after Charlemagne's day, however disorganized the empire might become, however incompetent its rulers might be, something more had been added, both in the sphere of political and social organization and in that of art. Not only had a new breath of life inspired the development of culture; even more important, a new unity had been imposed, a new and controlled centre of development provided by Charlemagne and his court at Aachen, and for the next century, however many schools arose in the monasteries and cities of southern Germany and northern France, it was towards Aachen that the gaze of all of them was directed. If any single factor is to be regarded as affecting the development of the new culture more than another, it is probably that of centralization.

The new art grew to maturity with astonishing rapidity, and already by the end of the first quarter of the ninth century, only twenty-five years after Charlemagne's coronation at Rome as Emperor of the West, the old Germanic and barbarian elements had to a great extent been cast aside and a new art had been established in their place which was to leave its mark on Europe for many centuries to come. Indeed, on the continent the whole of Ottonian art and a great deal of Romanesque would never have been possible had not the Carolingian style been previously developed, while in England Carolingian influences on later developments were well nigh as considerable, and it is impossible to understand later Saxon art without taking them into account. Their importance is the reason for the last paragraph which seems at first glance to be concerned entirely with the continent and not with England.

The eighth and ninth centuries in Britain, on the other hand, presented a very different picture. Northumbria had been extremely prosperous, and art of a very high quality, the art of the Ruthwell and Bewcastle crosses and of the Lindisfarne Gospels, had flourished there during the last quarter of the seventh and the whole of the following century. Cultured life had also developed and fine work had been executed in the south of England at much the same time, though independently, while in Ireland the art which we know as Celtic had reached astonishing heights of excellence round about the year 800, especially in metal-work and manuscript-painting. But just as there was no unified rule in the British Isles, so there was no centralized patronage, and as a result no unified style; and though, from the point of view of sheer quality, individual Northumbrian, south English, or Irish works were but seldom equalled on the continent, the Carolingian culture there was far more highly organized. Purely because of this cohesion the Carolingian style was not only more uniform, but also exercised a far greater influence on subsequent developments in Britain.

In the political sphere the lack of unity in Britain was an even more vital factor than it was in art, for it made defence a wellnigh insuperable problem, and when the Norsemen, restless and pushed on by a developing sense of power, began to seek for new lands and ready loot, Britain was the area to which they turned rather than the continent, where Charlemagne's disciplined armies and centralized control were more than they could cope with. In Britain in the ninth century there was no properly organized defence; rule was divided and weak, and the country seemed to offer to the rapacious invader a convenient and ready field for his activities; the prosperous state which had been achieved in the previous century, moreover, had made the country rich enough to be a tempting prey.

Nor does the year 800 represent as definite a turning-point in art in Britain as it did on the continent. There the year of Charlemagne's coronation at Rome may be taken as that of the inception of the new Carolingian style. In Britain the art of the ninth century, though not as fine as that of the eighth, was yet its direct descendant. No new elements had come to the fore, little subsequent growth of a creative character had taken place, and any changes that are to be observed between the products of the eighth and those of the ninth century are to be attributed to decadence rather than to creative effort; they are to be regarded as the result of Norse ravaging and destruction and not as the outcome of any internal aspirations towards civilization or changes in taste. If, then, a period is to be selected as a turning-point in Britain it is rather the last quarter of the ninth century, when Alfred came to the throne and set the star of Wessex firmly in the ascendant, than the commencement of the century, as on the continent.

Even so, the emergence of Wessex was a slow process, for a new culture cannot be evolved with as much suddenness as an enemy can be defeated. The process had, in fact, no doubt, begun in the indiscernible way in which such things do begin, even before Alfred set about his wars against the Danes. But it was accelerated by his political activities, and it was helped in a material way by the direct and active support that Alfred gave to artists, craftsmen, and men of learning, welcoming strangers from abroad and encouraging the liberal arts at home. Schools were opened and churches built; new monasteries were founded, notably St. Mary's

abbey at Shaftesbury (880) and St. Mary's at Winchester, and
considerable benefactions were made to others such as Glastonbury.
Scholars were brought from the Frankish area to preside over the
new schools and monasteries, and men of learning were collected
from all over England; most of them were probably Mercians, for
under Offa (757–96) this region had seen a period of prosperity
while Wessex was still a backwater.

Though more than one of Alfred's successors was incompetent
as a ruler, these developments continued after his death, and in the
political sphere the ascendancy of Wessex was complete by about
the middle of the tenth century; the end of the northern kingdom
in the year 954 may be taken as a turning-point. From then on the
king of Wessex controlled all England from Channel to Clyde,
except for certain areas such as East Anglia, which remained outside his actual realm. All through these years a new cultural life was
developing, and with it what was virtually a new art came into
being. It would in many ways be more exact to call this new art
the art of Wessex, and to distinguish the earlier as Northumbrian,
rather than to group the two together under the term Anglo-
Saxon, as is usually done.

In the social sphere the gradual merging of northern ideas into
the old Anglo-Saxon structure was something of very considerable
importance and gave a new turn to the life and thought even of
southern England. But in art the fusion was never very complete;
a number of Norse monuments were set up, but they are isolated
and sporadic, and can nearly all be omitted from any analytical
survey as intrusive; that is to say, they were left by raiders whose
stay was brief, and not erected by the permanent inhabitants. They
are, therefore, not to be regarded as expressive of the dominant
character of the civilization. Such raids were nevertheless an
extremely important feature of ninth-century history. Norwegian
landings on Northumbria's coast had begun in the eighth century;
in Mercia attacks started rather later, but from about 835 a series of
extensive plundering expeditions had been made, which had more
or less laid the whole of the province waste by about 880; even the
south of England, especially Kent, suffered, but the west country
as a whole escaped serious devastation. At much the same time the

continent was similarly threatened; and though the Carolingian area was too strong to be seriously affected, the French coast was repeatedly raided; in 841 the Norsemen attacked Rouen, in 845 Paris, and for the next half century that part of the continent nearest to England was ravaged as much as England herself; raids were even made as far southwards as Toulouse.

The development of English internal history runs in close parallel with the extent and direction of the Norse attacks. Thus the importance of Northumbria, which was the principal centre of culture in the seventh and earlier eighth centuries, gradually waned and that of Mercia grew. But Mercia, prominent and prosperous for a time, was soon to give place before Wessex, again primarily because of their respective geographical positions. And as the centre of culture drifted southwards, so contacts with the continent, and more especially with the Mediterranean area, were developed and cemented.

Though it was set in action primarily by Norse raids, this southward drift was also affected from outside in other ways. First, the old Celtic form of Christianity which had dominated in Northumbria gradually declined in face of the new and more vigorous form introduced from Rome, which was linked with the cultural and political centres of the continent by numerous ties. Kent, with its ecclesiastical town of Canterbury, was the centre of this contact, and as a result this area gradually acquired a new importance while the old monasteries of Iona and the north, when they were spared by Norse raids and devastations, faded into insignificance. Secondly, Northumbria was rent by internal feuds which weakened the government, while in the south contacts with the continent were not only responsible for the introduction of new cultural elements, but also for raising the standards of administration and government.

Finally, there was the question of personality. External causes, whether geographical, political, or religious, all had their part to play, but for any single region to acquire predominance in a society like that which characterized England in the ninth century, the influence of a leader, a single individual, was equally essential. To achieve unity and progress something more has always been necessary than communal effort, however ardent, however active that effort. The word unification must, in fact, be interpreted in its most literal sense, for where centralized control has been achieved, this has invariably been the outcome of the work of a single individual.

In the course of the eighth and ninth centuries three such individuals had a role to play, and with each of them we can associate a school of art as well as a period of political tranquillity. The first two of them fall outside our period, namely, Offa (757–96) and Egbert (802–39), but their rules had considerable effect on subsequent events. Offa was the first to establish a strong centralized government, with its centre in Mercia, and he was able to resist the invasions of the Norsemen on the one hand and the Welsh on the other. The stability he brought about seems to have been reflected in art in the establishment of an important school of sculpture of which the most outstanding work is that at Breedon in Leicestershire (see pp. 86 f.). The second, Egbert, was a Wessex man, and about 829 under his leadership that province was extended to include all the country south of the Severn and the Thames. To his reign are to be assigned a number of works of art of very high quality, freer and more 'baroque' than those of Mercia, though they do not yet show quite the same polish, one might almost say the same international standards, as those which are to be assigned to the period of the last and greatest of our three great men, namely, Alfred (871–99).

Alfred was, above anyone else, the true unifier of southern England, and he was, further than that, the first conscious patron of a national art and culture. It is to him that we owe the final defeat of the Norse invaders, for he showed them that England was no longer defenceless and weak, but a power to be respected. It was he who established a new security and a firm government, and it was he who codified and enforced a new series of laws and a new system of social administration. Finally, but by no means least, it was he who was responsible for the veritable renaissance in art which began during his reign and left its mark on southern England for more than a century and a half. It was, indeed, one of the outstanding events in the art history not only of England, but also of western Europe as a whole in the age between the close of the Carolingian phase and the birth of the Romanesque, and its influence was in the end exercised on the continent almost as much as continental influence affected the art of England. We shall have much to say of this renaissance, but for the moment the lovely Alfred jewel in the Ashmolean Museum at Oxford may be cited as the visual expression of all that it stood for.

The events which led up to the age of Alfred were exciting enough. All through the later eighth and earlier ninth centuries the Danish incursions had been in the main plundering raids, devastating in their collective or long-term effect, but individually considered, neither large nor really disastrous. But in 850–1 a Viking army for the first time wintered in England, so indicating a more permanent threat, and in 865 an attack on a far larger scale was launched. It was in fact a great invasion, as large in actual numbers as that which came from France in 1066. But unlike the Norman invasion it lacked an historian—naturally so, one feels, for unlike the Norman invasion it was destructive rather than constructive in object. The Danish army first concentrated in East Anglia and then moved north, in 866 winning a victory at York; by 867 Northumbria had been completely overrun, and close contacts between Scandinavia and Scotland were established; they remained important for many centuries. With the north secure, the area to the south was then attacked. East Anglia was looted during the next two years, Edmund, King and Martyr, was defeated and slain in 870, and the war carried into Wessex. It was there that Alfred made his first important entry on to the stage, for he met and checked the Norsemen at Ashdown in 871. But the same year King Æthelred was slain, and it was still on a note of Danish victory that the campaign ended.

In Yorkshire, Durham, and Cumberland the Danish invaders were able to settle down and adopt a peaceful life; by about 900 they had become part of the stable population and were themselves subjected to a separate wave of Norse attacks at a rather later date. These attacks came by way of Ireland and the Isle of Man, and were responsible in the end for a transformation in a good deal of the art of the region (Fig. 1). In East Anglia again the Danish invaders had in the main settled down and become a tranquil element in the population. This area was afterwards to become the more or less independent Danelaw. But over the rest of England the character of the Danish invasion was far from that of a peaceful penetration. It took on the role rather of a devastating conquest, which might have carried all before it and eventually have destroyed England, and perhaps also, with England no longer there, the whole of the rest of Christian Europe had not Alfred, after Ash-down, been granted a brief respite by the disbanding of the Danish army; it only reassembled in 876.

Alfred had still not been able to carry his reforms far enough to permit of full benefit being reaped from this respite. The extent of his control was still uncertain; allies were suspicious and unwilling to co-operate fully, and for the first two or three years things went against him. But at Ethandun, in 878, he was able to defeat the Danes fairly decisively, and from then on the situation was changed. In the first place Alfred substituted for the customary violence and slaughter of victory a practice of alliance and friendship, and in the second his adversary Guthrum signed a peace and was baptized. Though oaths were frequently broken and confidences betrayed, Alfred's policy in the long run served to settle the country and to strengthen his own position at the same time. The next years were given over to consolidation of the power of the crown and its supporting nobles, so far as the political sphere was concerned, and to the active re-establishment of culture in that of daily life.

It was in this, perhaps, that Alfred's true genius lay. Other men might have won his victories; other men might have consolidated the power of the crown and so left a sound political legacy to the future; but only a truly great man would at the same time have attempted to set art, literature, and learning on a sound footing, not so much by borrowing on a large scale from outside as by fostering activities at home. There were, of course, borrowings; the Alfred jewel, though essentially English, shows clearly the influence of Byzantine art; in the minor arts we can very often detect the influence of the Carolingian tradition; the litera-ture which was made available for all those who wished to read was practically all either of classical or European origin. But Alfred's real aim was to foster indigenous art and thought, and the borrowings were done with this essential object in view. He realized that he could not create a new world outright; he did not even attempt to construct and embellish a new capital by importing architects and collecting works of art on a large scale from the most famed sources abroad. He tried rather to develop that which was good in his own world, and borrowed to stimulate this development, not to eclipse it by something more brilliant and spectacular. In this his action was the very opposite of Charlemagne's, and when Alfred brought artists or works of art from overseas, he did so with quite other aims than those which had inspired the great continental unifier.

Alfred's zeal as a patron of art is further attested by Asser, who states that a sixth of his revenue was devoted to the support of artificers of various sorts, and to these divers works were entrusted.[1] A gold object called an 'aestel' was sent to each bishop; gold shrines, elaborately decorated, were presented to numerous churches and monasteries; architects and builders seem to have been kept as busy as the workers in precious metals, and the records speak frequently of Alfred's work as a patron of architecture. Though many of these craftsmen and builders came from abroad, their duties seem to have consisted primarily in teaching the local men rather than in producing works of a purely foreign style. There is in any case something essentially English about the most important piece of sculpture of this age that has come down to us, namely, the cross at Codford St. Peter in Wiltshire (Pl. 6). The influence of Italy and Byzantium which is often so marked in the sculptures from the seventh to the eleventh centuries has here been completely subordinated to the native idiom; the hieratic convention which characterizes the Mercian sculptures at Fletton, Castor, or Breedon, where close east Christian inspiration is obvious, is strikingly absent, and the whole style of the work is fresh and quite distinctive. In the almost dancing attitude, the strange but elegant contortion of the figure and the lovely balance of the

[1] *Asser's Life of King Alfred*, ed. W. H. Stevenson, Oxford (1904), sect. 101, or J. A. Giles, London (1900), 83.

composition, there is something quite new which seems to herald the style of the Winchester school which was to dominate Anglo-Saxon art from the third quarter of the tenth century onwards.

The close of Alfred's reign was, however, not to be devoted to such peaceful activities alone; a large Viking invasion, directed against France in 885, showed that the old enemy was still powerful, and in 892 a new attack was launched against England, two fleets being assembled, one of 250 and the other of 50 vessels. This threat, though menacing, seemed, however, to lack something of the drive of the earlier ones; it was resisted, and Alfred's death in 899 occurred simultaneously with the termination of the first period of Viking expansion, which had begun as long before as 793 with a raid on Lindisfarne. But even if the energy of the old Norwegian Vikings had abated, the northern menace was still alive, for both the Swedes and the Danes began to seek for new territories, and the effects of their respective expansions soon made themselves felt. Swedish attacks were mainly directed against Germany and France, where they had serious results; in 997 they even penetrated across the former country and reached as far eastwards as Novgorod. The Danes, on the other hand, moved mainly towards England, and from around the year 900 onward they exercised a very important influence on the course of the history of this country. At first the English were able to resist, and a Danish army was defeated by Edward the Elder near Wolver-hampton in 910. At the same time the Viking colonies in the north also lost their independence, and Edward, when he died in 925, was the first king to rule a fully united England.

His successors, however, were less fortunate, and soon the Danish invasions took on a new form, for unlike the old Vikings, who had come as plunderers, these new peoples came as settlers, and by quite early in the tenth century what was virtually a Danish province, the Danelaw, had become established in East Anglia. It enjoyed its own laws and customs, its own system of organization, its own ideas of monetary computation, its own method of land distribution, and so firmly did these and other cultural factors become established that they survived for many centuries even after the Norman conquest had given a new unity to England.

And though the influence of Danish art on future developments was rather less strong, the art of the Danelaw was, until the Norman conquest, of a quite distinct character, as we can see from the cross shafts of the region, which show none of the Mediterranean or continental characteristics which are so marked in the rest of Saxon art. The art and culture of the Danelaw were, however, developed more or less independently in the province, and there were no very considerable cultural exchanges with Mercia and Wessex. So long as the Saxon rulers were strong, the Danes remained quiet and friendly; if ever the rulers showed signs of weakness, the Danes took instantaneous advantage of the situation, and throughout the latter half of the tenth century they demanded, and procured, very extensive sums in the form of Danegeld, which was little more than a bribe to keep them quiet.

But this was to come later. Edward the Elder was a strong king, under whom England as a whole enjoyed tranquillity and prosperity. He set out as well to carry forward the intellectual reforms set on foot by Alfred, and he seems to have been especially fond of literature and poetry. His reign was a period of real progress and brilliance. His successor, Æthelstan (925–39), carried on the same traditions. He received the homage of the British king of Strathclyde and of the king of the Scots, though the latter broke his oath of allegiance in 933 and as a result was attacked and defeated by Æthelstan at Brunnanburgh in 937. The Viking kings who controlled York from about 918 to 950, on the other hand, in general remained peaceful subjects throughout.

Æthelstan was also distinguished as a patron of art. He was a keen supporter of the Church, and that his court was a centre of culture and civilization is clearly attested by the number of manuscripts which survive from his time; one of the most interesting is a treatise on chess now at Corpus Christi College, Oxford (MS. 122). The king was a generous donor, and many libraries benefited by his gifts. Stone crosses were erected in large numbers at this period. The old Northumbrian type, modified by Danish and Manx influence, penetrated to the south, and the tranquil state of internal affairs is reflected in the fact that we find such crosses in the tenth century in the midlands as well as in Wales and Cornwall.

But more important than the southward spread of the old northern style in art was the growth of the new southern style which is first to be traced in the Codford shaft. This style developed throughout the first three-quarters of the tenth century, which must have been a vital period for its growth, even if but few monuments survive to illustrate its progress.

This same age was also one of progress on the continent. The tremendous innovations of Charlemagne had, it is true, been followed by a period of comparative quiescence in the mid ninth century, but new ideas had already taken root and were soon to blossom forth with great vigour as a result of the foundation of the Ottonian Empire in the early tenth century. The death of Louis the Child in 911 had brought an end to the direct Carolingian line, and by 919 a new Saxon kingdom had been established in eastern Germany under Henry I (919–36). It was, however, from the name of his son and successor, Otto I, that the new empire took its name, and Otto is of special interest to us, first because he married as his first wife Edith, an Anglo-Saxon princess—tangible proof of the contacts between England and the Central Empire—and, secondly, because it was under the Ottonian rulers of Germany that Byzantine influence became for a second time of vital importance on the continent, and by way of the continent it reached this country; how considerable was the role it played will be shown in the pages that follow.

Otto I (936–73) set out with the idea of modelling his empire on that of Charlemagne, and for this reason had himself crowned at Charlemagne's old capital, Aachen, thereby indicating in the first place that he hoped to be considered as Charlemagne's successor, and in the second that he wished his empire to be regarded as something wider and more extensive than his father's old Saxon kingdom, for Aachen was outside its bounds. After various campaigns of solidification, he was crowned for a second time in 962—but on this occasion as Emperor of the West by the pope at Rome; in the same way Charlemagne had been crowned 162 years before. Eleven years were still to elapse before Otto's authority could be fully asserted in Rome, and, even so, it never extended over more than a part of Italy where Moslems, various independent Christian rulers and, most important of all, the Byzantine emperors, continued to control large tracts of country. Otto and the Byzantines were indeed intermittently at war till 969, when the Byzantine emperor Phocas died, and better relations were established with his successor John Tzimisces; in 972 Otto I's son married the Byzantine princess Theophano at Rome.

Within a year Otto I was dead and Otto II (973-83) had come to the throne. His reign was short and, politically speaking, far from easy, for he was faced with struggles against the Byzantine forces and the Moslems in Italy, as well as against Norse and Slav invaders in Germany. Yet culturally speaking it was none the less a decade of stabilization at home, when foreign, especially Byzantine, influences were much to the fore, most notably in the realm of art. Theophano indeed seems always to have remembered her Byzantine heritage, and Ottonian art displayed a marked influx of Byzantine ideas and styles at this time; the ivory in the Cluny Museum showing the coronation of Otto and Theophano by Christ, closely modelled on a famous Byzantine ivory showing the coronation of Romanos and Eudoxia, may be cited as an example.[1] This period of Byzantine cultural preponderance no doubt continued with increased vigour when Otto III came to the throne, for from his accession in 983 until 994, when he passed out of wardship, the government was conducted first by his mother Theophano and his grandfather's widow Adelaide, together, and then by Theophano alone. Theophano, it must be remembered, was a princess of great culture, personality, and determination, who was intensely proud of her Byzantine heritage. The future king was brought up with great reverence for Italy, and it was there that he felt his spiritual home to be. Yet he did not neglect Germany from the cultural point of view, and a number of churches were founded by him at Aachen and elsewhere. His enthusiasm in this direction was no doubt stimulated by the early influence of Bishop Bernward of Hildesheim, who, in association with Theophano, had been responsible for his education. And there is no single name at this period that testifies to an interest in

---

[1] H. Jantzen, *Ottonische Kunst*, Pl. 1, p. 88, or H. Goldschmidt, *Die Byzantinische Elfenbeinskulpturen*, vol. ii, Berlin (1934), no. 85, Pl. xxxiv.

art and culture to compare with that of Bishop Bernward. To this day he is remembered for the extent of his patronage; and the superb metal-work doors and curious Easter column decorated with relief sculpture which he set up at Hildesheim are still known under his name.

Theophano and Bernward of Hildesheim were, indeed, between them, probably responsible more than any other individuals for the great developments in art that characterized the later Ottonian age, and the art of Hildesheim no doubt exercised an influence in this country just as did the Byzantine art patronized by Theophano. And if we have delayed at some length over the story of the Ottonian world, it is because both these trends of influence have usually been neglected by art historians and archaeologists in favour of that binding Britain with the Viking world. In reality the role of the Germanic area, and of Byzantium beyond it, was far more active than that of Scandinavia, for the continental elements were fundamental in Anglo-Saxon art in southern England, where-as northern ones were only superficial; they are, indeed, hardly to be found at all in manifestations of fully accomplished art, such as the manuscript-paintings or the best of the sculptures in stone and ivory.

This continental influence was probably intensified and accentu-ated by the inspiration of three very remarkable individuals, all of whom were in close touch with the continent at this time, namely, St. Dunstan, St. Æthelwold, and St. Oswald. Of the three St. Dunstan was the most important. Born in 909 he was brought up in close association with the court, where he appears to have learnt something of continental thought and ideas, though this acquaintance was to develop extensively later on in his life. It was only after considerable soul-searching that he actually decided to adopt monastic life, but no sooner had the decision been taken than his new vocation began to have its effect upon his daily life. He was soon famed as an ascetic and visionary, and so great was his reputation that at the age of 22 he was made abbot of Glaston-bury by King Edmund (939–46). As abbot he brought not only reforms but also great prosperity and culture to the monastery. In addition to being a distinguished ecclesiastic and a thoroughly able man of affairs, he was also a singer and a harpist, a skilled worker in metals, and a keen patron of the arts. It would seem that he was in touch with the continent at this time, for his rule was based on that of St. Benedict and the monastic reforms that he set on foot were more or less exactly contemporaneous with those that were being enacted by the Benedictines on the continent, marked, in the sphere of art, above anything else by the foundation of Cluny in 910. But when banished by King Eadwig in 956 it was not in a Benedictine house that Dunstan sought refuge, but at the monastery of Blandinium at Ghent, which had been reformed independently by Gerard of Brogne. Its abbot, Wormar, remained Dunstan's close friend, and subsequently is said to have paid him a visit in England. On Edgar's accession in 957 Dunstan was recalled and appointed bishop of Worcester; in 959 he moved to London and in 960 was made archbishop of Canterbury; in the same year he visited Rome. He remained at Canterbury till his death in 988. It was probably in these twenty-eight years that his most important work was accomplished, for the reforms which had been set on foot were then made nation-wide, receiving, no doubt, fresh impetus from what had been learnt overseas.

St. Dunstan was aided in these activities by his close friend and contemporary, Æthelwold, who had been born and ordained in the same year as Dunstan and who had been made abbot of Abingdon by King Eadred (946–55). He was apparently of a more violent temperament than Dunstan and took a stronger line in effecting the reforms sponsored by King Edgar (957–75). He was made bishop of Winchester by that king in 964, a position second only in importance to that of archbishop of Canterbury; in his case his office was especially powerful from the monastic point of view in that the abbeys of Ely, Peterborough, and Thorney also fell under his control. He remained there till his death in 984. He, too, was in close touch with the continent, especially with the Benedictine abbey of Fleury, which had been reformed from Cluny in 930. It was probably through Fleury that he became familiar with the rule of St. Benedict, which he subsequently translated into English.

Oswald was of Danish origin, and played in the north much the same role as Dunstan and Æthelwold in the south. He had been in

similar close contact with the continent, and when he founded
Ramsey abbey he appointed as its first prior a man whom he had
known at Fleury. Indeed, he borrowed much from there in the
reforms which he instituted whilst archbishop of York. His friend,
Abbo of Fleury, one of the most important of the continental
ecclesiastics of this period, had actually spent two years in this
country, from 986 to 988, and after his return to France he seems
to have remained in close contact with Oswald until he died in
992. Abbo survived the archbishop by eight years.

Thanks to the efforts of these men more than thirty monasteries
for men and six for women had been established in England
by about 1000, and all were developed along a single line from
then onwards. A few, such as Tavistock which was burnt in 997,
were destroyed by Danish incursions; others, such as Bideford,
for one reason or another, disappeared. But under Edward the
Confessor there was a great period of expansion; Norman ecclesiastics were introduced even before the days of William, and in
some of the monasteries subsequent development was thus unbroken in spite of the conquest. The continuity in art and culture
after the Norman conquest, to which we shall call attention as we
proceed, was no doubt to a great extent due to the unifying
influence of the monasteries, and their role in the formation of
English art at this time was enormous.

The close monastic and cultural links with the continent that
had been established by Dunstan, Æthelwold, and Oswald were
carried further by political events, for from about 975 onwards the
Danes of the north had once more begun to get restive, and during
the reign of Æthelred (978–1014) raids on the English coast were
fairly numerous. North Devon and Somerset were thus overrun
in 988 and further attacks were delivered in 990 and the following
years. The fact that the raiders sought refuge in the ports of
Normandy and made that area their striking base led to serious
disagreements between the English and the Normans which,
though temporarily patched up by a peace negotiated by the pope
in 991, served, nevertheless, to throw England and the central area
of the continent into the same camp. Had there been a more
competent and determined king on the throne of England than

Æthelred, a strong alliance with the Ottonian Empire might have been brought about as a sequel; it might have had a lasting effect on European history. As it was, success eventually fell to the Danes, and it was only by annual payments of the Danegeld that they were kept within bounds at all.

The completion of Danish successes was probably almost as much due to diplomacy as to direct action, for it was diplomacy above anything else that led to the coronation of Canute the Dane in 1017 as king of England and Denmark; it was diplomacy that caused him to marry Æthelred's widow, Emma, in 1019, and it was diplomacy that led him to visit Rome in 1027 to be present at the coronation of the Ottonian ruler Conrad II. While on the way to Rome Canute negotiated for privileges for English traders and pilgrims with the king of Burgundy, and while in Rome he arranged with the pope for the remission of taxes on the Schola Saxonum, an institution in Rome which had previously benefited from the interest of earlier visiting sovereigns, notably Alfred. Trade between the continent and England seems to have increased as a result of these contacts, and a number of commodities are mentioned in Ælfric's dialogues as imported by England, namely, brocade, silk, gold, ivory, wine, oil, spices, and glass; many of these same things seem to have been re-exported to Scandinavia along with English products such as jewellery, metal-work, woollen goods, and embroidery.

These facts serve to prove the wise and liberal policy of Canute as a ruler, and he seems to have played just as active a role as patron of the arts. In any case he not only built a church as a kind of common war memorial after his victory at Assandun in 1016 and gave a rich pall embroidered with peacocks to the tomb of his former adversary Edmund Ironside, but also honoured the English saints and gave rich gifts to numerous abbeys. There is reason to believe that his reign was one of great artistic prosperity, and some of the finest pieces of sculpture, such as the Romsey Rood (Pl. 13) and the York Madonna (Pl. 22) are in the writer's opinion to be assigned to it. Their evidence is important, for such things were more dependent on royal patronage than the manuscripts, which were done in the main in and for the monasteries.

The good relations with the continent which were set on foot by
Canute's visit to Rome were extended to an actual alliance by the
marriage of Conrad's son Henry to Canute's daughter Gunnhild.
Henry was crowned at Rome in 1046. But he soon met with
difficulties in Germany, and the situation was by no means solved
when he died and was succeeded by his six-year-old son as Henry
IV (1055–1106). Henry IV was a minor until 1067, and the in-
competence of his regents led to a further deterioration of the
situation. Things were little better in England, for the period of
stability and cultural progress brought about by Canute's firm
rule came to a sudden end with his death in 1035, and the political
situation remained confused till Edward was crowned at Winchester in 1043.

It is, however, improbable that this political confusion affected
the social or artistic life of England very deeply; it was of a superficial rather than a basic character and did not last long enough to
interrupt the tenor of life as a whole. As a result the entire period
from Canute's accession in 1016, or even before then, till the
Norman conquest was one of continuous cultural and artistic
progress, and though during the first part of it there were close
relationships between England and Denmark, there were throughout links of a more fundamental character, so far as art was
concerned, with the continent, and even if Edward's pro-Norman
policy—he had lived in Normandy from his thirteenth till his
fortieth year—went some way towards weakening the bonds with
the Ottonian world, contacts were maintained none the less
through the monasteries. It was in reality the Norman invasion of
England in 1066 that finally shattered them, though they would
doubtless have broken of their own accord before very long
owing to the vigour of the new style of architecture and sculpture
which was growing up, for Norman architecture was but a branch
of the great western style which we call Romanesque, and which
we now recognize as one of the greatest phases of the world's
history in architecture and sculpture.

Here, however, for the first time we see national bonds breaking
through those of political tutelage, for French Romanesque art
was something very distinctive, and though local stylistic groups

soon developed, for example in Burgundy, in the south, or in Normandy, all were closely related and were distinguished by features clearly different from those that characterized the arts of contemporary Germany or Italy. The old Ottonian Empire on the other hand cut across national boundaries, for it included south Germany and Lorraine, and at times also most of Burgundy and parts of Italy. It was reserved for the next age to see a national culture, a national political power, and a national artistic style linking hands together to become one of the dominant factors in the history, art, and culture of the world; the centre of this new effort was the Île de France, its guiding spirit Louis, son of Philip I (1060–1108), who assumed control in 1100.

In England the reign of Edward the Confessor (1042–1065) was a period of artistic prosperity even if, in the political sphere, the monarch showed a lack of energy and little inclination to take the reins of government firmly in hand. As already stated, links with Normandy were close; the Confessor's abbey at Westminster was virtually a Norman building, and during his reign a number of Norman ecclesiastics were appointed to important positions, notably Mannig at Evesham, who was a keen patron of the arts, and did much to improve and decorate the church of his monastery. And after the conquest the Norman abbots, who in most cases replaced the Saxon ones who had supported Harold, made their monasteries the centres of the new culture which they imported from their homeland. But it was not a clean sweep, quite a number of the old Saxon abbots stayed on, and in general the community remained unchanged even if the abbot was new.

So far as art is concerned, three facts stand out with regard to the Confessor's reign. First, the Danish contacts of Canute's day waned progressively in importance. Secondly, new relations of a very far-reaching character were set on foot with Normandy. Thirdly, whatever the contacts, the English element in art continued to develop, and survived even in face of the terrific inrush of new ideas resulting from the Norman conquest.

Of the Norman conquest itself little need be said here; its course is too well known to demand detailed description. It must be noted, however, that it was absolute in that a new culture and a new art were introduced by the conquerors who sought to impose both on England forthwith. Centuries before the Norsemen had brought their art with them, and elements of it had remained to be blended with the indigenous art as the years went by. Subsequently, the Danes had given something of their culture and social organization. The Carolingian heritage and links with the Ottonian and Byzantine worlds had been responsible for the introduction of numberless art forms, ideas, and other aspects of national life. But never before had England been subjected to a systematic, organized domination, the aim of which was constructive rather than destructive. It was an age of great brilliance, 'splendid in painting, sculpture, architecture and glass, promising in poetry, acute in thought; an age of art and an age of heresies'.[1] The foundation of this new age must concern us here; its full fruits will fall for consideration in the next volume. But brilliant though it was in England, the fact remains that the twelfth was pre-eminently a French century, while the eleventh and tenth were essentially English.

Two final events of outstanding significance on the continent, and not, perhaps, without repercussions in England, may be noted. The first was the final rupture of relations between the churches of Constantinople and Rome in 1054, which came about as a result of the growing power and importance of the popes. It was to have a vital effect in later years, preventing the possibility of any understanding between east and west in face of the Moslem advance; more immediately it favoured the policy of the Normans in Italy by hindering any alliance against them, and so helped to establish Norman ascendancy in general; and it also effectually cut off, for a time at least, the Byzantine from the western world. The second was the departure of the First Crusade which reached Constantinople in 1096. Its conception marks more clearly than any other single factor the beginning of a new age, that of chivalry and adventure, and the close of the century was perhaps a more important turning-point in the history of west European culture and thought than any date since the foundation of the New Rome by Constantine in 323.

[1] Clive Bell, *Twelfth Century Paintings at Hardham and Clayton*, 10.

II

ENGLAND AND THE CONTINENT

THE numerous instances of links with the continent in the political, social, and religious spheres that characterize the centuries preceding those with which we are dealing here have been fully examined by Levison in his book *England and the Continent in the Eighth Century*; they are, moreover, outside the scope of this volume. But as far as art is concerned, the legacy that was left by the Carolingian world in England a century or so later is so important that some attention must be paid here to the links that bound the two areas at the time of the empire, even though they were forged a century before the period with which we are dealing. One instance of the presence of Carolingian elements in the eleventh century may be cited at the outset to justify this excursus. In his discussion of the Benedictional of St. Æthelwold, Warner notes the Carolingian character of the lettering; a similar influence is present in other Winchester manuscripts, and Carolingian elements in the stylistic character of the miniatures are numerous. Warner regards this as possibly due to Æthelwold's intercourse with Fleury and Corbie when he was at Abingdon,[1] and this may well be the case. The important fact, however, is that the influence is that of the Carolingian style, and not the Ottonian, though at the time that the Benedictional was produced and the Winchester school was flourishing, namely, the latter part of the tenth and the first half of the eleventh century, Ottonian art had already replaced the earlier Carolingian on the continent, and the stylistic features that distinguish it so clearly from the earlier style had been fully developed.

These Carolingian survivals are in many cases extremely important, and the nature and true degree of originality of later Anglo-Saxon art can often only be fully evaluated when the Carolingian elements have been taken into account. But their presence is in

---

[1] See the *Chronicles of Abingdon, Chron. Monast. de Abingdon*, i. 129, ed. J. Stevenson.

the main something that can only be disclosed by a stylistic analysis
of an actual work of art, and here it is rather the more concrete
evidence of contacts in the political, economic, or social spheres that
must be dealt with, for they serve to substantiate the artistic ones.

In the political sphere, then, the most obvious evidence of inter-
relation is that offered by records of marriages, usually engineered
for diplomatic reasons. Levison lists a number of these (p. 112) and
in addition it may be noted that Egbert lived under Charlemagne's
protection before he became king of Wessex in 802. Contacts of
this character often had an immediate effect on art in that objects
were taken from one country to the other as presents or as part of
a marriage dowry, and these were at times used as models by the
craftsmen of the country to which they were taken. An obvious
instance is the copying of Byzantine ivories and other precious
objects at the Ottonian court at the time of Theophano's marriage
to Otto II. Similar presents were, however, also sent at other
times; Byzantine textiles, for example, were given to most of the
Carolingian rulers,[1] and textiles and other treasures from the
continent were sent to England by Charlemagne and others.
Textiles seem to have been the most usual objects for presentation
by more easterly to more westerly powers at this time, partly, one
would suppose, because they were easy to transport, and partly
because the Byzantine world excelled in their manufacture. But
on one occasion at least, English stuffs were sent to the continent,
for it is recorded that Charlemagne asked Offa (757–96) for
'English cloaks' and he sent him an Avar sword and silken mantles
in exchange.[2] The inclusion of silks in the consignment suggests
that the English textiles were probably of wool.

Saintly relics constituted another class of object that was frequently exchanged, and it is likely that these were often enshrined
in cases of metal-work, decorated with precious stones and enamels.
Books were given with these, and their bindings were often no
doubt of the finest work of Byzantine or Germanic craftsmanship.
Weapons again were transported, and several examples of Carolingian origin have been found at various times in England. An

[1] J. Ebersolt, *Les Arts Somptuaires de Byzance*, Paris (1923), 56 f.
[2] W. Levison, *England and the Continent*, 112.

iron spear-head found at Henley, 18 inches long, with cross-bar below the blade, another of the same type from Nottingham, and two from London may be cited as examples.[1] All are of a type previously unknown in this country, and must have been imports from the Carolingian world.

Journeys to the continent, made for the purpose of acquiring books, were undertaken by numerous leading English ecclesiastics, and, as is well known, Irish and English monks also frequently settled overseas from the eighth century onwards. The Saxon monk Willibald thus assisted at the end of the eighth century in the revival of monastic life at Monte Cassino, and English monks held a predominant place in the Benedictine world as a whole. In the field of illumination the continent owed much to such men, and the influence of the Hiberno-Saxon school abroad was considerable. Books actually made in the British Isles appear to have been taken to the continent in quite large quantities, and they were copied locally as far afield as Italy and Spain. The same influence was exercised on sculpture also, and Kingsley Porter notes as an instance the Irish style of the sculptures of St. Michael's at Pavia.

In the same way continental monks had reached Britain, and throughout the course of the ninth century the power of the old Celtic church waned and that of Rome increased as a result of their influence. The popes sent their emissaries to the west, and in return numerous Englishmen made pilgrimages to Rome and even to holy places further afield such as Egypt, Constantinople, and the Holy Land. The names of some of these men have come down to us; such were Willibrod and Wynfrid in the ninth century, and there were many more in the centuries that followed. It was the duty of the English metropolitans to visit Rome to receive the pallium from the pope, and many actually did so. The city was in fact held in the greatest reverence in England from the end of the eighth century onwards as the centre of religion, the centre of culture, and perhaps most important of all, as the home of St. Peter who held the keys of Heaven—to the medieval mind, with its imaginative, visionary outlook, this had much more than a purely symbolic meaning; it had also a practical significance, for it would,

---

[1] Reginald A. Smith, 'Anglo-Saxon remains', *V.C.H. Berkshire*, i (1906), 246.

so to speak, introduce the individual on earth to the guardian of Heaven, and when the time came for admission, familiarity would accelerate entry. There was indeed a special Saxon quarter, the Schola Saxonum, between St. Peter's and the Tiber, where the pilgrims lodged.

Another source of contact was trade; first, the slave-trade, and secondly and more important, the international trade in goods. The latter was probably responsible for art contacts just as extensive as those resulting from religious or diplomatic intercourse. English coins were frequently modelled on Frankish or Byzantine prototypes, and hoards of coins, English on the continent and continental in England, have quite frequently come to light. Though some of the English ones might have reached the continent in the form of the yearly tribute to the pope which was initiated in the time of Offa (757–96), their presence at numerous places other than Rome suggests that trade was a more weighty reason for the presence of a large percentage of them.

Though the Danish invasions of the later eighth and early ninth centuries on the one hand, and the weakness of a series of puppet popes on the other caused serious interruptions in the continuity of these contacts, they would seem never to have been completely broken, and by the middle of the ninth century intercourse with Rome had once more been resumed on a regular basis. Æthelwulf (839–58) exported to Rome a great treasure which included English works of art, and even before the middle of the century he thought of making a pilgrimage thither for the purpose of prayer, believing that the Viking invasions came as a punishment for sin. In 853 he sent Alfred there as a child of four to pay respects to the pope; Alfred appears to have been confirmed by the pope, and in any case he received from his hands the robes of the consulate, in the old Byzantine manner. Subsequently, in 855, Æthelwulf himself went to Rome, taking Alfred with him for a second visit. In addition he took, according to Anastasius, numerous presents, which included a crown of purest gold, two basins of gold, a sword bound with gold, two small gold figures, four silver-gilt dishes, two palls of silk with golden clasps, and some silk dresses and hangings. While there the king restored the

Schola Saxonum near the Vatican. On his way home he spent
several months as the guest of Charles the Bold at the Frankish
court, and while there he married the emperor's daughter; as she
was only twelve years old at the time it would seem that the
match was arranged for political rather than personal reasons.

In the reign of Alfred (871–99), contacts with the continent
became even more important. In the political sphere a number of
marriages between leading personalities on both sides of the
Channel were arranged; Alfred's third daughter, for instance, was
married to Baldwin II of Flanders. In the religious field continental
ideas and personalities were eagerly sought by Alfred in the process
of his religious and cultural reforms. Some of his most prominent
supporters in his task of re-establishing culture in England were of
continental origin. When he founded the monastery of Athelney,
for example, he brought over 'certain priests and deacons' from
abroad, mainly from Gaul, and one of his foremost helpers,
Grimbald, came from the abbey of St. Bertin near St. Omer,
where a bastard son of Charlemagne had once been abbot. John
the Old Saxon, first abbot of Athelney, came from Corbie, and
he was in close touch with the archbishop of Reims.

No contacts were, however, more firmly established than those
with Rome itself. Records have been preserved of exchanges of
missions in the years 881, 883, 884, and 886–91; other missions
which have remained unchronicled were doubtless exchanged also,
for alms were sent yearly to Rome until 890. Pilgrimages to Rome
on the part of the devout and journeys thither by traders were
even more numerous, and the records tell us that in return objects
of trade and relics were brought to England; in 882, for instance,
Alfred received from Rome a fragment of the True Cross—it was
no doubt elaborately mounted. Gifts were also exchanged with
the patriarch of Jerusalem, who was at the time begging for
financial support to maintain the church of the Holy Sepulchre,
and envoys were even dispatched by Alfred to India; William
of Malmesbury records that they returned laden with jewels.[1]

[1] *Gesta Pontificum*, ii. 80. For a survey of the travels and trading journeys of this
period see W. Cunningham, *The Growth of English Industry and Commerce*, Cambridge
(1915), i. 80 ff.

Spices from the east were, like jewels, always an important item of trade; they came to England by way of the Mediterranean world. Important contacts were also made with the Byzantine emperor at Constantinople, and they were in all probability extensive. Their existence is attested by concrete evidence even more than in the records. Alfred's coins were thus clearly modelled on Byzantine originals, and those minted in London not only bear on the obverse the head and shoulders of the king, executed in a very Byzantine style, but also carry on the reverse a monogram which indicates London, and which is obviously a variant in Latin characters of the monograms in Greek lettering that were so popular in Byzantine art (Fig. 2). The rendering of Æthelstan's head was perhaps even more Byzantine than that of Alfred's, and the same style remained to the fore in the coinage right down to the conquest; even William the Conqueror's head was done in a Byzantine manner on his earliest coins.[1]

FIG. 2. *Monogram on Alfred's coins*

These contacts continued after Alfred's death. Five of Æthelstan's half-sisters were married to continental princes, so that Britain was in this way allied to most of the more important rulers on the continent. One, Eadgifu, thus married Charles the Simple of France and became the mother of Louis IV who was brought up at Æthelstan's court; another, Edith, married, as his first wife, Otto, later Otto I, the founder of the Ottonian empire; Eadhild married Hugh, count of Paris; a second Eadgifu married Louis II of Provence; and Ealgifu was married to a prince of Lesser Burgundy. There must have been much interesting diplomatic history enacted in connexion with these marriages, but no details of it have survived. Its extent is, however, reflected in the fact that Æthelstan sheltered at his court many foreign princes, notably Allan, count of Brittany, and the heirs of the count of Ponthieu. The degree to which their presence may have affected art is borne out by records of the embassy which came to arrange the marriage of Eadhild to Hugh of Paris. It was received by the king at Abing-

---

[1] See H. A. Grueber, *Handbook of the Coins of Great Britain and Ireland in the British Museum*, London (1899), especially no. 201, Pl. VI.

don in 926, and numerous presents were given, which included an onyx vase, a diadem set with jewels, the sword of Constantine the Great with one of the nails from the True Cross set in gold in its hilt, the lance of Charlemagne, said to have been that with which the centurion had pierced our Lord's side, fragments of the Cross and the Crown of Thorns, set in a crystal mount, and the standard of St. Maurice, captain of the Theban legion. Whether all these objects were authentic is beyond the point; what is essential is that the exchange of such things, many of them in contemporary mounts, took place.

Other gifts, of a more ecclesiastical significance, were also exchanged. In 929 Coenwald took presents to German monasteries, and the king received in return a number of books most of which he presented to monasteries all over the country. One, which he gave to Christ Church, Canterbury, and which is now in the British Museum (Cotton, Tiberius, A. II) was executed for Otto the Great at Liége; another, which he gave to St. Augustine's, Canterbury, again in the British Museum (Roy. I. A. XVIII) was also probably done in France. Another, known as Æthelstan's Psalter (B.M. Cotton, Galba, A. XVIII), was done in part on the continent and in part in England. Æthelstan also entertained many foreign scholars at his court, and kept up contacts with several monasteries in France and Germany. His kingdom embraced Mercia as well as Wessex, and included the Britons of Cornwall on the one hand and Anglo-Scandinavians of the Danelaw and Norsemen in Yorkshire and Northumbria on the other, so that the influence of his court affected a wide area at home and, through the Norsemen, served also to link the Mediterranean with the northern world.

Up to this time the continent had been controlled by a number of rulers in different areas, all of more or less equal importance, but with the rise to power of Otto I a new phase began, or rather an old one was re-enacted, for in founding his empire Otto had constantly in mind the aims and ideals that had inspired Charlemagne a century before, and he too regarded himself as emperor of the west, peer of the great east Christian ruler at Constantinople. Like Charlemagne, he looked to the east for ideas and inspiration, like Charlemagne he too turned to the past glories of Italy as a basis on which to build. But, unlike Charlemagne, he could also look back to the past glories of his own land, and in many ways Ottonian culture was in reality a re-creation of that of the old Carolingian age. But in the century and a half that had elapsed since Charlemagne was crowned, ideas in art had changed and styles had evolved, and the new art that was to flourish so bravely under the Ottos was in many ways very distinct from that which had preceded it. On the one hand the influence of the classical element was less in evidence, and on the other the legacy of barbarism had been well-nigh entirely eliminated—or rather perhaps so completely assimilated that it is possible to discern it only after a very comprehensive analysis. In ivory-carving and manuscript-illumination, for example, the large, majestic figures showing a real feeling for modelling and plasticity, which were characteristic of the former age, had given place to figures of a more linear character where ideas of modelling were little understood, while in the spheres of ornament and metal-work the vigorous, though basically barbarous, heaping together of precious stones or brilliant enamels which was so usual in Carolingian work had been succeeded by a subtler, more ordered system of arrangement, and the setting of the stones had become simpler.

Byzantine influence again had become very important in metal-work and enamelling at this time, and we see the polished elegance which characterizes the art of Constantinople in the tenth and eleventh centuries gradually exercising a growing effect on the west. Byzantine ivories were thus often used to form a part of Germanic book covers at this period, and Byzantine enamels, or local copies of them, were similarly employed. The Matilda cross at Essen or the Imperial crown of Conrad in the Schatzkammer at Vienna are thus closely related to Byzantine works of art; the treasures of Queen Gisela from Mainz show clearly the influence of Byzantine models in style, colouring, iconography, and decoration. The construction of the eleventh-century bronze doors at Augsburg is again of a Byzantine character. Another interesting instance of this Byzantine influence is to be observed in the nature of the Imperial costume, for the lorum or superhumeral, a jewelled collar worn on the left shoulder with broad strips hanging from it down the breast and back, was introduced into the west from the Byzantine world by Theophano. It is worn by Otto II in a painting at Chantilly, a leaf of the Registrum Gregorii; and it also appears on one of the enamels of the necklace in Queen Gisela's treasure at Mainz. Other Byzantine fashions in dress were probably introduced to the Ottonian court at the same time.

This Byzantine influence was uppermost in arts which were in the main connected with the court; in more out-of-the-way regions or in classes of art which were primarily monastic, Byzantine elements were far less to the fore. This was especially the case with painting, and Ottonian miniatures in the main are completely un-Byzantine in style. Even the iconography is at times distinct, and the Bible scenes quite often show an entirely different system of arrangement. A comparison of the rendering of certain non-biblical subjects in Ottonian and Byzantine art also serves to bring this out; an interesting instance is to be found in the different renderings of the scene of the coronation of a king and queen by Christ; Ottonian versions appear in the Pericope Book of Henry II at Munich (Cod. Lat. 4452) of about 1012, where Christ is shown crowning Henry II and Kunigund, or in the Evangeliary at Upsala of about 1047, where He crowns Henry III and Agnes. The crowning of Otto II and Theophano on an ivory in the Cluny Museum, which exactly follows a Byzantine model, is represented in a rather different way.[1] As regards style, the Ottonian miniatures are in general very Germanic, or rather they show for the first time in pictorial art those features which were later to become characteristic of Germanic art as a whole. They are thus essentially 'expressionist', they lay great stress on the play of the imagination and little on the clear, straightforward narrative; even less do they seek to reproduce nature. Like the Byzantines, the Germans always sought to interpret rather than to record, but their interpretation was usually of a more nebulous, hazy character, lacking the logical approach so typical of the Greek mind.

Very similar characteristics appear in a great deal of Ottonian sculpture, and much of the work has an emotional appeal which

[1] For the Cluny ivory see H. Jantzen, *Ottonische Kunst*, Munich (1949), Pl. 1; for the Byzantine model see F. Vollbach, G. Salles, G. Duthuit, *Art byzantine*, Pl. 33.

is quite foreign to Byzantine and also to Anglo-Saxon work. Examples do, however, exist which show on the one hand a distinct Byzantine influence, and which on the other are akin to Saxon work in this country. The wooden doors of St. Maria in Kapitol at Cologne, which are close to some Byzantine model both in style and in iconography, may serve as an example.[1] In one of the panels our Lord is shown on the Cross with a soldier on either side; the loin-cloth and the general arrangement of the scene are of Byzantine character, yet at the same time are quite Saxon; though more accomplished, it might almost have served as a model for the sculptured slab of the crucifixion at Daglingworth in Gloucestershire (Pl. 14 a). In ivory-carving the more Germanic and the more Byzantine styles seem to have existed side by side, and a number of the plaques of ivory or pieces of metal that survive, where single saints in niches are shown, must have been closely inspired by Byzantine models. The metal binding at Essen, associated with Abbess Theophano, and dating from about 1050, may be cited as an example.[2]

The Ottonian age saw a remarkable extension of trade with Britain, and there are documents which indicate that foreign merchants visited this country in comparatively large numbers and that our own traders travelled abroad as far as Rome quite regularly, even before the time of Canute, who, we know, obtained new concessions for these travellers. A treaty of 991 indicates the extent to which trade was carried on along the sea-board; it suggests that a Viking fleet entering any foreign port was likely to find an English trading-vessel there. Trade between England and France was particularly important,[3] and it was also carried on with Scandinavia; by the eleventh century, indeed, English coins were not only normal currency there but were also used as models for the national coinage. English merchants also almost certainly travelled along the two great trade-routes of the continent, via

[1] See R. Hamann, *Die Holtztür der Pfarrkirche zu St. Maria in Kapitol*, Marburg (1926).
[2] Illustrations of all these Ottonian works are given by H. Jantzen, *Ottonische Kunst*, and of most by H. Picton, *Early German Art*, London (1939).
[3] See E. Sabbé, *L'importation des tissus* (1935), 1262.

the North sea and the Baltic to Russia, and via the Low Countries and the Rhineland to Italy. The latter was, from their point of view, the more important, but an interesting piece of evidence regarding the use of the former route is offered by the fact that Vladimir Monomachos, king of Russia 1113–25, married Agatha, daughter of King Harold of England, and some of his family seem to have found asylum in Russia after 1066. Vladimir, incidentally, was the grandson of the Byzantine emperor Constantine Monomachos.[1]

The route to Russia was thus important, and it probably also provided a link with regions farther to the east, most notably Armenia. The exact role played by this country in the development of European art has not yet been fully determined, but it may be noted that many of the plans and ideas that later characterized the architecture of the fully developed Romanesque period were anticipated there by more than a century, as were many of the motifs and designs of the sculpture. How far such intangible things as ideas in art were carried along the trade-routes it is hard to say, but the similarities between Armenian sculpture on the one hand and Anglo-Saxon and Romanesque on the other are at times astonishingly close, and the fact that many of the motifs or ideas which are found both in Armenia and in the west are not present in the Byzantine area suggests that the northern route via Russia may at times have been even more important than the southern one by way of the Mediterranean world. The southern route served no doubt to link Constantinople and the Holy Cities of Palestine with the west, but it was less important as a through route to the Caucasus, to northern Asia Minor, or to central Asia.

Records of actual contacts brought about by travellers at this time are comparatively numerous. Dunstan visited Rome in 960, and Sigeric, archbishop of Canterbury from 990 to 994, went there to receive the pallium on his appointment to the archbishopric. One of his followers has left for us a full account of the journey, together with a description of the churches that they visited in the Holy City; the manuscript is now preserved in the British Museum

---

[1] G. Verdansky, *Kievan Russia*, New Haven (1948), ii. 336.

(Cotton, Tiberius, B. v).[1] Canute made a pilgrimage to Rome in 1027, accompanied by Lifing, abbot of Tavistock; on the way out he stopped at the abbey of St. Bertin. One bishop and two abbots were sent by Edward the Confessor to the Council of Reims in 1049, and in the following year two bishops were sent to Rome. In 1062 Pope Alexander III sent two legates to Canterbury, the first to go since the time of Offa. Rather later a Canterbury monk named Joseph went to Rome, and a full record of his journey has survived.[2] Throughout the whole period the annual contribution known as Peter's pence was more often than not paid to Rome each year. A hoard of coins found in the Forum in 1883 gives some idea of the form that this tribute took, for it has been shown that it was more probably part of this tribute than a trader's hoard. It comprised 834 coins, of which as many as 829 were Anglo-Saxon dating from between 944 and 946.

In addition to connexions brought about in this way, an extremely important role, so far as the nearer portion of the continent was concerned, was played by the monasteries. Presents were exchanged between them, when Winchcombe abbey sent a manuscript to Fleury at the end of the tenth century—it is still preserved at Orleans (MS. No. 105)—or when Ramsey abbey, it would appear, sent one to the same place between 1010 and 1020—it is now in the Bibliothèque Nationale (Lat. 987). Further, monks themselves moved, and German names are prominent in later Anglo-Saxon monastic rolls, and English monks were often attached to continental houses just as they had been in Carolingian times. In the sphere of scholarship the English church, thanks to a great extent to the reforms of Ælfric, abbot of Eynsham, was revered on the continent, and the English monasteries were looked to as important centres of book production. English manuscripts found their way to a number of continental monasteries at this time. So far as the available evidence goes, it would seem that in this respect links with Flanders and France were perhaps even more important than those with the central Ottonian sphere. Dunstan, the leader of the reformed monastic movement in England, was

[1] Published by F. P. Magoun in *Harvard Theol. Rev.* xxxiii (1940), 267.
[2] See C. H. Haskins in *E.H.R.* xciii (1910), 293.

at Ghent between 956 and 957; in 960 he became archbishop of Canterbury. A number of other prominent monks, including Oswald, afterwards archbishop of York, lived and studied at Fleury. Abbo of Fleury spent some time in this country at much the same date, and rather later, between 1033 and 1066, we find three men from Lorraine as bishops in England. Edward the Confessor, as is well known, established close relationships with Norman houses, especially Jumièges, well before the conquest; Robert of Jumièges thus became bishop of London about 1044. Artisans seem to have moved almost equally freely; thus Saxon architects were famed on the continent, and one, Gauthier Coorland, was responsible for work on St. Hilaire-Le-Grand at Poitiers, which was consecrated in 1049.

As in earlier days, the current of influence was at this time not entirely directed from east to west. The English monastic reforms under Dunstan were independent of those at Cluny and may have influenced the continent even if later the Cluniac ideas came to exercise an important effect on Britain. And in the sphere of manuscript-illumination there was a good deal of English influence in France, even if it was hardly as considerable as it had been in the case of the Hiberno-Saxon school. Thus the school of St. Omer was obviously affected by this country, and the Winchester manner is apparent in much northern French work of eleventh-century date. It may even be that the sudden growth in the importance of sculpture on the continent at this time came about to some extent as the result of English inspiration, for this country was in advance of the continent at least with regard to the quality of the work that was being produced.

Yet in this last phase of Saxon culture it was probably with the Byzantine world that the closest affinities existed, and the links that bind later Saxon sculpture to Byzantine art are very strong indeed. They will be discussed in detail in connexion with particular works, but it may be said here that the evidence suggests that these links were both direct and indirect—that is to say, English craftsmen made use both of Byzantine models and of models from the Ottonian world which were themselves closely inspired by Byzantine originals. English craftsmen may even have worked under Byzantine masters, either in the east, or in Germany; indeed, so far as pottery is concerned, there seems to be no other possible explanation for the presence of a distinctive glaze of Byzantine type in this country (see p. 247). We know that Byzantine objects and probably even Byzantine craftsmen were taken to Germany by Theophano when she married Otto II, and it is possible that these or other craftsmen penetrated to this country.

Direct links between the Byzantine and Anglo-Saxon worlds were of very old standing. Angles had visited the Byzantine court in the time of Justinian, and contacts seem to have been maintained from then onwards. England was important as a source of zinc and lead, and legend records the exchange of these commodities against grain and Byzantine silverware. Commercial contacts were, as we have already seen, intensified in the tenth century, and the importance of the links is borne out by legal evidence, for there appear to have been certain borrowings by the Byzantines from Anglo-Saxon law at this time. In the next century we find more than a few Anglo-Saxons as well as Norsemen serving in the Byzantine royal bodyguard, and such men, when they came home, may well have brought with them objects, or perhaps also at times even a Byzantine friend or two. Witness to the closeness of the personal links in the first half of the tenth century is borne by the readiness with which those who sought to escape from Norman overlordship after 1066 took up service in Constantinople, and eventually formed the English company of the Varangian guard.[1] The Byzantines, being enemies of the Normans in south Italy, were for a time at any rate especially ready to welcome the English, who were enemies of the Normans in the North Sea area.

Similar contacts with the Byzantine world continued in the Norman period, and English manuscripts of the twelfth century are often very Byzantine in style. There seems indeed to have been a new wave of Byzantine influence in England in the twelfth century, though it was of a far less fundamental character than that which had characterized the tenth. Its effect is to be seen most clearly in the style and iconography of a number of miniatures in manu-

[1] A. A. Vasiliev, 'The Anglo-Saxon immigration to Byzantium', *Seminarium Kondakovianum*, ix (1937), 39–70.

scripts of the period, but it is also at times apparent in points of detail. Even in the early Norman wall-paintings at Clayton in Sussex the type of crowns worn by some of the figures is essentially Byzantine, though they may well have been copied from examples in Germany, for such crowns had also been adopted there under Byzantine influence.

It was these contacts with the continental world, first with the Carolingian and then with the Ottonian empires in the central region, with Italy and France more to the south, with Byzantium to the east, and perhaps even with the Caucasus at greater distance, that had the most important effects on art, but the effects were felt mainly in the south of England so far as area was concerned, and in the more elegant work of the court and the principal monastic centres so far as art was concerned. But art was not confined to these areas or these circles alone, and work, even if of a ruder character, was also produced in the midlands and the north, and sculptures, even though less accomplished, were executed under the patronage of the peasants and the population as a whole just as much as under that of the court and the larger monasteries. Much of this work was produced in direct imitation of the more aristocratic art of the court, as we shall see when we come to deal with the sculpture. But much of it was also distinct, in that the elements that went to compose it, both formal and spiritual, emanated from the Norse and not from the Mediterranean repertory. The Norsemen, indeed, left a considerable artistic legacy to Britain, even if the documents do at times suggest that their activities were confined to pillage and destruction on the grand scale, and it would be completely erroneous to deny the importance of this legacy, even if its role has, in the writer's opinion, sometimes been overstressed. Its effect would have been apparent in the art of the tenth and eleventh centuries whatever the political situation might have been, but as it was, it was intensified, for the cultural contacts with the northern world were continuous. The Danelaw thus looked to Scandinavia throughout the greater part of the period with which we are dealing; there were marked phases of Norse ascendancy in Yorkshire and Northumbria (see Fig. 1); and Canute, though he became very much anglicized, was a

Dane by birth, and he ruled England and the Norse world simultaneously.

The source of inspiration was, in later years, Denmark, whereas at an earlier date it had been Norway and Sweden, and though it was based on the same elements, the new Danish art was something quite distinct. When one is dealing with fairly accomplished works in England, therefore, it is not difficult to distinguish the Danish influence. But when the works are very primitive, it is sometimes hard to say whether they are to be regarded as the result of contemporary Danish influence or as due to the copying of some old Norse model which had penetrated to the area many years before. The Danish influence was, of course, the more important and the more creative. At the outset it mainly affected Yorkshire and the neighbouring counties, the invaders penetrating along the Ouse, Tees, and other river valleys. But soon East Anglia became even more important, and in the tenth century the Danelaw was virtually a Danish colony on English soil. Sporadic instances of the penetration of Danish art also occur elsewhere all over central and southern England. It was probably chiefly as a result of the close links with Denmark at the time of Canute that a number of monuments in what is known as the Ringerike style are to be found in the south-western counties.[1] The most important of these Ringerike finds from the artistic point of view are the stones from St. Paul's churchyard, now in the Guildhall and British Museums in London, which date from the second quarter of the eleventh century (Pl. 23 a). The beast which decorates the largest of the stones is well-nigh identical with one on an ivory casket from Bamberg, now in the Munich Museum, which is known as the Kunigund casket. The casket was probably brought to Bavaria from the north by Queen Kunigund, wife of the emperor Henry II (1002–24). Another casket, at Cammin, is again similar.[2] The prototype for all must ultimately have been of Scythian inspiration.

Other examples of the Ringerike style in England are quite numerous, as are those of the next phase of Norse art, the Urnes style. Many writers on Saxon art, notably Kendrick and Shetelig,

---

[1] For a discussion of this and other Norse styles see p. 127.
[2] A. Goldschmidt, *Elfenbeinskulpturen*, ii, nos. 189 and 192.

have indeed regarded these northern works as of greater importance than those inspired by the continental or Mediterranean worlds.[1] Norse influence in England was undoubtedly considerable even in late Saxon times, and it was felt in the south as well as in the north. But it was the Mediterranean elements that were the more vital and that had on the whole the most significant and lasting effect on the development of English art.

With regard to the northern world the exchanges were once again of a dual character, and English influence was in return exercised on Scandinavia just as it had been on France. English missionaries, we know, played an important part in the conversion of Norway and Sweden to Christianity which was taking place from about the middle of the tenth century, and it is likely that art products, especially manuscripts, were taken thither by the preachers. In the twelfth century a whole group of fonts were carved and set up in Västergötland which show clearly the inspiration of English prototypes of the early Norman period.[2] Other works were no doubt similarly inspired at a slightly earlier date.

What may be termed the Celtic trend in art was naturally enough associated in the main with the western portions of the British Isles, namely, Cornwall, Wales, and Scotland, where the old Celtic elements of the population were dominant. The most important art was sculpture, and large numbers of crosses covered with crude interlacing ornament survive all over the area from the south of Cornwall to the north of Scotland. Apart from the decorative motifs that characterize this style, namely plaits, interlacings, and spirals, the sculptures can often also be distinguished from those of other groups on technical grounds. The tool-marks that survive on a few crosses in Wales, for example, show that a pick or pointed chisel was the most usual implement; a half-finished cross at Kells, Co. Meath, offers evidence that a similar tool was used in Ireland. It also shows how the design was dealt with; the stone was squared and the design roughly set out upon it; the ground was then cut away to leave the figure-subjects in relief, and the detail

[1] T. D. Kendrick, *Late Saxon and Viking Art*, London (1949); H. Shetelig, *Viking Antiquities in Great Britain and Ireland*, Oslo (1940).
[2] J. Roosval, 'Swedish and English Fonts', *Burlington*, xxxii (1918), 85.

of these was sculptured last of all. Such technical evidence is valuable, and, when it has been fully studied, will no doubt eventually help to determine the place of origin of certain styles and types.

Ireland is important in this connexion, and so far as sculpture of the Celtic group is concerned, it is there that we must look for prototypes. In Ireland an art descended from that of the eighth- and ninth-century illuminations flourished in stone and metal in the tenth and eleventh centuries. Two important dated examples in metal-work may be cited, the Maelbridge bell shrine of 954 and the St. Patrick bell shrine of between 1091 and 1105; the ornament of numerous stone crosses is to be assigned to the same stylistic group. But other influences had also begun to affect Ireland itself, and most objects in metal, croziers, book shrines, reliquaries, and so on, are in a distinct manner, and hints of Scandinavian influence are often apparent. The figural work on the crosses shows a greater diversity of style, and in addition to the northern motifs others of Syrian or Coptic origin also appear. If Syrian or Coptic influence is to be discerned in England at all, it was probably by way of Ireland that it came.

The foregoing will suffice to give some idea of the great extent and wide diversity of the external contacts that characterize the culture of the period with which we are dealing. We are so prone to imagine that in early times contacts across wide areas were rare and journeys extremely difficult. Yet the exact contrary seems to have been the case. A perusal of the annals brings out the ease of movement within England itself. In the Mercian Chronicle, for instance, we find that Edward the Elder was within only a few months successively at Towcester, at Huntingdon, at Stamford, at Nottingham, and at Bakewell in the Peak district. The same is true of the movements of others, and it is consequently to be assumed that artisans could move about with similar freedom. Overseas contacts seem to have been no more difficult. Journeys to Rome, to the near East, and even to farthest India were quite usual; trade was vigorous and extensive and international contacts were astonishingly free. These facts have often been forgotten, and as a result there has been a tendency to treat English art in the later Saxon period either as an offshoot of that of the Norse world or as a purely isolated manifestation showing now and again perhaps some sign of links with the outside world but pursuing in the main a course of development interrupted only by the vicissitudes of political history. This was actually very far from the case. Quite apart from the destruction wrought by wars or the contacts brought about by major political events, there was continual give and take between the west, north, east, and the south which began in Carolingian times and never ceased for more than the briefest of spaces to affect the development of English art. What is really the most remarkable factor of English art, its very individual character, springs out of this. National arts that are virile and progressive have invariably benefited from contacts with the outside world, as have the peoples that practise them. They have learnt new ideas, new themes, new idioms, and have made these new elements their servants, working to their advantage. Only when a country is artistically weak have such close contacts tended to bring about cultural and artistic subordination. Such servitude was rare in the history of English art, and throughout the Saxon period, however considerable the outside contacts may have been, the art of the country remained above anything else English. And even when the Normans sought to superimpose a new style—lock, stock, and barrel—the old English traditions in architecture, sculpture, and ornament soon assimilated and transformed it, and before the end of the eleventh century English Romanesque had begun to take the place of Norman art. The brilliant age of the twelfth century, in many ways one of the most individual and personal in the whole of English art history, had already dawned, even before the turn of the century, and it was built not only on the foundations that had been laid at Cluny and in Normandy, but just as much on those established by Alfred, Dunstan, Æthelwold, and others in Wessex.

III

LATER ANGLO-SAXON ARCHITECTURE

I. DEVELOPMENTS ON THE CONTINENT

THOUGH the ninth and tenth centuries were marked by nothing like the same creative genius as characterized the eleventh and twelfth, buildings of considerable importance were, nevertheless, being erected in most parts of Europe. In the Mediterranean world a new, well defined style, in some ways related to, but also completely distinct from, the Byzantine of east Christendom had been evolved. Originally regarded as well-nigh the prerogative of Lombardy, it is now generally recognized that the style was developed more widely, and it has recently been accorded the name of First Romanesque, initiated by Puig-i-Cadafalch.[1] It is characterized by plans of rectangular or basilical form with projecting apses, by the use of blank arcading to decorate the exteriors of the apses or sometimes even the whole of the outsides, by the use of transverse round arches to support the roof, and sometimes by barrel-vaulted interiors. The churches are usually small and plain, and no new or very important architectural problems were either tackled or solved by their builders, but the churches do, nevertheless, constitute a definite group. The style was probably first developed in northern Italy, but it is in Spain that the most important early examples survive to this day, unaffected by later additions. St. Michael's at Cuxa (971), St. Cecilia's at Montserrat (957), and St. Martin's at Canigou (1009) may be cited as examples. The style was also important in the south and centre of France; the nave of St. Philibert at Tournus (980–1000) is to be included in the group. In Italy the most considerable remains are probably those of San Giorgio at Valpolicella (c. 730)

---

[1] See his *Le Premier Art roman*, Paris (1928), and *La géographie et les origines du premier art roman*, Paris (1935). Both contain references to a number of other relevant works, mostly in Spanish.

and portions of the churches of SS. Tosca and Tenteria (*c.* 875) and San Stefano (899) at Verona.

In central Europe, as opposed to the Mediterranean area, a great deal of work was also being produced in the tenth century, and though much of it was at first of a rather eclectic character, and there was no style as definite as the First Romanesque, a number of buildings of greater size and with more ambitious ground plans than those usual in First Romanesque architecture had been erected even during the Carolingian period. One of the most striking characteristics of this architecture was the great variety of the ground plans, many of which were extremely original, ovals, trefoils, octagons, or variants of these forms occurring, in addition to three-aisled basilicas often of considerable size, and usually with an apsidal termination at the west as well as at the east end. The eastern end was usually dominated by a large transept, and similar transepts with towers at the crossings marked the western as well as the eastern terminations. Sometimes a western gallery with an altar in it took the place of the western apse; it was none the less a western sanctuary.

In the Ottonian period the diversity of plans was less considerable, and cruciform basilicas or single-aisled hall churches became the most usual forms. The former plan was unquestionably taken over from Italy; the latter no doubt owed a great deal of its popularity to the old wooden stave-built halls which had existed in Germany since early times, though it is only in Scandinavia that examples have survived till today. Churches of both types were characterized by a marked feeling for space, and are distinct on the one hand from Byzantine buildings, where great complexity of plan dominated, and on the other from the Carolingian, where stress seems to have been laid on length. Similarly, the absence of vaulted roofs or transverse arches in masonry differentiated the style from the First Romanesque. In addition the German buildings were usually large, whereas First Romanesque invariably and Byzantine usually were small.

Another element that has by many been attributed to German developments is the conception of the tower as a decorative feature, forming an intrinsic part of the whole architectural conception.

Such towers are quite distinct in appearance, as well as in the ideas that inspired them, from the bell towers of Italy. These were essentially isolated structures, standing quite apart from the buildings to which they belonged. They were, moreover, plain and simple and circular in shape. The German towers on the other hand were square and were usually built in a series of receding stages with open arcading to decorate them. Round towers were, however, also used in Germany to contain staircases, but they were attached to the buildings, being symmetrically disposed on either side of them, often at both the east and west ends. The question of the origin and evolution of towers is a very complicated one, but it need not concern us here, for there is nothing in Britain that can claim to antedate German examples, and the idea, if not the actual system of construction, in all probability came to Britain from there.

These various constructional features were developed in the area which formed the nucleus first of Charlemagne's and later of the Ottonian empire, and their full evolution into a style took place in the ninth and early tenth centuries. The style itself may best be termed Ottonian Romanesque. If, in the Carolingian period, architecture was eclectic, by Ottonian times it had developed into a clear and distinctive style and was sufficiently elaborated to play an important part in the formation of true Romanesque at a subsequent date. Indeed, though Germany was eventually to become something of a cul-de-sac as far as architecture was concerned, quite a number of the changes that marked full Romanesque and which were later pushed to their furthest development in Gothic had become apparent there as early as the tenth century. In northern France progress was even more marked. A distinct group of churches built on the apse and ambulatory plan had, for instance, already made its appearance in the tenth century, and the churches even had, in certain cases, chapels for minor saints radiating around the apse in the manner of the fully fledged French Romanesque cathedral or monastic church. Examples of such buildings existed at Orleans (990), Tours (994), Nantes (992), le Mans (Notre Dame de la Couture, 995), and Tournus (St. Philibert, end of the tenth century). Equally progressive developments with regard to vaulting had also been made elsewhere, though the problem of roof-ing the main aisle with stone had, of course, not yet been tackled on a large scale. Pilgrimage to Santiago de Compostela had begun in the tenth century—one of the first was that of Godescalc, bishop of Puy, in 951—and the conveyance of artistic ideas and motifs over the country-side through the medium of pilgrimage had already been set in motion.

These developments in architecture were in the main peculiar to certain areas of France, notably Burgundy, and are distinct from those associated with the First Romanesque style in the south of France, Italy, and Spain. While they were taking place in France, however, Germany's initial role had been played out; and from the mid tenth century onwards buildings in the German area remained static so far as invention was concerned, and influence from there ceased to be of a vital or creative character. It was, therefore, to France that the English builder of the late tenth century turned for inspiration, whereas previously he had looked to Germany.

2. DEVELOPMENTS IN ENGLAND

In England the more or less complete surviving buildings that are to be assigned to the later Saxon period, and more especially to the later ninth and tenth centuries, are few and far between. This is to be attributed to a number of causes, most obvious of which was the fact that the age was followed by a series of periods of remarkable building activity, all of which saw developments of very great consequence in architecture. The Norman, the Early English, the Curvilinear, the Perpendicular, and even the Tudor styles were all new, all vigorous, and all creative, and during each of them the churches of previous ages, which were found for one reason or another inadequate to serve contemporary needs, were destroyed to give place to new and grander edifices. It is not sur-prising that such Saxon churches as were not replaced, as many of them were, during the century following the Norman conquest, were in most cases pulled down to make way for something more commodious and elaborate at some subsequent date.

But there were, no doubt, other causes also. A distribution map (Fig. 19) of the churches in which Saxon elements are to be found is particularly suggestive, for the majority of examples either cover an area running from the south-west to the east-central part of England, from the region of Bristol to that of Lincoln, or are in the north or extreme south. Now this distribution is not very closely related to that of the population which, with certain exceptions in the extreme west, was fairly evenly distributed in any case all over the non-mountainous portions of the island. The distribution of the churches does, however, correspond closely to the lie of the limestone belt, the central portion of which is formed by the Cotswold hills, and their prolongations northwards and southwards. It is in fact clear that the surviving churches are mostly to be found in the regions where good building-stone was available, and it is only reasonable to suppose that those of other areas were constructed in some more perishable material, namely, wood or wattle. There is no evidence that brick was made during Saxon times, either early or later; where it was employed, as at Dover and Brixworth, it was Roman brick that was re-used.

There are a few literary references to these wooden churches—Æthelric, bishop of Durham, for example, pulled down a wooden church at Chester-le-Street and replaced it with one of stone; the same was done at Wilton, and St. Pancras's at Lewes was a wooden church. Domestic buildings also seem practically all to have been of wood. But it is by no means easy to reach a conclusion as to what the wooden churches were like, and only one example remains, that at Greenstead in Essex, which is not necessarily typical. It is a building of stave-work, that is to say, it consists of sections of tree trunks set vertically (Pl. 2 *b*). This method of construction was certainly important and many of the churches of the 'wood' area were no doubt of similar appearance. But there remain other methods of construction in this material, and there is circumstantial evidence that two at least of these were known, namely, half-timbering and block-work.

Any direct evidence with regard to block-work, that is to say, wood construction where baulks of timber are laid horizontally, the ends overlapping as in a Canadian log-cabin, is unfortunately well-nigh non-existent. Such construction was, however, known in Denmark and Norway at this time, and certain authorities, foremost among them Strzygowski, have asserted on the grounds of analogy that similar churches must also have been built in England. The contention is possible, but little more, for to make satisfactory buildings in this way, long, straight trees are necessary, and though these were easily procurable in the pine forests of northern Europe, they were not readily forthcoming in the deciduous woods of England, where short, fat trunks, much more suitable for use in the vertical position, as at Greenstead, were all that was available.

Evidence regarding the prevalence of half-timbered or framework is a good deal more convincing, though here again no actual examples have survived. The theory that churches were indeed built in this way is based on the fact that wattle was certainly used in secular work, and it is supported by the prevalence in stonework of types of construction that seem to copy more or less exactly those proper to wood. The late-tenth-century towers at Earl's Barton (Pl. 1) or Barton-on-Humber are the most striking examples. It is held that the pilaster strips to be seen so clearly upon these towers are direct imitations in stone of the frame of an original timber construction. The form that the strips take at Earl's Barton is especially significant, for they are not merely vertical pilasters, but show a criss-cross disposition, which is peculiarly reminiscent of construction in wood, such as we know in medieval half-timbered-work so familiar today in such counties as Cheshire. At Barton-on-Humber and elsewhere the criss-cross disposition is absent, and round- and triangular-headed arcades appear together, the former below, the latter above.

It is, however, not only in England that these triangular-headed arcades are to be found; they are to be seen in eighth-century buildings at Poitiers and at Cravant in France, and in the famous abbey gateway at Lorsch in Germany (ninth century), and they seem to have been quite usual in Carolingian architecture. Their presence in England can thus be accounted for by continental influence and it does not necessarily imply that wooden prototypes were actually copied in this country in Saxon times; the whole idea might equally well have been introduced from abroad. The triangular-headed arch is found as an ornament sculptured on Roman sarcophagi, and arches of the shape, formed by splaying out one brick above another, were used in Roman architecture both on the continent and in Britain; there is a good example in the villa at Chedworth in Gloucestershire. The idea might thus have been adopted from Roman art either at the time of the Roman overlordship or later.

The use of pilaster strips as a purely ornamental feature, as at Earl's Barton, may also have been derived from the continent. The feature was common in Ottonian, First Romanesque, and Carolingian work, being no more than a variant of the blank arcading which is one of the most important distinguishing elements of the First Romanesque style. It was, together with other features of the style, apparently adopted from near Eastern prototypes in brick, more especially in Sasanian Persia. Here again the influence of wooden prototypes was no doubt ultimately important, but it was probably too distant to be of concern to us here. But far more often, as Jackson and Fletcher have shown, the pilaster strip in Saxon England was functional and not merely ornamental, for it served to hold together the rough work of the walling. In such cases its use is more likely the result of indigenous evolution.[1]

Another feature in Saxon architecture that bears witness to a more immediate derivation from a style proper to woodwork is the nature of the baluster-like pillars which often appear in many Saxon churches as dividing columns in windows or niches. Though of stone, they seem unquestionably to be copies of lathe-turned prototypes, and lathe-working is a technique proper to wood rather than to stone. But Baldwin Brown has shown that the lathe was used in making stone columns, bases, and capitals in Britain during the Roman occupation,[2] and its use in Saxon times for working stone, therefore, does not necessarily indicate the presence of any immediate wooden prototype; it might have been due to the survival of a method conceived during the days of the Roman occupation.

The frequent use of a flat impost block in place of a capital, or above it, is again a form of construction proper to wood. A good example survives at Wickham in Berwickshire. Such blocks are shaped like planks and they would seem, ultimately, to be due to

[1] See the very important papers by these writers, *Journ. Brit. Arch. Ass.* ix. 12, and xii. 1.   [2] *The Arts in Early England*, ii. 9.

the copying of a wooden prototype. The copying may have been done at a much earlier date in its initial stages, though there are no examples and the evidence here favours local evolution rather more than foreign influence. The predominant style of Anglo-Saxon mouldings and architectural carvings is again one proper to woodwork, whereas in the Gothic period the reverse is the case. The plank-like arrangement of the stonework of the great western arch at Barnack, for example, is strikingly suggestive of wooden construction (Pl. 4 b); without some such model in view it is hard to see why it was done.

More definitely conclusive evidence of the use of wood in church building exists with regard to the upper stories of towers. At St. Riquier in Picardy, St. Wandrille at Fontenelle, Cologne, and elsewhere on the continent, towers which were entirely or partly built of wood have been recorded, and there is equally reliable evidence to show that they were also known in England. A seal of the chapter at Chichester reproduces a tower of similar type which must have stood either there or at Selsey, and the stone sub-structures of the crossings at Deerhurst, Breamore (Hants), and elsewhere are so slight that they could not possibly have supported stonework structures above them; they would, however, have been adequate to uphold wooden towers. It would seem, therefore, that wooden towers were quite common in Saxon times.

Partisans of the theory that the Saxon pilaster strips and arcades reproduce in stone forms adopted from contemporary wooden architecture in England have conducted a very polemical defence of their theory—or rather attack against those who refuse to admit the importance of wooden prototypes. But though their reasoning has often been brilliant and their arguments extremely forceful, they have, nevertheless, failed to produce any completely con-clusive proof. The case in fact remains 'not proven' in either direction. If it could be shown that the examples of these various types of construction were in Britain confined to the fringe of the stone area and that they did not occur in the centre of it, it would be permissible to conclude that the copying was the result of the immediate proximity of wood-building styles. But this is not the case, and in default of such evidence it is hard to refute the contention that the copyings of the wooden prototypes first took place elsewhere on the continent of Europe or in Asia, and that the ideas came to England ready formed from overseas. Such copying did, for instance, take place in architecture in Greece in very early times, for the classical temple of stone was ultimately to a great extent derived from a prototype erected in wood. Farther to the east, again, as Strzygowski has shown, a similar copying of wooden forms in brick or stone was responsible for the origin of the whole idea of domical construction.[1] We may thus conclude that, though these features of Saxon architecture show the influence of wooden construction, the initial transition to masonry was in all probability not made in this island.

Alongside stone, however, wood construction no doubt remained extremely important over large areas of Britain, and in these areas stave-work was probably the favourite technique. But even if we admit that the pilaster strips and similar features were not derived locally from wooden prototypes, we need not necessarily conclude with Baldwin Brown[2] that block-work was the only type of wood construction known and that frame-work was only introduced at a much later date. Even if it did not influence stone, the technique may well have been practised, and it was quite probably extensively used for domestic building in Germany, and as England's debt to that country was in other respects considerable, lessons in that direction may well have been learnt also.

More definite links with the continent, and more especially with Germany, are to be traced with regard to stone building, and there are several important features in Anglo-Saxon work which can be attributed to German influence. Most notable, probably, is the western apse or sanctuary. Though this was by no means as common in England as it was in Germany, there is evidence that it was used in this country. Thus there was probably a western as well as an eastern apse in the first plan of Canterbury. At Deerhurst the disposition of the west end suggests that there was a gallery there containing an altar; and at Barnack there survives to this day a

---

[1] See particularly his *Origin of Christian Church Art*, Oxford (1923), and his *Early Church Art in Northern Europe*, London (1928).
[2] *The Arts in Early England*, ii. 39.

niche in the west wall and two smaller ones like aumbries on either side of it, which support a similar usage; the traces of seats found around the walls in 1854–5 would not preclude such employment, for they might have been sat in by ecclesiastics, as were those of eastern apses in the Byzantine world. The west tower of Barnack, with its wide opening to the church (Pl. 4 *b*), would thus have been virtually a western apse, though square instead of round. This is a far more likely supposition than that proposed by Baldwin Brown

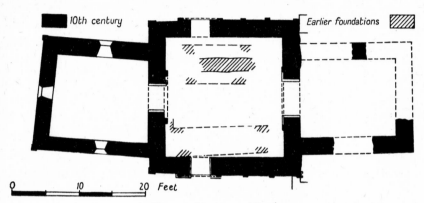

FIG. 3. *Barton-on-Humber*

that the lower story of the tower was intended for legal purposes.[1]

The plans of certain churches, e.g. that at Barton-on-Humber (Fig. 3), where a tower originally formed the central section of a three-chambered edifice, may perhaps also denote German influence, for this is the layout of the important church at Werden, on the Ruhr. The usual English disposition was that of a two-chambered church, a rectangular body with a rectangular chancel to the east of it and a chancel arch between. In the smaller churches this arch was often very narrow, and the width of the chancel arch appears to have been determined primarily by the importance of the church; in the smaller ones they were narrow, in the more considerable ones wide. The width does not appear to be correlated in any way with questions of dating. Additional chambers, called porticus, were also usual in the more elaborate churches, and they often developed into transepts in the later ones; it is indeed hard to

.[1] Ibid. 207.

say whether the idea of the transept in this country was evolved locally from the porticus or whether it was imported, along with other features, from the continent.

German influence was important with regard to windows, and it is probable that the double-splay window was introduced at a comparatively late date from the Rhineland. In any case it does not appear before the Danish period. Originally a slab of thin stone or a wooden board, pierced with holes geometrically disposed, was placed at the narrowest part; at Barnack, where the stone slabs survive, the openings constitute an intricate interlaced design (Fig. 4). Usually such windows have but one light, but sometimes they are double with a pillar at the centre, and a large cantilever capital above it. A good example of such a capital is to be seen at Forncett St. Peter in Norfolk, though the window there is a single-splayed one. This type of pillar and capital follows a Byzantine prototype, which, according to Clapham, reached Germany in the ninth century and England probably in the tenth. Quite a different system was employed in France. But double or even triple openings were known in Italy, and it is possible that the idea came to England from there. Italy was, of course, an important centre in the development of architectural ideas at this time, and although farther away than France and Germany, contacts were, as we have shown, frequent, and pilgrims went there in quite large numbers; they may well have brought back architectural ideas or plans or even stonemasons with them when they returned home. Marble columns and wall facings in the church of St. Riquier in Picardy were thus imports from Italy; there may have been similar imports in England.

Apart from the numerous extraneous influences that were exercised during the ninth and tenth centuries, however, the question of direct evolution from the earlier styles of stone building in Britain must also be considered, for even if architecture in Northumbria in the seventh and eighth centuries had not reached the same heights as had sculpture and illumination, work of quality and originality was produced, and even if complete churches are few and far between, there are quite a number of plans of seventh- and eighth-century structures to guide us. In

Northumbria the churches were usually small, and the chancels narrow and short, but the naves were comparatively long; thus that of the church at Monkwearmouth was 63 feet in length, while

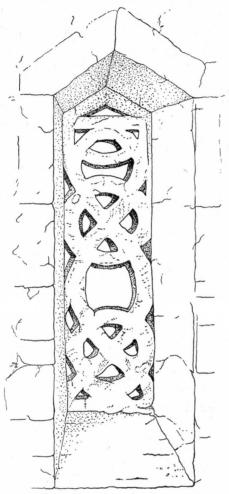

FIG. 4. *Barnack. Pierced window slab*

the church at Hexham was 150 feet long; it was described by Eddius as the most splendid church on this side of the Alps, so was perhaps exceptional. The most distinctive feature of all these churches was the great height as compared to the width; Bradford-on-Avon shows this very clearly (Pl. 2 *a*). Chancels were usually nearly as wide as the body of the church, and the two were often connected in the larger buildings by a triple opening.

Another important feature of early Saxon architecture was the porticus. These consisted of one or more additional chambers, added outside the church. Sometimes there was one on the north and one on the south, as at Bradwell, which combined to give the effect of a cruciform plan. Sometimes there was one on either side near the east end, the one on the north opening into the chancel and the one on the south into the aisle, so forming chambers like the prothesis and diaconicon of Greek churches. Sometimes they were carried all round the edifice, constituting what was virtually an enclosing frame and suggesting, on plan, a three-aisled basilica, though in reality the idea is a distinct one, for the porticus connect with the main aisle only by a few small, narrow openings, and not by means of an open arcade. And if the small chambers at the east end were inspired by the eastern prothesis and diaconicon, these surrounding chambers may have been inspired by another eastern construction, which has been termed by Baltrusaitis the 'partitioned' building. This idea seems first to have evolved in the near East, partly as a result of limitations imposed by building materials and partly owing to the demands of cult or esoteric tastes in the Persian-Mesopotamian sphere.[1] The conception spread thence to other regions, and Saxon buildings may represent a farther westward extension of the idea or it may have been evolved locally as the result of a similar lack of good roofing material, which would permit a wide span, coupled with a similar ignorance of the possibilities of pillared supports: it is hard to say. In any case the 'partitioned' type of church was probably copied occasionally in later Saxon times, though the general trend of the age was towards a far more open type of building and a less esoteric conception. In fact here, as with many other of the features characteristic of the early styles, the Danish invasions seem to have produced a marked break, and the debt of the later Saxon churches of the south to the early ones of Northumbria was not very considerable.

[1] J. Baltrusaitis, *L'Église cloisonnée en orient et en occident*, Paris (1941). D. Talbot Rice, 'The origin of the complex church plan in Cyprus', *Byzantinoslavica*, vol. ix, pt. i, Prague (1947).

Another constructional feature occasionally to be found in England, which may have been evolved locally or may have come from the east, is the horse-shoe arch. Examples which suggest this form are to be found at Clee in Lincolnshire, and at Langford in Oxfordshire, and at rather an earlier date at Limpley Stoke in Wiltshire and possibly at Brixworth. There are also arches which approximate to the horse-shoe form in the early Norman work in the cathedral at Winchester. In none of these cases, however, is the horse-shoe form very marked, and it may have been arrived at by chance, rather than copied intentionally from some foreign model. If a foreign model was used, it was probably from Moslem Spain that it came.

One further feature that must be noted is the use of long- and short-work in the masonry at the corners of the buildings. This consists in the employment of large monolithic blocks laid alternately horizontally and vertically. Often they stand out slightly from the face of the wall, and it would seem that the rest of the wall was covered with stucco or plaster, while the monoliths were left plain. The method of construction was extremely popular in later Saxon times. It may be that it was invented by the later Saxon builders, mainly for the purpose of strengthening the wall; as such it was linked with the use of pilaster strips. The system is essentially English and continental prototypes cannot be considered in this case.[1]

3. THE MONUMENTS

As already noted, but few Saxon churches have survived, and of the available examples the majority are small buildings in out-of-the-way places. Yet there were larger and more ambitious ones, and Clapham even goes so far as to suggest that had there been no Norman conquest a style akin to the Carolingian Romanesque of the continent might well have developed in England.[2] The larger Saxon churches that were destroyed by the Normans must have been very fine buildings, and Clapham shows that the truest ideas

[1] For a discussion, with a distribution map, see E. D. C. Jackson and E. G. M. Fletcher, *Journ. Brit. Arch. Ass.* ix (1947) and xii (1949).
[2] *English Romanesque Architecture before the Conquest*, 77.

of them are not to be gathered so much by studying the smaller churches that have survived in this country as by paying attention to the larger and more extensive edifices on the continent. Most important, in this respect, is probably the church of St. Riquier in Picardy.[1] It had a double transept and a single apse, and there was a staged tower at each crossing, and two round staircase towers at each corner of the transepts. The church was elaborately decorated, and the decoration included reliefs in stucco depicting the principal subjects from the New Testament.

Nothing so elaborate survives in England, but two groups of the larger buildings are, nevertheless, to be distinguished, an earlier, covering the period from the end of the ninth century till about 950, and a later, from then till the conquest. The most outstanding example of the former was the religious portion of the construction undertaken by St. Swithin at Winchester (d. 862). His work was, however, considerably altered by Bishop Æthelwold in 980. To the latter period, which is by far the more important, belong the extensive buildings done by Dunstan, Æthelwold, and Oswald, under the inspiration of Edgar (959–75); by Canute, who built and restored numerous churches and monasteries; and finally those resulting from the pious enthusiasm of Edward the Confessor. Records exist of fine cathedrals at Canterbury, rebuilt by Archbishop Odo (940–60), Winchester (980), Durham (999), and Worcester (tenth century); and of abbeys at Ely (c. 1000), Ramsey (970), Thorney (972), and Glastonbury, which was extended by Dunstan in the tenth century. Among those of which parts survive Elmham (c. 1000) and Peterborough (970 and earlier) may be mentioned.

We know the church at Canterbury, presumably the edifice resulting from building done by Archbishop Odo (940–60), from Eadmer's description only.[2] It had a nave, with two aisles and two square porticus at the middle, one on either side, like small transepts; there was a semicircular apse at the east and probably a similar one at the west, as was usual in Germany. Odo may also

---

[1] *English Romanesque Architecture before the Conquest,* 79, and Fig. 19.

[2] *De Reliquiis S. Audoeni,* Corpus Christi College, Cambridge, printed in *Gervase of Canterbury,* i, Rolls Series (1879), 7. For a summary see C. E. Woodruff and W. Danks, *Memorials of the Cathedral and Priory of Christ in Canterbury,* London (1912), 19.

have been responsible for the lofty crypt which was built to afford a satisfactory sanctuary for the numerous relics that the cathedral possessed. In general, however, crypts were after this time much rarer in England than on the continent.

Winchester, as rebuilt by Æthelwold about 980, had a number of chapels, an atrium of considerable size, and a great five-staged tower, presumably of wood, which is depicted in St. Æthelwold's Benedictional (fol. 118v). The 'White church' at Durham, which

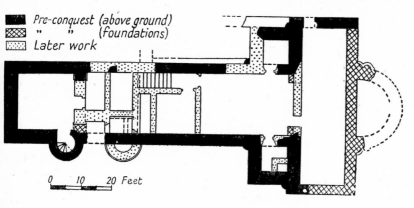

FIG. 5. *Elmham abbey*

was completed in 999, had two towers of stone, one at the west end, the other over the choir, probably at a crossing. The great church at Worcester was dedicated to St. Mary and was set up by Oswald beside the old one of St. Peter. It was pulled down in Norman times to make room for the new cathedral dedicated to St. Wulfstan; it was its very greatness that necessitated its destruction; had it been as small as St. Peter's, state the records, there would have been no necessity to pull it down. Ramsey abbey (968–74) had two towers; one apparently stood over the crossing and was supported by arches over the projecting arms. Thorney (c. 972) appears to have had altars at both ends, and was thus of the double-ended German type.

Of the cathedral at Elmham in Norfolk quite extensive portions remain and its plan can be clearly traced (Fig. 5). It is to be dated to the late tenth or early eleventh century. The nave was without aisles but had a transept at the east end, giving the building the form of the letter T. There was a semicircular apse projecting from the centre of the transept, a large tower at the west end, and two smaller ones in the angles between transept and nave.

At Peterborough parts of the church of Æthelwold, built between 970 and 972, have been discovered below the present cathedral. This building had a transept, with a small presbytery projecting from it. Remains so far excavated at Glastonbury do not give much help in explaining the very scanty textual references, but the church appears to have had a tower as well as a crypt.

All these were longitudinal buildings with separate nave and chancel; some, as for example Elmham and Ramsey, had transepts and apse as well. In fact the most usual plan for buildings of importance seems to have included a transept at the eastern extremity of the nave or choir, with a projecting presbytery beyond. The plan appears on a smaller scale in the church at Deerhurst. Though some of these churches were far from small, none appears to have approached the contemporary continental churches either in size or in the spatial conception of the edifice.

In addition to these larger buildings, which we would now class as cathedrals or abbeys, there were numerous smaller churches and today nearly 200 examples, which are wholly or in part Saxon, survive. Many more, such as that at Kingston, which served as the coronation church of the Saxon kings from the time of Alfred onwards, are known from the records. Those that survive are mostly in smaller villages or in out-of-the-way districts where large churches were not required in subsequent times or where no money was forthcoming to pay for reconstructions. The most important are probably those at Bradford-on-Avon in Wiltshire, at Deerhurst in Gloucestershire, at Wing in Buckinghamshire, at Stow in Lincolnshire, and at Great Paxton in Huntingdonshire. There are towers of outstanding quality at Earl's Barton, Barton-on-Humber, Barnack, and Sompting, and there is a very lovely crypt at Repton (Pl. 3).

Bradford-on-Avon is particularly interesting, for though small, and consisting of only two rectangular chambers end to end, it is very beautifully built of finely squared ashlar blocks, and serves to give an indication of the type of workmanship that one would doubtless have found in the larger cathedrals and abbeys, anyhow in the limestone region (Pl. 2 *a*). It must date from the earlier part of the tenth century. Like the older churches of Northumbria, it is unusually tall in relation to its length and breadth, and has few and small windows, set high up in the walls.

The church at Deerhurst is again fairly complete (Pl. 4 *a*). It belongs mainly to the mid-tenth century, and consists of a nave,

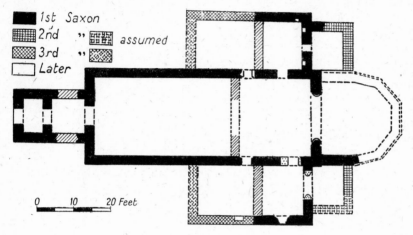

FIG. 6. *Deerhurst*

transept, transeptal chapels, polygonal apse, and a western tower (Fig. 6). If there was a tower at the crossing it must have been of wood, for the walls are too thin to have supported a superstructure of stone. The habit of placing two towers axially along the building which we see here appears to have been a general one, and it survived even into Norman times in spite of the wholesale introduction of French ideas, one of the most striking of which was the construction of twin towers at the western end on either side. As has already been noted there was at Deerhurst a gallery at the western end, which probably contained some form of altar, and so acted as a western sanctuary. The polygonal apse at Deerhurst is paralleled in the smaller tenth-century church at Wing in Buckinghamshire, and the form was probably a popular one at the time whenever an apse was included in the plan. At an earlier date semicircular apses were more usual. Deerhurst shows a number of features which were probably to be met with in several of the medium-sized, even perhaps in some of the larger churches of later Saxon times, and it is especially important from this point of view. For example, the church of St. Mary at Dover shows a similar disposition, with two towers in echelon along the axis of the building, and those at Winchester and Ramsey were similar in plan. The church of Great Paxton in Huntingdonshire shows work of eleventh-century date in the nave arcades, and the great arches that marked the crossing are very fine;[1] the transept has, however, disappeared. Of transeptal churches the best-preserved example is that at Stow in Lincolnshire, where the transepts are complete and where there are also handsome arches at the crossing. The church is additionally important because it is clearly dated to the time of Eadnoth, bishop of Dorchester from 1006 till 1016.[2]

The towers at Earl's Barton (Pl. 1) and Barton-on-Humber have already been discussed in connexion with blank arcading, but their very beautiful lines and proportions may be stressed here, for they serve to illustrate the charm of this late Saxon building. The Tower of St. Bennets', Cambridge, is similar; that of Barnack is very effective from inside because of the wide opening between its lower story and the body of the church (Pl. 4 b). The tower at Sompting may also be mentioned, for it is the only one that retains its original Saxon roof. This consists of a pyramidal tiled roof, set above a four-gabled square. Such roofs were usual in Germany in medieval times, and they appear to have been even more character-istic of Carolingian and Ottonian building in that country. It is likely that the form was also a usual one in England in Saxon times, though it was probably an import from Germany.

Lastly, the crypt at Repton may be cited (Pl. 3). It has a stone-vaulted roof set on four columns. Cross arches spring from the columns, and the vault is rudely groined. It must have been set up shortly after the year 1000, and though the crypt existed before that time, the capitals and columns are presumably of the same date as the vaulting. The capitals are very roughly carved, and the columns are decorated with a spiral moulding which is interesting

[1] R.C.H.M., *Huntingdonshire* (1926), 198 and Pls. 108–10.
[2] *Arch. Journ.* ciii. 168.

in that it heralds the more proficient and accomplished decoration on the great Norman columns at Durham.

A few buildings of more complicated shape than these churches, which are all little more than variants on the rectangle, may also be mentioned. One of the first, so far as we are concerned, must have been a church set up by Alfred at Athelney, which, according to Asser, had four columns in the centre. It is uncertain whether it was of stone or wood; if of stone, it may have been similar in plan and conception to the Repton crypt. Byzantine prototypes at once spring to mind. Asser says that Alfred built it after his own design, but this of course does not necessarily mean that he invented the plan but rather that it was something unusual at the time. Asser adds that the churches built by Alfred were in general 'more venerable and precious' than those which his predecessors had erected. This phrase would seem to imply not only that they were more elaborately decorated and contained more precious objects, but also that their plans were of a more ambitious and more poetic or spiritual character, and a centralized building is certainly not only more elaborate, but also more moving, emotionally speaking, than one of longitudinal plan.

Unfortunately, not one of Alfred's churches survives, but one very interesting building of centralized plan has been fully excavated, namely, St. Augustine's at Canterbury. There were originally two churches of rectangular plan on the site, the more westerly dedicated to SS. Peter and Paul, and the more easterly to the Virgin. They stood on the same axis but with a space in between. Abbot Wulfric (1047–59) set out to join them by constructing between the two a centralized building, octagonal outside and circular inside. One side of the octagon took the place of the western wall of St. Mary's, its opposite side that of the eastern wall of SS. Peter and Paul. On its north and south faces there were semicircular buttress towers, which projected like apses. Within these was a second circle consisting of eight piers which supported the roof. It would thus seem that this stood on a drum and was higher than that of the surrounding area; whether or not it was domed in the manner of Sta. Constanza at Rome it is impossible to say.

This singular and extremely ambitious edifice was left unfinished at Abbot Wulfric's death, and the whole complex of buildings was pulled down to make way for a new structure in the time of Abbot Scotland (1070–87). Luckily the foundations were left practically untouched by Scotland's workmen, so that now that the site has been excavated the plan can be exactly traced. Though somewhat simpler, the disposition is very close indeed to that of St. Bénigne at Dijon, which was erected by Volpiano between 1011 and 1018. There appear, however, to have been quite a number of buildings of similar plan in Carolingian times of which the most important was Charlemagne's church at Aachen. Wulfric must have been inspired by one of them; perhaps it was Dijon, for he very probably passed through that place when he visited Rome in 1047; or perhaps it was even Sta. Constanza itself, which he could easily have seen whilst he was in Rome.

The general character of all Saxon churches, more especially with regard to the nature of many of the details, the presence of bell towers, and the love of the western sanctuary, savours strongly of the Carolingian world. Even the great popularity of the single-aisled plan is paralleled in the hall churches of Germany. But still the actual buildings have an essentially English character. A number of features which are characteristic of this island above anything else can be distinguished and tabulated, and they are listed below. But well-nigh equally important are the more intangible factors of style, which it is often very hard to define in exact terms. One can do little more than say that there is something about the style and spirit of the buildings that distinguishes them as English, even if the intrinsic elements that go to compose them can all be traced to some part of the continent.

Of the more definite English factors, the most important is probably the great popularity in the smaller churches of a plan consisting of two rectangles end to end, the eastern one smaller than the western; the two are usually separated by a comparatively narrow chancel arch. But there are other features, which though less obvious, are equally important. Such are a love of placing windows high up in the walls, an affection for the old porticus or side chamber communicating with the main body of the church by a small opening only, and the predominance of the square east end which was present in nearly all the smaller churches and in some of the larger ones also. These features have an added significance, for they not only appear as characteristically English in Saxon times but tend to crop up again and again long after the Anglo-Saxon style had given place to Norman or Gothic. Thus the square east end is often found in Norman churches of large and elaborate type as well as in the smaller ones; it supplanted the French form with projecting apse, usually with chapels radiating from it. Small chapels of a

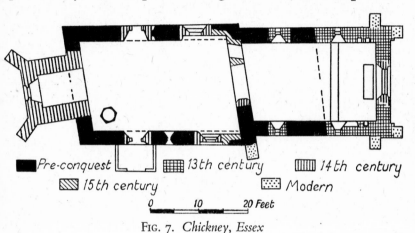

Pre-conquest   13th century   14th century

15th century   Modern

0   10   20 Feet

FIG. 7. *Chickney, Essex*

semi-detached character, and not intrinsic parts of the edifice, are again far more usual in the Gothic churches and cathedrals of England than they are in France. And though windows grew in size and came nearer to the ground as time went on, the wall space was never eliminated in this country to quite the degree that it was in France where Gothic buildings became practically all window and no wall. Another feature which may also be claimed as typically English is an irregularity or absence of care in setting out the plan. A close study of Anglo-Saxon plans shows it in a large number of instances; the plan of the small church at Chickney in Essex may be cited as an extreme example, for there is hardly a true right angle in it (Fig. 7). And irregularity, if not inexactitude, is apparent all through Norman and Gothic work in this country, and indeed survives as a distinctive feature till even more recent times. The English builder always loved to do things free-hand; his more logically minded continental confrère preferred to have recourse to mathematical proportions and measurements. Yet it is perhaps this very irregularity that constitutes much of the charm of Saxon architecture. The rather clumsy detail of the mouldings of arches and windows, the rough masonry of the walls, the somewhat top-heavy circular columns that separate the bays of the windows, and the rather dumpy windows; all these things go together to constitute both the character and the attractiveness of the style. The churches seem to grow out of the landscape, with all the irregularity, yet all the natural beauty of a plant or tree. More finished or more exact workmanship would rob these buildings of a great deal of their charm and their spontaneity.

IV

EARLY NORMAN ARCHITECTURE IN ENGLAND

I. ECCLESIASTICAL ARCHITECTURE

QUITE early in the eleventh century a very distinctive type of large church, in the construction of which a number of new and important architectural ideas were involved, had become usual in Normandy. Such buildings were characterized by long-aisled naves usually with two western towers, transepts usually with one or more apsidal chapels in each arm, and short aisled choirs terminating in apses. None of these characteristic features was in fact indigenous to Normandy, for they appeared at an earlier date in central and southern France, and the ambulatory type of apse, which we see fully developed at Jumièges before the middle of the century, was also probably taken over from the south, where the plan had been developed by the Benedictines for their pilgrimage churches. Whether these features were first evolved there or in Lombardy is a problem that does not concern us here; it suffices to accept the fact that it was in central France that they were most fully developed.

It was, however, in Normandy that a series of constructional features and further elaborations of great importance, affecting the upper structure of the buildings, were first extensively developed, most notably the full triforium and clerestory. Wall shafts from the floor to the roof of the aisle, usually at alternate bays, also appeared some time before the problem of throwing a vault across the main aisle had ever been tackled; they were doubtless intended to support diaphragm arches, i.e. large arches thrown across the aisle to aid in the construction of the wooden roof and also to buttress the high walls of the nave on the insides; the outsides were upheld by the side aisles. By the early eleventh century, the side aisles were often already roofed with stone vaults, and in a few churches were topped by half-arches inclined against the walls of the main aisle like obscured flying buttresses.

These features, combined and developed in Normandy, found their way to England even before 1066, for Edward the Confessor's church at Westminster, built between 1045 and 1050, was already in the new style. Thus, had there been no Norman invasion, this style would no doubt have penetrated gradually, but it would never have completely ousted the Saxon style in the course of two decades in the way that it did. As it was, a period of tremendous activity in church building followed upon the Conquest, and in the next thirty years the reconstruction of practically all the more important Saxon cathedrals or monastic churches had been put in hand and the building of cathedrals for a whole series of new foundations had been begun.[1] This activity only slackened off in the last few years of the century as a result of William Rufus's anti-ecclesiastical policy and a consequent lack of funds; there was, however, renewed activity in the early twelfth century, and it is to that century, rather than to the eleventh, that the accomplishment of the works set on foot by the Conqueror is to be assigned. Indeed, the original eleventh-century schemes were frequently enlarged and elaborated in the twelfth.

The majority of the larger buildings in the new style were composed of purely Norman elements, and we have to wait until the twelfth century before ideas and constructional systems that were characteristically English and not importations once more came to the surface. Sculpture and painting, on the other hand, remained of a more conservative character, and in these arts works which were purely Saxon in style continued to be produced till well after 1100. This was principally because the Normans, though great builders, paid less attention to figural sculpture, whether in the tympana or on the capitals, than did the Romanesque builders of the rest of France; in the south and centre of that country the case was very different; sculptures in the area were of the finest from the very inception of the Romanesque style. In Normandy, in the eleventh

[1] For a particularly clear account of how the new abbeys rose up see M. M. Morgan, 'The abbey of Bec-Hellouin and its English priories', *Journ. Brit. Arch. Ass.*, 3rd series, v (1940), 33.

century on the other hand, there was little but ornamental work of a non-representational or stylized character. The difference in taste between the regions is no doubt to be accounted for by the prevalence of Norse blood in the one and of Latin blood in the other area; the Norsemen, even though in many respects completely Frenchified, nevertheless, in others remained faithful to the old tastes of their national breeding, to which figural art was something entirely foreign.

But even though all the elements that composed these churches were completely Norman, England soon succeeded in one way or another in putting a national complexion upon them. Edward the Confessor's church at Westminster, though its plan was close to that of French examples, was, with its twelve-bayed nave, much longer than any contemporary church in Normandy, and at St. Mary's, York, St. Albans, and elsewhere, five or sometimes seven eastern chapels were set in echelon to the east of the choir and transepts in place of the three usual in Normandy. Both of these features, a love of length, and an elaboration of the square east end, underwent great developments and soon became perhaps the most essentially English characteristics of the new style. The English builders, again, were less exacting with regard to towers, and the system of one at the crossing and two at the west end, over the side aisles, which is so typical of Normandy, was not generally adhered to in England, even in theory, and it was still less often followed in practice, for plans which included this feature when originally drawn up seem to have been frequently changed during the progress of building. We see the Norman disposition for instance at Southwell, but elsewhere the old Saxon habit of placing two towers axially, one over the crossing and one at the western end over the nave—followed for instance at Deerhurst and St. Mary's, Dover—made an early reappearance. Ely, Bury St. Edmunds, Winchester, and other buildings thus followed this disposition. It is, however, impossible to dogmatize on this point, for many of the earlier towers of the Norman period in England have fallen owing to the poorness of the masonry, and subsequent restorations in many cases swept away all trace of them. Norman walls, though invariably thicker than Saxon—the latter are never more than 3 feet thick and often less—were seldom as well built or as strong. It would seem that the great building activity of the years immediately succeeding the conquest set a demand on craftsmen and skilled masons which the supply was inadequate to fulfil.

As we have already noted, a number of constructional features which were essentially English came once more into prominence in the twelfth century: such are the square eastern end, found both in the main building and in the 'choir', and the small rectangular presbytery, as at Southwell (c. 1120). They contrast markedly with the two more elaborate types of eastern termination, the apsed and ambulatory, and the tri-apsidal. A larger number of churches of both types were erected here shortly after the conquest. The most important examples of the apsed and ambulatory plan were the Conqueror's abbey at Battle (1067–94), Bury St. Edmunds (c. 1070), St. Augustine's, Canterbury (c. 1073–99), Winchester (1079), Worcester (1084), Chichester (c. 1092), Norwich (c. 1096), Old St. Paul's (1087), Chester (1092), Gloucester (1089), and Tewkesbury (1087). The tri-apsidal plan was employed at Westminster (1045–65), Canterbury cathedral (1070), Lincoln (1072), Old Sarum (c. 1076), St. Albans (1077), Rochester (1077), Ely (c. 1090), St. Mary's, York (1089), and Durham (1093).[1]

It is also tempting to explain the love of inordinately tall columns which characterizes a group of west-country churches, notably Gloucester (1089) and Tewkesbury (1087), as being the result of a return to ideas prevalent in Saxon times when tall, narrow interiors were favoured; Bradford-on-Avon is an example of the tenth, Monkwearmouth of the seventh century. The disposition of Tewkesbury is especially interesting, for there were four instead of the usual three stories; the same was true of Pershore, and M. Bony has shown that these English examples antedate the earliest known on the continent.[2] Nor is it necessary to go to the continent, or even to the Near East with the Crusaders,

---

[1] The dates are those of commencing work; in many cases the buildings were not completed for quite a number of years; but in many of them the original disposition was adhered to, even if the buildings were made longer.

[2] 'Tewkesbury et Pershore', *Bull. Mon.* (1937), 281 and 503.

to explain the presence of centrally planned churches, for, as we have shown above, examples were known in England before the conquest. But the most spectacular churches of this type, the Temple in London and similar buildings at Cambridge and Northampton, are so closely associated with crusading knights that the church of the Holy Sepulchre at Jerusalem must in their case be accepted as the most direct source of inspiration.

Of the actual eleventh-century churches that survive to this day, the two that are earliest in style, if not actually in date, are the chapel in the White tower of the Tower of London, and Blyth priory in Nottinghamshire. The former, so far as the outside is concerned, is entirely concealed within the fortress-like construction of the Tower (see p. 78); inside it is severe and plain, but its balanced proportions are of very great beauty. The latter, Blyth priory, has been altered considerably at various periods, but much of the original work survives, and though the priory was only founded in 1088, its style is conservative, and suggests a comparison with Jumièges in France, one of the earliest of Norman buildings. Like the chapel in the Tower, it is very plain and severe, and contrasts markedly with the more ornate Durham, though the latter is actually only a few years later in date.

No study of early Anglo-Norman architecture would be complete without due consideration of the question of the development of vaulting: this was indeed perhaps the most important contribution that the Romanesque style brought to the art of building as a whole, for it was thanks to the tentative efforts made by the Romanesque builders in France and Lombardy that the superb achievements of Gothic vaultings were possible at a later date. The diaphragm arches of the early eleventh-century buildings are the first indications of what was in the architects' minds, and though most early Norman churches were roofed with wood, the systems of buttressing that survive at several places on the continent and at Norwich (c. 1096), Chichester (c. 1092), and Gloucester (1089) in this country, suggest that the intention had been to throw a groined vault over the main aisle, even if in practice the builders did not dare to take the risk or had to substitute a wooden roof for reasons of economy. And at Durham the whole church was intended to be roofed with an elaborate system of ribbed vaults from the very day that its construction began in 1093. Other examples followed it in the early twelfth century. Durham is in fact the earliest example, in England and on the continent alike, of the employment of fully developed ribbed vaulting on a large scale, and it marks a vital stage in architectural history.[1] It is, in addition, one of the most beautiful churches in the world both with regard to its interior and its external proportions, in no way marred —perhaps even improved—by the more recent central tower.

This question of superficial appearance, using the word literally as applying to the surface and not in the accustomed rather scathing sense, is an extremely important one, for though the Norman style is almost invariably described as strong and solid, it did, nevertheless, owe a good deal of its delight to the quality of its mouldings and arcadings and to the decorative treatment of its façades, and did not depend for its appeal purely and simply on line and proportion. The great central tower of Tewkesbury, which belongs to the twelfth century, serves as an admirable example of the fullest culmination of this idea; its whole conception is ornate, and the interplay of light and shade on its intricately arcaded surfaces is a thing of very rare beauty. The treatment is far more plastic and aesthetically finer than the purely linear ornament of Saxon façades as seen for instance on the tower of Earl's Barton. The same thing is obviously true of the more ornate interiors such as Durham or Dunfermline, and even if Gloucester, Tewkesbury, or St. Albans seem at first severe and plain, further examination discloses that the mouldings and the capitals, though simple, are, nevertheless, extremely forceful, and the triforia are almost always of an essentially ornamental character. And when we come to the sculpture of the doorways, though figural work is rare, the conception was often a decorative one in spite of apparent plainness. This is, of course, especially true of

---

[1] French authorities are prone to disregard Durham; it affords, however, the earliest surviving instance of the system. The evolution probably actually took place in Italy—Pavia and St. Ambrogio at Milan may be noted—or in south central France. The fullest development was, of course, in the Île de France a generation or so later. See J. Bilson, *Arch. Journ.*, lxxxix, 1922, p. 101.

twelfth-century work, such as the south porch of Malmesbury, but it is apparent even in early Anglo-Norman work as, for instance, in a door in the north transept at Winchester (*c.* 1080) now walled up, which dates from the time of Bishop Walkelin (1079–93). The Norman may have been inept as a figural sculptor, and he may have left his capitals plain as often as not; yet he had, without doubt, an innate feeling for architectural ornament even if a detailed stylistic analysis of the elements of this ornament, chevrons, cables, beak-heads, and so on, is hardly possible before the twelfth century. The same subtle sense of the decorative effect to be achieved by simple mouldings also characterizes the monastic, as opposed to the strictly ecclesiastical, work, and it is even apparent in the most sober of all styles, the Cistercian.

The change over to the new Norman architecture was much less sudden with regard to the smaller village churches, and in the more out-of-the-way districts there was quite a considerable over-lap of styles; it was probably most marked in the west country and along the Lincolnshire borders. Even in these places, however, it was never as considerable as at subsequent periods, that is to say, the overlap of the Saxon style over the Norman in time is much less considerable than that of the Norman over the Early English or of the latter over the Decorated phase of Gothic. By 1080 or thereabouts, in fact, buildings which were intrinsically Saxon had ceased to be erected, and the new Norman style had become prevalent. And with it there came, in the smaller churches, a few distinctive systems of construction, which seem to have been absent in the more sumptuous buildings. Most obvious is the use of herring-bone masonry, which was very rare in Saxon times, and became unusual once more after about 1100.[1] Rough stone-work, and in ashlar construction the use of very thick joints, were again typical of Norman building in the eleventh century; with the development of the style in the twelfth century the joints usually became finer in the ashlar and the stones were more

---

[1] The system was occasionally used in pre-Romanesque work on the continent, especially in Spain, but in England it was probably indigenous, rather than introduced. For its use in Spain as early as the mid-tenth century see Puig i Cadafalch, *Le Premier Art Roman*, 12.

carefully laid; such work was only possible when the requisite number of properly trained masons was forthcoming.

2. SECULAR ARCHITECTURE

In a work which is mainly concerned with art, little need be said of secular architecture, in the first place because we know very little about it, and in the second because there is nothing in what we do know that suggests that it is worthy of separate consideration from the artistic point of view; in so far as it rose above mere building, it became allied to ecclesiastical architecture, and is to be considered with it. This is especially true of the Norman period when castles show the same type of masonry, arching, vaulting, and surface decoration as do the churches; the keep at the Tower of London known as the White Tower may be cited as an example.

Castles built of masonry and involving elaborate constructional problems were unknown in Saxon times, when fortified places were no more than mounds topped by a stockade. The idea of combining a fort and a dwelling place in one building seems to have been brought to this country from France shortly before the time of the conquest, probably as a result of the contacts with France initiated by Edward the Confessor, but no remains of pre-conquest date survive and the earliest structures that we know are to be attributed to the building policy of William I. The foundations that go back to his day are numerous, but many of them were doubtless no more than earthworks like that at Dinan shown on the Bayeux tapestry. Only at Exeter, Colchester, and in the White Tower in London does masonry survive which is probably to be assigned to William's reign. Work at Corfe, Richmond, Tamworth, and Durham is, however, probably eleventh-century; at Tamworth there is a great wall of herring-bone masonry like those in some of the churches of the period.[1]

The White tower at London, founded by the Conqueror and completed by William Rufus in 1097, is by far the most important piece of pre-twelfth-century secular architecture. Though it was subsequently much altered, its form seems in the main to have

---

[1] For a list of these early castles see A. H. Thompson, *Military Architecture in England during the Middle Ages*, London (1912), ch. 3.

been much the same then as it is now, that is to say, it was four
stories in height even then, and was divided internally into two
parts by a dividing wall. One half was again subdivided at right
angles to form two unequal sections, the larger occupied by St.
John's chapel, its sub-crypt on the lowest floor and the chapel itself standing on the second floor but rising through the third. The
rest of the building may have been divided into smaller rooms by
wooden partitions, but these have now gone. They were, however,
probably few in number, so that the maximum use could be made
of the large hall-like rooms. These today seem somewhat gaunt,
but St. John's chapel, though very plain and simple, is truly
architectural and an effect of great beauty is achieved. It is especially
interesting as it is the oldest complete Norman church in this
country. The great keep at Colchester was of the same date as the
White tower and followed the same plan, though it was larger;
its two upper stories have unfortunately gone. As at the tower, the
eastern apse of the chapel jutted out to form a bastion-like tower
on that face. Though a number of other square keeps, such as
Rochester or Dover survive they are all of twelfth-century date,
and so fall outside our period.

Another important secular building of this time was Westminster hall, which was William Rufus's most important contribution to architecture. The fact that it was in building at the same
time as the White tower suggests that, though the keeps were
certainly used for residential purposes, they were primarily intended
for defence, and that anyhow in the capital, the keep was resorted
to only in case of necessity. A palace, which was basically a dwelling rather than a fort, had existed at Westminster in any case
since the beginning of the century; it stood between the abbey
and the river. It is figured thrice in the Bayeux tapestry, where
Edward is depicted seated on his throne in a hall, giving instructions
to Harold, and again near the middle, where the death of Edward
is shown as taking place in an upper story of the palace (Pl. 95).
The hall was large with a wide-spanned roof, and the outer walls
appear to have been of rough stone; a small staircase tower stood
at either side of the main façade and this was two-storied. Two-
storied buildings appear indeed to have been fairly usual in late

Saxon times, for it is recorded in the Anglo-Saxon Chronicle that in 987 the Witan met at Calne in an upper room, the floor of which collapsed, killing some, wounding others, and leaving St. Dunstan, who was present, suspended on a beam. If Calne could boast a two-storied building, many other places could no doubt do so also.

The Saxon palace of Westminster was destroyed to make room for a new one by William Rufus, and his edifice remained in being till the reign of Richard II when it was remodelled, though the original ground plan and a considerable part of the walling of Rufus's great hall was not affected and survives to this day. This building was of stone and, like that of today, it was 240 feet long and 67½ feet wide, though it was probably not as high as the present structure.[1] This building must have been very striking; it was the first great secular edifice in the country and William Rufus—by no means a liberal patron of the arts—is reputed to have expressed regrets that it was not even larger. It also seems to have stood alone; in any case we know practically nothing of any other secular building of the same character at this time.[2] The majority of such buildings were no doubt of wood rather than stone and as a result of fires they have failed to survive.

[1] I. M. Cooper, 'Westminster Hall', *Journ. Brit. Arch. Ass.*, 3rd series, i (1937), 168. Lethaby, 'The Palace of Westminster in the eleventh and twelfth centuries', *Archaeol.*, 2nd series, x (1906), 131.

[2] For a full survey of domestic architecture, most of which falls outside the period of this volume, see Margaret Wood, 'Norman domestic architecture', *Arch. Journ.* xcii (1935), 167–242. She cites thirty-nine examples.

V

SCULPTURE

I. GENERAL

A GENERATION ago the accepted view was that the most glorious sculpture ever produced in the western world was that of the Gothic cathedrals; more recently the quality of French Romanesque has come to be realized, and more recently still the excellence of what was done in Northumbria around the year 700 has been admitted. But in addition to these great ages, there was another period when large-scale sculptures of high quality were produced, though it is less well known and the surviving works that are to be assigned to it are extremely few owing to the devastations of time. This period comprises roughly the generation on either side of the year 1000, and works of quality were produced on the continent and in this country alike. On the continent the best work was mainly in metal; it is associated with the name of Bernward, bishop of Hildesheim in Germany from 1008 till 1052. In the British Isles, so far as we know, work was mainly in stone, but wood may also have been important though no examples have survived. But of the stone-work enough material of high quality exists not only to attest that England was in the forefront as a centre of religious sculpture at this time, but also to suggest that it was likewise the home of a number of innovators to whose experiments the great achievements of the twelfth-century sculptors of France are perhaps to some degree to be attributed. There are thus stylistic resemblances between work in England which, in our view, should be assigned to the Saxon period, and work in France which belongs to the twelfth century. At times, indeed, the resemblances are so close that it is tempting to suggest the movement of actual craftsmen; at others they are to be seen more with regard to the nature of the ornament than in style or technique, and are thus more probably to be attributed to the employment by French sculptors of manuscript models of English origin than to the transit of actual workmen.

The evidence, indeed, suggests that English manuscripts were quite extensively used for this purpose on the continent. Worringer has called attention to the fact that the famous St. Peter of Moissac and the Isaiah of Souillac, both of the first quarter of the twelfth century, reproduce exactly the conventions and idiosyncrasies of tenth-century English miniatures such as one in the British Museum (Roy. 1 E. VI);[1] and Kingsley Porter has noted the fact that some of the capitals at Cluny (c. 1094) and Vezelay (c. 1120) must have been inspired by a manuscript or manuscripts of the Winchester school.[2] The facial type of the figures is, in fact, closely similar, the fluttering draperies so characteristic of the Winchester school also appear on the capitals, and the surfaces of the costumes show the same conventional folds which suggest the inspiration of the old spiral ornament of northern art rather than any feeling for the modelling of the form beneath. The long slender feet and hands which characterize the sculptures of Autun again appear to be modelled on those of such a manuscript as St. Æthelwold's Benedictional, while the aedicular canopies, flying angels, and aureoles which we see in King Edgar's Charter were copied in sculpture at Cluny; indeed the sculptor there really translated into stone the types and manners of Winchester illumination. The tympanum of St. Julien de Jonzy shows clearly the influence of Winchester ornament; the figures of Cain and Abel at St. Gilles have a very Saxon appearance, and a group of the Virgin and Child at Donzy in the Nièvre is again similar. So close are all these in style to Anglo-Saxon works that it would even seem possible that there may at times have been some more direct exchange, affecting sculpture itself. Perhaps some such work as the Barnack Christ (Pl. 19 a) even reached France early in the eleventh century; it is surprisingly close in appearance to a sculpture

---

[1] 'Über den Einfluss der Angelsächsischen Buchmalerei auf die frühmittelalterliche Monumentalplastik des Kontinents', in *Schriften der Königsburger gelehrten Gesellschaft*, 1931.

[2] *Romanesque Sculpture of the Pilgrimage Roads*, i. 98.

of the same subject at Poitiers (Pl. 19 *b*; see pp. 114 f.). Even so, however, an indirect influence by way of manuscripts must have been more important than a direct connexion, if such ever existed, for manuscripts can be easily transported, whereas sculptures cannot. Nor, though some of the individual examples are very fine, was there ever a distinctive school of sculpture in England in the way that there was in miniature painting. With regard to the illuminations, the term Winchester school does convey a definite impression of a class of work which, wherever it may have been done, bears a clear stylistic hall-mark; and, further, apart from the work of this type, little of importance was produced. But in sculpture there does not seem to have been any such universal style; the sculpture of crosses intended to stand out of doors is generally quite different in appearance from that of slabs meant to stand indoors; work done in the more cultivated centres is quite distinct from that of the outlying districts; sculptures of a monumental figural character are quite different from those of a decorative or ornamental nature. The play of a number of diverse streams of influence is to be seen, and the sculptures in which the role of one of them was in preponderance are often so absolutely distinct from those which show the workings of another that one would hardly attribute them to the same age or country; the Romsey Rood (Pl. 13) and the slab from old St. Paul's in the Guildhall Museum (Pl. 23 *a*) may, for example, be contrasted. The two are of much the same date and both were carved in southern England, yet they are completely different in every other respect.

Because of this diversity, the problems of dating are immeasurably complicated. In the first place, the repertory of ornament was so similar in Britain and in northern Europe that it is at times hard to distinguish the effects of a new, imported inspiration from those of an old one that had long lain dormant; in the second, work was sometimes so crude that it is hard to tell whether a newly imported model had been copied by an incompetent craftsman or whether the scheme of some old Northumbrian sculpture had been followed after it had undergone a long and progressive decadence. And thirdly, work was sometimes so accomplished and finished that it is tempting to suggest that foreign workmen as well as foreign prototypes must at times have penetrated to this country. Indeed, so excellent is much of the work that more than one authority has questioned whether it should not be assigned to Norman art and to the late eleventh or twelfth century rather than to Saxon art and to the tenth or first half of the eleventh. Nor is the geographical distribution of the various styles very consistent. The best late Saxon figural sculpture is undoubtedly to be associated with Wessex, but some of it is to be found in Mercia or even in southern Northumbria, and we here and there also find in the south monuments which are completely northern in spirit. When this is the case, the monuments are not always to be dated to the same period as would apply if they occurred in the north, for there was often a considerable time-lag between the penetration of an idea and its adoption in a far distant area.

In spite of such difficulties, however, certain generalizations may be permitted. First, Scandinavian influence appeared slightly before the time of the Danish settlements and remained predominant in the north from then until the Norman conquest, though works showing it quite clearly are to be found distributed sporadically elsewhere. Nor did works of Scandinavian type entirely cease to be produced at the conquest. In his survey of the crosses of Westmorland and Cumberland, Collingwood concludes that the Norman conquest was, in that area at least, more a peaceful penetration than a deluge.[1] The old art remained unchanged for at least a century, and only then did new motifs come in; but even so the old interlacings and key pattern motifs survived in popular art almost till the present day. Norman stylistic elements did not appear before the twelfth century, and it is thus not easy to date Saxon material precisely to a pre- or post-conquest date. What Collingwood says of Westmorland and of Cumberland also holds good in great part for Yorkshire, Lancashire, and Derbyshire, and except in architecture changes as a result of the Norman conquest were far from rapid even in the southern counties.

Secondly, it is probable that the centre of high-quality production

[1] See his introduction to W. S. Calverley, 'Notes on the early sculptured crosses in the diocese of Carlisle', *Cumb. & West. Ant. and Arch. Soc.*, extra series, vol. xi (1899).

gradually moved southwards. The best work in the seventh
and eighth centuries was thus produced in Northumbria. Then,
around the year 800 the most important centre was Mercia;
finally, in the tenth century, Wessex became the main centre,
though today many more sculptures of the period actually survive,
if the crosses are included, in the north of England than in the
south.

A third and important conclusion that may be drawn is that
there was in existence, even before the days of Alfred, what may
for the sake of convenience be termed a 'court' school which was
responsible for a number of better-finished, more sophisticated
works than were executed in general. From early days the Breedon
slabs serve as examples; from later ones such sculptures as the
Romsey Rood are outstanding. Products of this class are found all
over the country; they are usually slabs or individual figures,
intended to be set up inside buildings rather than crosses for
erection out of doors, and the work, even when on a small scale,
is of an essentially monumental character, whereas that of the
crosses is much more detailed and ornamental. The former are,
in fact, in what Sir Joshua Reynolds called the 'Great' style, the
latter in what he called the 'Ornamental'. The work of the
'court' group shows far closer links with the continent than does
that of the provincial schools. Here too, however, distinctions
can be made between works like the Inglesham Madonna (Pl. 15 a)
and the Wormington Crucifixion (Pl. 11 b), which follow continental models crudely and at a distance, and works like the mid-
tenth-century cross in Leeds parish church (Pl. 24 b), which, even
when they are accomplished and finished, are in the direct line
of descent from the crosses of the eighth century; if Mediterranean
influence is present here it was conveyed by way of the old
Northumbrian school and not from the contemporary continent.

Finally, it should always be borne in mind that our picture of
the sculpture of this age is lamentably incomplete. There was
probably a great deal of work in wood and perhaps also in metal
and stucco, and all this has now perished, while even of the
stone-work only a very small proportion now remains. We
have already alluded to the importance of wood in English

architecture (pp. 52 f.), and in Germany, in France, and especially in Italy the material was widely used for sculpture also. The famous Volto Santo at Lucca may be cited by way of example. In Germany and Italy, again, much work of high quality was done in metal,[1] and it may also have been used much more widely in this country than surviving examples suggest, though it is hardly likely that anything on quite the same scale was done in England as in Germany. In France and to some extent also in Germany there is, again, evidence that stucco was probably used quite frequently in Ottonian and more especially in Carolingian times. Carolingian influence counts for so much in Anglo-Saxon art that the taste for stucco sculpture may well have penetrated along with other fashions; indeed, fragments of carved stucco were found in the Saxon layers at Glastonbury, and there are some carvings *in situ* on the capitals of Milborne Port in Somerset.

Though the period dealt with in this volume begins with the age of Alfred, there are certain sculptures, which have usually been assigned to a date in the ninth century before his accession, that must be considered at the outset, for they show the same marked continental affinities that are apparent in later Saxon work as a whole. The most notable examples are the slabs at Breedon in Leicestershire; they have sometimes even been dated to the eighth century. Though all the Breedon work is probably of the same date, it is to be assigned to at least three distinct hands. The first was responsible for the largest slab only. This slab is 3 feet high and shows an angel standing full length in a niche, the right hand raised in blessing; the manner of blessing is that of the Greek church, with the fourth finger bent to touch the thumb, and not that which was used in the west (Pl. 5 a). The relief is fairly high and very incisive, and the style rather classical—the same kind of classicism that one sees in Carolingian ivories. The whole feeling is essentially continental, and it is tempting to regard the slab as altogether outside the line of normal development from Northumbrian prototypes; its classicism is likely to be due to a contemporary trend of influence from Europe, conveyed by means of an ivory or a manuscript

[1] For a list of German metal-work sculpture at this period see A. Kingsley Porter, *Spanish Romanesque Sculpture* (1928), 42. For Italy see his *Lombardic Architecture.*

illustration. The style and iconography are close to those of the ivories of the Ada group in the Carolingian world, and our sculpture may have been inspired by one of these; a small plaque in the Victoria and Albert Museum bearing the annunciation and the nativity (No. 267—1867) may be compared. The idea of placing a figure under an arch in this way was common to both Carolingian and Byzantine art. If a Carolingian model was indeed used, the Breedon slab could hardly date from before 820 or thereabouts at the earliest, and a dating in the eighth century would be precluded. But if a Byzantine prototype had been employed, an earlier dating would be possible even if improbable; in this case the similarity of the Breedon sculpture and the Ada group ivories would be accounted for by the east Christian elements in both.

The second Breedon style is to be seen in a number of smaller slabs bearing figures; most important is one 2 feet high and rounded at the top, so forming a niche, in which is a half-length figure with draped head; the left hand holds a book; the right, which is very large and clumsy, is extended across the chest (Pl. 5 b). Kendrick compares it to a figure in the Book of Cerne (818–30), but the style of the figure in the Book of Cerne is much closer to Celtic art, and the resemblance is hardly to be attributed to anything more than a common descent from the same remote ancestor. The iconography of the figure is, however, puzzling; the head and drapery are those proper to the Virgin in Byzantine art; the attitude is more similar to that usually associated with Christ. The figure may, however, be taken as representing the Virgin, and the model followed by the English sculptor must have been either a Carolingian or a Byzantine ivory of a type very common from the ninth century onwards. One of the panels of an ivory casket in the Museo Nazionale at Florence, which was probably made in Constantinople, may be compared;[1] though it is of later date (twelfth century) it reproduces well-nigh exactly an iconographic model of a very much earlier period.

The same hand that worked this Virgin was probably also responsible for the friezes, which show a number of small figures standing in niches or arcades; they represent the Apostles. They

[1] F. Volbach, G. Salles, G. Duthuit, *Art Byzantin*, Paris (1932), Pl. 36.

have the same large clumsy hands and the same rather frozen appearance as the plaque bearing the Virgin. Kendrick notes that the capitals of the columns from which the arcades spring again show relationships to the Book of Cerne.

A third and softer style is apparent in a rectangular plaque, 19 inches high, bearing two persons standing in a light, dancing attitude, with heads in higher relief; their appearance is distinctly Romanesque. Work that is closely similar appears at Fletton, near Peterborough, where two plaques, each bearing single figures in niches, have been built into the walls of the church. They have usually been dated to the eighth century, primarily because ornamental friezes, obviously of that date, exist in the same church. But as the slabs are built into later walling, they need not be of the same date. At Castor in Northamptonshire a small slab, again built into a later wall, is of the same type; it bears a standing figure in a niche. The detail of the costume is here more elaborately indicated and the style as a whole is more linear. A number of crosses[1] and a small gabled sarcophagus known as the Hedda stone at Peterborough belong to the same group.

Now the geographical situation of most of these stones, taken in conjunction with the quality and character of the work, suggests that they can only have been carved when Mercia was prosperous. From about 830 till after 880 the region was hardly in the state one would deem necessary; there was no unified control, and even the monasteries were more or less extinct. Before that time the region saw great prosperity under Offa (757–96); after that time it participated to some extent in the renaissance of Alfred and his successors. One would thus at once suggest a date either in the second half of the eighth, or in the early tenth century, but hardly one in the full ninth. Concensus of opinion has favoured the former conclusion, and on the basis of the ornamental work it seems on the whole the more likely; but the continental character of the slabs is in agreement with the trend of influences that we believe characterized art in the tenth century, so that a later dating cannot be absolutely

[1] Notably those at Sheffield, at Bradborne and Wirksworth in Derbyshire, at Stapleford in Nottinghamshire, at Ilkley in Yorkshire, at Edenham and at Bishop Auckland. See A. W. Clapham, *English Romanesque Architecture*, i. 70.

precluded. Apart from this possibility, however, these stones concern us, for they point the road to the part played by prototypes which were ultimately of Byzantine origin, and it is a road we shall have cause to travel again more than once as we proceed.

A small gravestone known as the Lechmere stone, preserved at Hanley Castle in Worcestershire, may also be noted here, for it, too, shows continental affinities. It is of local stone, 1 foot 8 inches high, and bears on one face a standing figure of Christ, holding a Bible in one hand, and with a cruciform nimbus. The peaky face and deep-set eyes are essentially Mercian, but the position must have been inspired by a Byzantine model, even though the second hand is not raised in the attitude of blessing as was usual there. The edge of the stone, which is 3–4 inches thick, is decorated with a graceful scroll, and on the reverse there is a cross head in a circle with a plant rising up on either side of its balustre-like shaft. It may be regarded as a western variant of the eastern leaved-cross motif. A similar motif, cruder and more roughly carved, appears on a cross at Whitchurch in Hampshire. If these motifs do indeed represent the leaved cross, they constitute the most westerly example of a motif which was popularized by Nestorian Christians, and was not only adopted from them in Armenia and the Byzantine world, but was also carried by them to India and China. It was particularly important in the Byzantine world in the iconoclast period, and in this country could hardly date from before about 800 and is more likely to be later.[1]

One further monument which has usually been dated before our period must also be examined before we pass on to a discussion of stones which are universally regarded as post-Alfredian; it is the lovely 'cross' at Codford St. Peter, between Salisbury and Warminster, and it is particularly important for it helps to define a distinct and outstandingly fine style in early English art (Pl. 6). If the decorative work of Breedon and Fletton has been described as retrospective and the figural as continental, the Codford St. Peter sculpture may be aptly described as in essence completely

[1] G. Millet, 'Les Iconoclastes et la croix', *Bulletin de correspondance hellénique*, xxxiv (1910), 96. The distribution of this interesting motif has recently been examined by the author—see 'The Leaved Cross', *Byzantinoslavica* (1950), vol. x, Pt. i.

English. The work is of a quality not only far above that of
Breedon, but also far above that of the general run of sculpture in
the eighth and ninth centuries. The style is distinctive, and shows
on the one hand no hint of the old northern manner, and on the
other no similarity to that of the Mercian work which has just
been examined. The ornamental portion of the Codford St. Peter
cross is similar to the decoration of some slabs which adorn the
chancel arch at Britford in Wiltshire. These have been dated to
about 800, and a similar or slightly later date has usually been
assigned to the Codford sculpture.[1] The reigns of Egbert (802-39)
and Æthelwulf (839-58) are certainly both possible. During that
of the former the revival of Wessex had just begun, while the latter
monarch was renowned as something of a connoisseur; his finger
ring of gold inlaid with niello, which was found at Laverstock in
Wiltshire, and is now in the British Museum, is of very fine
quality, and when he went to Rome in 855 he took with him a
number of artistic products as gifts to the pope. It may be that one
of his reasons for doing so was to establish abroad the reputation
of English art, and one hopes that the bowls, the golden crown,
and the other things which he took with him were of the same
quality as the Codford sculpture. But even in face of this evidence
it is tempting to suggest that the Codford stone, and probably
the Britford ones also, were produced at a rather later date when the
renaissance of Anglo-Saxon art was in full swing. The figure on the
Codford stone in fact savours of Wessex in every turn and attitude
and seems to herald what was later to become the Winchester
style. The position of King Edgar on his Foundation Charter for
the New Minster at Winchester (B.M. Cotton, Vespasian, A. VIII)
is thus almost identical (Pl. 46), and we see the same attitude once
more at a considerably later date in a figure on the stem of the
ivory crozier in the Victoria and Albert Museum which has usually
been regarded as Saxon though some claim it as Norman (Pl. 41;
see p. 170). The attitude is indeed the characteristically Anglo-
Saxon one that was seized upon by Lewis Carroll to describe the
messenger Haigha in *Alice through the Looking Glass*, and even if

---

[1] T. D. Kendrick, *Saxon Art to 900*, 179. He was the first to recognize the outstanding importance of this monument.

the crozier is to be dated after the conquest, the attitude is one of the elements that help us to distinguish English work from that done on the continent.

As regards the ornamental part of the Codford slab, links with succeeding periods seem closer than with those that went before, and the style is experimental rather than retrospective. In addition to the fine scroll above the figure's head, there are further scrolls on the two side faces of the stone,[1] and these are distinctly suggestive of ornament of the Winchester school. On their evidence, as well as on that of the attitude of the figure, I suggest that the Codford stone is to be assigned to the reign of Alfred. It was at that time, more than at any other, that one would expect to find such fine work; it was at that date rather than before that Wiltshire was an important enough region for work of outstanding excellence to be produced there. Both the Codford and Britford carvings are, indeed, of very high quality, and they are by no means the sort of thing one would associate with a local craftsman in an out-of-the-way area, or that one would assign to any period other than one of marked artistic progress.

These are but selected monuments chosen to illustrate the highest degree that was reached in sculpture, first in Mercia and then in Wessex, to stress the importance of continental influence and to bring out the differences between the English and continental styles. But by no means all the work was of such high quality. At this time much crude carving was done in the smaller places, and even in the more important centres poor sculpture was not necessarily absent; conversely, work of outstanding quality was sometimes done in quite small places. It would seem, in fact, that sculptors moved about comparatively freely, and that accomplished craftsmen were hired to do work all over the country. Such men must have been trained in some central court or school, and in many cases it is probable that they not only had before them models from abroad, in the form of ivories or sketches, but also that foreign masters actually worked on English soil and taught the native sculptors something of their lore. Only on this assumption can the

---

[1] For illustrations of the side faces see J. Baron, *Wilts. Arch. and Nat. Hist. Mag.* xx (1882), 138.

markedly east Christian or continental affinities of some of the sculptures be explained, and only on this assumption does the sudden renaissance of sculpture about the time of Alfred seem conceivable.

It is, on this basis, possible to distinguish work of three types of sculpture, namely, that produced in the 'court' schools, where foreign tuition was available, that executed by local men who had come in contact with the Englishmen who worked in the 'court' schools, and that done in more out-of-the-way areas by local men who had seen little from outside and followed perhaps some sketch or ivory which had come their way more or less by chance. In discussing the sculptures, however, it will be more satisfactory to consider them under their various subjects, noting the quality of the work as we proceed, than to group works of the 'court', provincial, and primitive schools separately. Only in this way can the debt of one group to another be estimated. For the sake of convenience, however, the slabs and similar sculptures adorned with figural work, and originally intended for interior use, will be discussed first, the slabs with interlace or similar stylized ornament second, and the crosses, all of which were meant to be set up out of doors, third. These crosses were no doubt sometimes executed by the same sculptor as the slabs, but in general they show either cruder and more essentially local work or are distinguished by a decoration inspired by the old Northumbrian prototypes and conceived as a piece of formal pattern with no intent to model figural subjects. The crosses have usually suffered very seriously from weathering, so that it is often impossible to compare them, so far as style is concerned, with better-preserved work from indoors, some of which is almost as fresh as when it was executed.

The order of discussion will in the main be chronological, but so far as is possible the various iconographical themes will be discussed together, even if an exact chronological sequence is in this way broken.

2. THE FIGURAL SLABS

The first figured-slab that belongs without question to the age we are considering is the winged angel at Deerhurst (Pl. 8 *b*).

The head is in high relief, but the body and wings are more sketchily shown; stylistically the work is early rather than late, and as the church was founded around 910, it is probable that the angel is to be assigned to much the same date as the building. It must have been the work of a local sculptor, following some early, probably manuscript, model; as Kendrick says, it has a distinctly Celtic flavour about it. Yet the style of hairdressing, the appearance of the face itself, and the iconography and arrangement are all markedly influenced by Byzantine art; the face, wings, and disposition, for instance, are close to those on a Byzantine ivory of the Archangel Gabriel in Mr. Royall Tyler's collection, which is to be dated to c. 900.[1]

Kendrick suggests that this sculpture, together with numerous other works of art, most of which have disappeared, though a few, like St. Cuthbert's stole, worked probably at Winchester between 909 and 916, have been preserved, are the manifestation of a rebirth of art which was brought about by the enlightened and vigorous patronage of Alfred the Great. As with many a revival of subsequent times, two major elements are to be distinguished in its development; a renewal of native vigour, which had already begun to express itself before Alfred's day, and the introduction of fresh themes and models from abroad. The Deerhurst angel and St. Cuthbert's stole show clearly whence these models were introduced. It was Byzantine art, either by direct action or indirectly by way of Ottonian Germany, that was behind the tenth-century revival in Britain, just as classical art or the Christian style in Italy were the vital sources to which Charlemagne turned for inspiration when he sought to sponsor a new culture at the commencement of the ninth century.

Byzantine influence is again marked in the pair of flying angels at Bradford-on-Avon (Pl. 7). They are of considerable size—each about 5 feet long—and must once have formed part of a large rood. The treatment is linear and savours slightly of the north in the love that is displayed for rhythmical pattern as such, but the iconography follows closely the usual Byzantine rendering of the theme of flying angels. The theme was developed in the service of

[1] F. Volbach, G. Salles, G. Duthuit, *Art Byzantin*, Pl. 25 B.

Christianity from the sixth century onwards; before that it had been equally popular in pagan art in the form of the Winged Victory. In east Christian art the principal variant to be seen in its iconography is the presence or absence of veils in the arms of the angels; they are present at Bradford-on-Avon and also, for example, on a tenth-century Byzantine ivory showing the Forty Martyrs below with winged angels at the top in the Kaiser Friedrich Museum at Berlin.[1] The Bradford angels are probably to be dated about 950, though they may be rather later, for they are closely similar to the angels in the Benedictional of St. Æthelwold, which belongs to between 975 and 980.

A rather more vigorous yet no less Byzantine rendering is to be found at Winterbourne Steepleton in Dorset (Pl. 8 a); it is to be associated with the earlier rather than the later of these sculptures, that is to say it dates from nearer 910 than 950; it might even be assigned to the reign of Alfred. It is in high relief and though less flowing and elegant it shows a much more expressive rendering than either the Deerhurst or Bradford carvings. The face is full of vigour and life, and the knees are kicked up almost in glee; it is a particularly delightful work.

It is interesting to contrast the Winterbourne Steepleton angel with a late rendering of the same subject, this time in the vertical posture, at Stinsford in Dorset (Pl. 10 b). Sculptured in low relief, this figure has all the delicacy and charm of a Winchester school drawing, and is to be dated shortly after, rather than before, the year 1000. Unlike the others, it probably formed part of an annunciation group, and was not a supporting figure.

More primitive variants of this theme exist in other places, notably at Manchester, where there is an extremely poor and primitive relief; it is about 13 inches high and is cut in red sandstone— a rarity in this respect, for nearly all the sculptures known are in limestone. The angel holds a scroll and there is an inscription roughly cut partly on this and partly on the background which reads, 'In manus tuas dme commendo sp(iritum)', that is, 'Into thy hands, O Lord, I commend my soul'. It is probably to be dated

[1] W. Wulff and W. F. Volbach, *Die altchristlichen und mittelalterlichen, byzantinischen und italienischen Bildwerke, Ergänzungsband*, Berlin (1923), Pl. xiv, no. 574.

to the ninth century.[1] A fragment of sculpture recently discovered at Maiden Newton in Dorset may also represent an angel, though it is impossible to be certain, for so little remains.

So far as chronology is concerned, the oldest example of elaborate work after the Deerhurst angel is probably the much-damaged roundel at Gloucester bearing the bust of Christ enclosed within a guilloche border. The iconography is of Byzantine inspiration— it is the old theme of the Pantocrator which we see in so many mosaics and other works of art; the border is of a type which was very popular in Carolingian art; the style, so far as one can judge of it, in view of the very battered condition of the work, is as much Byzantine as English. It would therefore seem that we have here a sculpture executed by an English master who was making use of a Byzantine ivory for his model. The stone is probably to be dated to the first half of the tenth century.

Another stone showing Christ is preserved at Jevington near Willingdon in Sussex (Pl. 10 a). This time, however, our Lord is shown full length. He has a cruciform halo and holds a long cross. There are two interlacing beasts at His feet which represent the asp and basilisk, but they are purely northern in spirit, while the figure, though primitive and stylized, belongs rather to the Mediterranean family. A suggestion put forward by some authorities that the figure represents St. Michael or St. George slaying the dragon is not to be accepted, for the beasts are clearly intended for the asp and basilisk, and from the ninth century onwards Christ was frequently shown treading upon them. The work is obviously fairly late, and in spite of the northern element it should be assigned to shortly before the conquest rather than to the tenth century. A date around 1050 seems most likely.

With the exception of the Stinsford angel none of these sculptures shows to any marked degree those particular features that characterize the Winchester school in painting, they are all more continental in feeling; yet there are carvings that do show the delicate,

---

[1] J. J. Phelps, 'An ancient sculptured stone in Manchester Cathedral', *Trans. Lancs. and Ches. Ant. Soc.* xxii (1905), 172, dates it to the eighth or ninth century. See also W. E. A. Axon, 'The Angel Stone in Manchester Cathedral', *Journ. Brit. Arch. Ass.* xi (1905), 169–72.

linear manner and fluttering draperies of Winchester work, notably a figure of Christ at Beverstone in Gloucestershire and another at Bristol. It has been suggested that the latter (Pl. 12) is actually part of a cross shaft, but it seems on the whole far more likely that it was originally intended as a slab for internal use. Christ is shown standing erect, holding a cross in His right hand, and treading relentlessly on figures of the damned below Him, while He raises up Adam with His left hand. Though somewhat more rigid and clumsy, it is, nevertheless, close in style to a drawing of the temptation of Christ from a mid-eleventh-century psalter in the British Museum (Cotton, Tiberius, C. VI). Saxl and Wittkower date the sculpture to about 1100;[1] Kendrick regards it as completely Saxon. A Saxon date is by far the more probable; the fact that it is less light and fresh than the drawing, which Saxl and Wittkower put forward as evidence of its later date, is more probably to be accounted for because the sculpture belonged to a provincial school, whereas the drawing was produced at Winchester or a similar accomplished centre. A date around 1025 seems most likely.

The slab at Beverstone, now built into the south wall of the tower, is about 5 feet high, and again shows Christ full length, with His left hand holding a long stemmed cross.[2] Behind, His costume blows out like two fluttering streamers. His right hand is, however, raised in blessing, so the figure in all probability did not form part of the scene usually known as the harrowing of hell, where Christ is shown in Limbo, raising up Adam from the grave. Except for this, the Beverstone slab is similar to that at Bristol. It might even have been carved in the same workshop, though it is perhaps rather later in date; it is, however, hard to suggest any date more exact than the first half of the eleventh century.

Another important sculpture, or rather series of fragments of a sculpture, with Christ as its subject comes from Reculver in Kent; it has usually been assigned to a much earlier date. The finest of the fragments shows the lower portion of a standing figure (Pl. 9 *b*). The costume falls in a series of gentle folds; below, they

---

[1] *British Art and the Mediterranean*, Pl. 23.

[2] It has so far never been published and its position makes the taking of a good photograph very difficult.

terminate in loop-like undulations; above, the mantle is bound by a girdle; the figure's hand, holding a scroll, is preserved on one of the fragments, but the rest has perished. This sculpture has usually been assigned to the seventh century, and has been cited as the only surviving example of sculpture in the south of Britain at the time that the Bewcastle, Ruthwell, and other crosses were being done in the north. Records exist which mention other instances, notably a cross at Glastonbury, and others along the route of St. Aldhelm's funeral procession from Doulting to Malmesbury. Clapham sets forth the evidence for assigning the Reculver sculpture to about 670;[1] it is of a direct character, for the pavement of the church is stopped against the base of the cross, so that the base must have been there when the floor was laid; and the floor is indisputably contemporary with the church. The latter is dated by an entry in the Anglo-Saxon Chronicle under 669, which states that King Egbert gave Reculver to his mass-priest, Bassa, to build a church there. The church survived until 1805, when the walls were pulled down, but the remains were uncovered in 1926–7, and Sir Alfred Clapham, who was present, was convinced that what was left represented the original seventh-century building. The evidence would thus seem to be irrefutable with regard to the base. But it is still no more than circumstantial with regard to the cross; one would expect it to be of the same age as its base, but it need not have been; indeed the cross might easily have been destroyed and re-erected subsequently. And here the stylistic character of the sculpture is of great importance, for there is little about the fragments which remain that suggests, still less seriously supports, so early a date. The dignity and grandeur of Ruthwell and Bewcastle, the monumental feeling which predominates in the work there, or in the best work of the succeeding decades, like Easby, are completely absent. Instead one sees an elegant, subtle, flowing style, suggestive almost of Gothic. Yet if one places a photograph of the surviving fragment of the shaft beside one of so characteristic a Winchester work as the Stinsford angel, the two at once fall into place together. The delicate looped folds of the costume, the elegant pose, and the lightness of touch are essentially

[1] *English Romanesque Architecture before the Conquest*, 62.

features which we see in the manuscripts of the Winchester school. In fact, on stylistic grounds, there is every reason to date the Reculver cross shaft in the tenth century and to regard it as a monument of later Saxon art, which takes its place alongside the other fine sculptures of this period that show the same style, though it is no doubt rather earlier in date than the two that show the closest iconographic and stylistic parallels, namely, the Bristol and the Beverstone slabs.

A subject which was even more popular than that of Christ alone, and of which quite a considerable number of examples have come down to us, is the crucifixion. Variants occur where Christ is shown either singly or as one of the figures of a crucifixion group. By far the finest of them is the superb Romsey Rood (Pl. 13), which is probably to be dated between about 1000 and 1020. It shows the influence of the Winchester school of painting in the sophisticated elegance that characterizes it, but a Byzantine classicism is more marked than is usual in the illuminations. Christ is shown alone, whereas in western art at this time He was more usually accompanied by the two subsidiary figures of Longinus and Stephaton, bearing respectively a lance and a reed with the sponge at its end, or by the Virgin and St. John. Christ is, moreover, conceived as a figure of dignity and a symbol of strength, whereas most western crucifixions are less monumental and more illustrative in character. The conception we see here is exactly that which dominated in the central Byzantine area from the tenth to the twelfth century; a tenth-century Byzantine ivory in the Kaiser Friedrich Museum in Berlin may be compared.[1] So close are the similarities that one may conclude that once again the Saxon sculptor was following an imported model fairly closely. But he gave to it something that was definitely his own; he made in fact a great work of art which is in no way eclectic or second hand.

An entirely different conception of the crucifixion characterizes a small slab built in above the door of the church porch at Langford in Oxfordshire (Pl. 11 a). Though it has been incorrectly put together, it is obvious that Christ's arms were bent and contorted, and His neck twisted in agony; He is here clearly regarded as a suffering

[1] W. Wulff and W. F. Volbach, op. cit., No. 2393, Pl. xv, p. 37.

human being rather than a figure of heavenly glory whom pain could not touch. This is the conception that was in early times dominant in Syria and Palestine, but not in Constantinople or the central part of the Byzantine world where Greek ideas of elegance were never subordinated to eastern realism. That we should find this rendering in England is not surprising, for the eastern element, as opposed to the central Byzantine one, had played a considerable role in Ireland on the one hand and in France on the other. The important factor to recognize is that we have to do with two separate iconographical traditions, and that the character of the Langford slab is not merely due to a more primitive or more clumsy rendering. The same idea underlies the crucifixion at Wormington in Worcestershire (Pl. 11 b), where the severely contorted head and the thin straining arms once more bear witness to the eastern model; they are not to be attributed to the primitive workmanship alone. Both the Langford and the Wormington slabs may probably be assigned to a date between 1020 and 1050.

The same contorted position is to be seen on a large rood above the south doorway of the church at Breamore in Hampshire (Pl. 16 a). Christ is as it were silhouetted against the cross, and the Virgin appears on one side, St. John on the other, standing at some distance apart. The whole surface of the carving has been at some time hacked away, so that only the outlines of the figures can now be distinguished, but their swaying lines suggest that the detail was of Winchester character. Kendrick even sees in the work evidence of an appreciable change of style which took place in the middle of the century, and on the evidence of this he places the sculpture shortly before the conquest. He is probably right, and a date around 1040 would seem most likely. It is a major tragedy that this sculpture has suffered so terribly, for it must have been a work of outstanding beauty. If so superb a thing was to be found in a small parish church, one may imagine what the roods of the larger churches or cathedrals were like. The crucifixion at Romsey helps to complete the picture.

A second large-scale rood of the same type is preserved at Headbourne Worthy in Hampshire, though the conception is distinct, for Christ's arms are straight and stiff, and His head is only very slightly bent (Pl. 16 *b*). The figures of St. John and the Virgin are similarly firm and erect; that of St. John especially may be contrasted with the rendering at Breamore. If this rood, which is, alas, similarly battered, lacks the emotional appeal of that at Breamore, it has, nevertheless, a grandeur and a dignity which in their own way are none the less effective. The two show that there must have been some great sculptors at work in Hampshire at this time.

In addition to these two different conceptions of Christ, as a monument of dignity and grandeur, and as a vivid expression of suffering, the distinct iconographical traditions that characterize Constantinople and Syria–Palestine are further borne out by the identity of the supplementary figures. Thus in the Constantinopolitan tradition our Lord appears alone, or with the Virgin on one side and St. John on the other, whereas in the eastern tradition the figures on either side more usually represent Longinus and Stephaton. It was this disposition that was most usual in Irish art, and on the continent it seems to have dominated in southern Italy and Spain. We can trace in fact two distinct trends and routes of influence, the one from Syria–Palestine by way of southern Italy and Spain to Ireland, the other from Constantinople by way of northern and central Italy to the Carolingian and Ottonian spheres. Both exercised their influence in England, the effects of the latter being manifested primarily in the work of the 'court' school, those of the former in more primitive sculptures, most of which seem to have been associated with the west country. The eastern tradition no doubt penetrated from Ireland to the Isle of Man and was perhaps carried to parts of England from there.

Of three rather primitive but, nevertheless, interesting slabs at Daglingworth in Gloucestershire, one bears the crucifixion (Pl. 14 *a*), with Stephaton on one side of our Lord and Longinus on the other, and so represents this eastern tradition. The others show our Lord enthroned and St. Peter with an enormous key (Pl. 14 *b*). A smaller slab formerly built into the east wall on the outside bears a second crucifixion. On all of these slabs the heads are large, and the figures clumsy; the work must have been done by a local mason. It has charm, but little elegance. All are probably to be dated about 1050. The slab at Jevington in Sussex already noted

(Pl. 10 *a*) is in a similar primitive style which contrasts markedly with the more accomplished work at Breamore and Headbourne Worthy. Though found in London, another slab, which is now in St. Dunstan's church at Stepney, is perhaps on the whole closer to the primitive than to the accomplished group (Pl. 9 *a*). Our Lord is shown on the cross, with the Virgin and St. John on either side below, and with medallions, presumably of the sun and moon, above. The stone is small, and is framed by a border of stylized acanthus leaves like those usual on Carolingian ivories. Indeed, the whole sculpture looks, in photographs, very like an ivory, and the sculptor must have followed such a model very closely when he made it. The original was probably Carolingian rather than Byzantine or Ottonian, though the slab is to be assigned to the eleventh rather than to the tenth century. Around 1020 would seem the most likely date.

Another stone bearing the crucifixion may be noted here, for though it is not very accomplished, it has only once been published, and that a very long time ago.[1] It is very battered, but is probably Saxon, or in any case is to be assigned to the eleventh century. It shows Christ alone, on a double-armed cross beneath a curved canopy. The stone is now at Darrington near Pontefract in Yorkshire, but it was brought to its present place from the neighbouring village of Cridling Park.

A rendering of the crucified Christ which is completely distinct from all these appears on a larger scale on a fine relief now built into the east side of the porch at Langford (Pl. 17). This sculpture has special significance as being the only early example in England of a crucifixion where the Christ wears a long monkish robe, tied at the waist with a cord, in place of the more usual loin-cloth derived from the classical tradition in Christian art and universal in Constantinople and the central part of the Byzantine world. A somewhat similar robe is, however, worn by the enthroned Christ at Daglingworth;[2] it is secured at the waist by a four-

[1] R. Holmes, 'An ancient sculpture at Cridling Park', *Yorks. Arch. Journ.* xi. 17. There is a good photograph in the collection of the National Buildings Record.

[2] A. W. Clapham, 'Some Disputed Examples of pre-Conquest Sculpture', *Antiquity*, xxv, no. 100, 1951, Pl. VI.

stranded band and the knot in front looks like a piece of interlaced ornament.

Various explanations to account for the occurrence of the robed
version in England have been put forward, and Langford has been
assigned to various dates, depending on the prototypes that have
been considered. By most writers the rood has been regarded as
Saxon, and has been dated between 1000 and 1050; usually vague
Byzantine prototypes have been cited. Others have regarded the
sculpture as late Saxon, but have cited the wooden crucifix at
Lucca, known as the Volto Santo, as its iconographic prototype.
More recently Saxl and Wittkower, while accepting the Volto
Santo as the model, have dated the rood to the twelfth century.[1]

The Volto Santo is no doubt a possible prototype, for some form
of sculptured crucifix is recorded in legend to have existed there
since the eighth century or thereabouts, and Leofstan of Bury St.
Edmunds is said to have brought back a copy of it to England soon
after the middle of the eleventh century. He died in 1065, which
sets a definite terminus for the introduction of this copy. The actual
appearance of the Volto Santo of this period is, however, rather
uncertain, for there is reason to believe that the present crucifix
is of twelfth- or even thirteenth-century date, and that it took the
place of an earlier, presumably eighth-century, original. It is in any
case far freer than the Langford sculpture, and on purely stylistic
grounds, apart from considerations of material, place, or the aim
of the sculptor, one would expect it to be a good deal later. The
fame of the Volto Santo would, on the other hand, lead one to
suppose that the second sculpture would have followed the original
model closely, in any case with regard to the iconographical disposition of the figure, that is to say, the presence of the heavy
monkish robe rather than a loin-cloth.

The vague references to a Byzantine prototype for this form of
robed Christ which have been made by early writers are nonsense;
the robed Christ was unknown in Byzantine art properly speaking,
that is to say, the art which developed at Constantinople from the
sixth century onwards. The long robe was, however, quite usual in
the art of the region farther to the east, notably Syria–Palestine,

[1] *British Art and the Mediterranean*, 27.

and it is this area that should be borne in mind rather than the narrower Byzantium when ultimate prototypes are considered. Reil, in fact, in his exhaustive study of the iconography of the crucifixion,[1] distinguishes a special robed version in early times which he calls the Jerusalem type. Examples are afforded by a silver plate of the fifth or sixth century, and by a miniature in the Rabula Gospels, copied at Zagba in Mesopotamia in 586; there may perhaps have been a still older prototype. The model soon found its way to the west, and was used for the wall-paintings of Santa Maria Antiqua at Rome.[2] But both here and in the Rabula Gospels the robe is sleeveless and there is no cord at the waist.

Along with numerous other eastern, as opposed to purely Byzantine elements, this type was adopted in Germany, and long tunics, both with and without sleeves, were not unusual in German art in Carolingian times; an ivory in the Musée du Cinquantenaire at Brussels, of the important Liége group, may be cited. The type was also introduced into France, and became especially popular there in early Romanesque art, when crucifixes of this type, made of wood and painted in bright colours, were quite common. It also reached Spain, and a wooden crucifix of the late eleventh century in the Barcelona Museum, or another of the early twelfth century, at Belpuig, may be cited as examples.[3] From there no doubt the type travelled to Ireland, along the same route as the eastern variant of the crucifixion discussed above, and quite a number of examples were produced there. What appears to be a figure of Christ wearing a long-sleeved robe bound at the waist with a rope and closely similar in type to that on the Langford Rood, thus occurs on one of the great sculptured piers at Cashel (Fig. 8). It is dated to the eleventh century by Miss Françoise Henry,[4] but a date early in the century seems probable if other crosses with the same subject are compared, such as that at Kilfenora, Co. Clare.[5] At a later date the cross of Dysart O'Dea in the same

---

[1] J. Reil, Die frühchristlichen Darstellungen der Kreuzigung (1904).

[2] O. M. Dalton, Byzantine Art and Archaeology, Fig. 188, p. 308.

[3] A. Kingsley Porter, Spanish Romanesque Sculpture (1928), vol. i, pl. 34. É. Mâle, L'Art religieux du XIIᵉ siècle en France, Paris (1922), fig. 170.

[4] La Sculpture irlandaise, Paris (1933), 134.

[5] Proc. Roy. Soc. Ants., Ireland, 5th series, x (1900), 392.

county shows the motif once more.[1] A metal plaque in the Dublin Museum, known as the Athlone Crucifix, may also be cited; it is dated by Mahr and Raftery to the mid-eighth century on evidence which they regard as indisputable, and thus constitutes the earliest example of the type that has come down to us in the

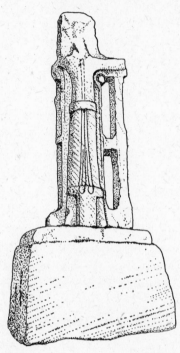

west.[2] The figure is very stylized and the long robe is adorned with superimposed spiral, interlace, and key patterns; inelegant winged cherubim appear on either side above, and below are very stylized renderings of Longinus and Stephaton; there is little understanding of figural art as such. Some other pieces of metal-work from Ireland show later variants, notably a plaque from Dungannon, Co. Tyrone, and a book cover of unknown provenance in the Dublin Museum. From Ireland the type was carried to the Isle of Man; we see it on a fragment of a cross of the early ninth century from the Calf of Man (Fig. 9), and it was no doubt by way of Man that it reached England.

FIG. 8. Figure at Cashel, Ireland

In view of this evidence the importance of the Volto Santo as a possible prototype for the Langford Rood is considerably reduced. Ireland on the one hand and Germany on the other are both more probable sources of influence; and the examination that has already been accorded to the distribution of the eastern type of crucifixion, where Longinus and Stephaton are present, further suggests that it is to Ireland that the eye should most probably be turned in the first instance. And, with prototypes available there as early as the eighth century, a dating of the Langford Rood in the

[1] H. S. Crawford, Carved Ornament from Irish Monuments, Pl. VIII.
[2] Christian Art in Ancient Ireland, ii. 106.

first half of the eleventh century seems more probable than one in the twelfth. There is nothing in any way comparable in the stone sculpture or indeed in any sort of art of the early Norman period

FIG. 9. *Cross from the Calf of Man*

in this country, nor are similar works known in the Romanesque sculpture of France. The rood must take its place, in fact, with the wide group of sculptures which Prior and Gardner regard as Saxon, but which French authorities and others, with French

Romanesque foremost in their minds' eyes, have tended, quite
wrongly, to place in the twelfth century. A date around 1020 seems
most likely.

With two notable exceptions such other sculptures as have survived, and can with reasonable certainty be assigned to Saxon
times, are all very primitive, and illustrate the work of local craftsmen rather than that of a master associated with some great
cultural centre. Of these more primitive works one of the most
interesting is a slab at Inglesham, near Lechlade, on the borders of
Gloucestershire and Wiltshire (Pl. 15 a). It has sometimes been
assigned to the twelfth century, but even if its actual date cannot
be regarded as eleventh century with quite as much confidence as
can that of other works discussed above, it can safely be said that
its style is essentially Saxon, and has nothing in common with what
the Norman sculptors were seeking to accomplish. In out-of-the-
way regions like this, old styles survived for many years after a
change had taken place in the more active centres, and the Inglesham slab may thus be post-conquest in date though pre-conquest
in style. That a Byzantine model was followed at anything like
first hand in this instance is most improbable, but that the ultimate
prototype was Byzantine seems equally certain, even though the
Virgin has twisted sideways and the Child has slipped off her knee
in the process of repeated copyings. The nature of the original
prototype for such a work as this is indicated by a lovely figure of
the Virgin and Child at Utrecht, again of eleventh-century date.[1]

A somewhat similar theme appears on a very roughly sculptured
slab of rather northern appearance at Deerhurst; it is probably to
be assigned to the very end of the tenth century, and represents
the work of a local craftsman who had more understanding of
ornamental than of figural sculpture. An even clumsier rendering,
much farther from the original model, appears on a stone, presumably a cross head, in the churchyard at Grosmont in Monmouthshire; it is probably of early Norman date though the
heritage is clearly Saxon. A slab in St. Alkmund's church at Derby
bears a seated figure which may represent the Virgin, but the work
is so clumsy that the subject may equally well be an evangelist as

[1] F. Volbach, G. Salles, G. Duthuit, *Art Byzantin*, Pl. 32 A.

Kendrick has suggested. This theme is, however, so far unknown in sculpture, though it was of course a favourite one in book illustration.

To a completely different iconographical heritage is to be assigned a plaque, bearing a figure that is presumably the Virgin, built into the eastern wall of the west tower at Deerhurst (Pl. 18 *a*). It has a curious flat surface, and it has been suggested that the detail has at some time been levelled off. It would seem more likely, however, that the sculpture was either never finished, or that the details were not sculptured, but were indicated in paint; very faint traces of paint survive to support this suggestion. A similar technique was employed on a slab at Shelford in Nottinghamshire, and a tombstone at Whitchurch in Hampshire, bearing the figure of our Lord, with one hand raised, holding a book, is similarly lacking in detail though it is sculptured almost in the round. A relief at Sompting showing a saint standing in an arcade, though in more moulded relief, is also rather similar (Pl. 15 *b*). It is hard to date, but may be as early as the Deerhurst slab, that is to say, about the year 1000. It is the work of some local mason, about as skilled— or as lacking in skill—as the man who carved the Daglingworth stones.

The step-shaped design which appears at the bottom of the Deerhurst slab is something completely Saxon. Of the figure of the Virgin there is enough to show that a Byzantine model of the iconographical type known as the Nicopea Virgin was followed. Here óur Lady stands holding before her, in the earliest stages of the theme, a medallion bearing the image of the Child Christ upon it, and, at a later stage, the Child Himself. A lovely mosaic formerly preserved in the church of the Assumption of the Virgin at Nicaea, but now destroyed, may serve as an example of the later type in Byzantine art.[1] No major work showing the earlier type survives, but it was particularly popular on lead seals, and it is quite possible that one such seal found its way to Deerhurst and was copied there in stone. Indeed, the curious technique of the slab, with its flat, rounded surfaces, somehow calls lead-work to mind.

The possibility that paint was used on the Deerhurst slab gives

[1] T. Schmidt, *Die Koimesis-Kirche von Nikaia*, Berlin, 1927, Pl. xx.

rise to the question of polychromy on Anglo-Saxon sculpture. Colour was very probably used quite extensively on full relief sculpture, as it was in later medieval times, though practically no

FIG. 10. *Byzantine plaque. From St. Mary Panachrantos, Constantinople*

traces of it have survived. A slab at Romsey, bearing the crucifixion, however, suggests that something more elaborate than mere painting of stonework was also done, for its background is cut away in such a manner that it would seem that it was meant to afford adherence to some coloured paste which was thickly applied, so giving the appearance of incrustation (Pl. 18 *b*). Work in this technique was quite common in Italy and in the Byzantine world from the ninth century onwards, and in this case again it may be suggested that the technique was introduced from those countries to the Saxon world. The appearance of the Romsey slab is closely akin to a marble plaque in the Byzantine Museum at Athens, where the background is in relief and where the figures are cut away and painted (Fig. 11). In the Byzantine world coloured stones were sometimes inlaid in the place of coloured paste or paint; the best-known examples of the technique are from the

FIG. 11. *Byzantine plaque. Byzantine Museum, Athens*

church of St. Mary Panachrantos at Constantinople, the finest of which bears St. Eudoxia; it has been quite frequently reproduced.[1] Another slab from the same place, which is only preserved in part, presents a closer parallel to our Saxon example, for the stylized plant motif that can be seen behind the cross on the Romsey slab appears in almost exactly the same form on that from St. Mary Panachrantos (Fig. 10). As regards iconography, a Byzantine prototype must again have been closely followed by the carver of the Romsey Crucifixion; the central panel of an ivory tryptich in the Kaiser Friedrich Museum at Berlin gives a clear idea of what it must have been like;[2] practically the only difference is that more

[1] The Panachrantos finds have not yet been fully published, but the St. Eudoxia slab is reproduced in F. Volbach, G. Salles, G. Duthuit, *Art Byzantin*, Pl. 72, and one of the other slabs is figured by S. Casson, 'Byzantium and Anglo-Saxon Sculpture', *Burl. Mag.* lxiii. 35, Pl. B.

[2] O. M. Dalton, *Byzantine Art and Archaeology*, Figs. 140, 229.

figures are included on the ivory. It is probably to be dated to the
early eleventh century.

A number of other sculptures may be mentioned here, the dates
of which are more open to doubt than those dealt with above. All
are of high quality, and even if Norman in date, they show hints
of the Saxon tradition and so attest the Saxon heritage. Very near
to Saxon art in style and to the Saxon period in date are two panels
at Chichester, one showing the raising of Lazarus, the other Mary
and Martha greeting Christ at the gate of Jerusalem (Pls. 20 and 21).
The latter was carved by an accomplished sculptor who sought for
polish and finish in his work; the former is in a more expressionist
style, and the emaciated figures are quite distinct from those
of the first slab even though the two, iconographically and stylistically, are undoubtedly to be assigned to the same school and
date. The differences are due to individual hands, not to date or
locality.

The panels had been cut up at some time before being set in
their present position, and it has been suggested that they were
brought from the old church at Selsey together with certain
treasures and other works of art which are known to have been
moved to Chichester. They were discovered there behind the
choir stalls in 1829. Other fragments of the same type in the
Cathedral Museum suggest that originally there were more panels;
they may have formed part of a screen.

The style of the reliefs calls to mind that of wall-paintings in
various Sussex churches, especially that at Clayton, and on this
evidence certain authorities have assigned them to the twelfth
century. A Norman date was originally proposed when the sculptures were first published by W. de Gray Birch, who based his
arguments for the late date on the similarities between the Chichester
sculptures and those of the Norman font in St. Nicholas's church
at Brighton, as well as their relationship to a number of twelfth-
century seals and to the miniatures of such twelfth-century manuscripts as Egerton 1139 (fol. 4b), Harley 1810 (f. 61), Add. 17738
(f. 4), and Arundel 157 (f. 7b), all in the British Museum.[1] His

---

[1] 'The ancient sculptures in the south aisle of the choir of Chichester cathedral',
Journ. Brit. Arch. Ass. xlii (1886), 255–62.

conclusions have been followed by a number of more recent writers, notably Saxl and Wittkower.

There are, on the other hand, important factors which militate against the later dating. First, such Norman sculptures of the raising of Lazarus as we know are quite distinct as, for instance, one at Lenton in Nottinghamshire. Secondly, Kingsley Porter has called attention to the similarities that the Chichester slabs show to the sculptures of Santo Domingo de Silos, which are dated by him to between 1073 and 1076.[1] He suggests that Silos may have been influenced by manuscripts of the Winchester school; the close resemblance that they show to the twelfth-century Bury St. Edmund's Gospels is, he thinks, due to the fact that both followed the same model closely. If Kingsley Porter is correct, the Chichester slabs could hardly be later than the early part of the last quarter of the eleventh century. The work is, however, too good to belong to one of the peasant schools which were working at the end of the eleventh century, and on the ground of quality alone a date nearer the middle of the century would seem more likely than a later one—unless the slabs are assigned to the full twelfth century.

Another important factor with regard to their dating is the presence of the favourite Carolingian acanthus border on one of the slabs. This occurs in manuscripts of the Winchester school in the tenth and earlier eleventh centuries, and on the slab at St. Dunstan's, Stepney, bearing the crucifixion which has been noted above, as well as on numerous continental ivories. It constitutes an instance of continental influence which was in stone sculpture normally associated with the Saxon and not with a subsequent period, and although the evidence of its presence is not irrefutable as a dating-point, it is, nevertheless, of importance. Nor can the suggestion that the slabs were brought from Selsey be completely disregarded; Selsey was a Saxon foundation, and any sculptures that decorated the cathedral there would be of the same period.

---

[1] A. Kingsley Porter, *Romanesque Sculpture of the Pilgrimage Roads*, 55. Others, however, do not accept such early dates for the Silos work; see W. M. Whitehill, *Spanish Romanesque Architecture*, 168. For a summary of the question see Clapham, *Romanesque Architecture in Western Europe*, 129.

If the panels did indeed come from Selsey, they would thus certainly be of pre-conquest date.

More weighty still, however, are the stylistic arguments put forward by Prior and Gardner, namely, the subtle and profoundly penetrating expression of the figures, which is quite foreign to early Norman work, the architecture of the background, which is Saxon rather than Norman, and the delicate, fluttering draperies, which are clearly of Winchester type. Yet the draperies are not completely Saxon, being heavier and more metallic than was usual in the best work of that period. Similarly, the attitudes of the figures are more angular. Though not approximating completely to what we know as typically Norman in the twelfth century, the work has, nevertheless, a slightly French touch about it, and this is shown more clearly if works of French origin are compared. The illustrations of an eleventh-century life of St. Aubin, in the Bibliothèque Nationale (Lat. 1390), for instance, show quite close similarities, and such details as the sloping shoulders, the bands at the wrists, and the rather metallic folds are common to both. The manuscript is definitely north French, a product of what has sometimes been termed the Channel school.

The wall-paintings at Clayton show similar traits, which have been explained as the result of contacts with other north French or Flemish works. Their nature affords yet another proof of the close links that from the middle of the eleventh century or thereabouts bound the art of Kent and Sussex with that of the neighbouring districts across the Channel. These links must, it would seem, have existed independently of the Norman conquest; they were first forged several decades before it took place, and they continued for a generation after it. It was to the art of north France and the Flemish world that this country was bound in this case, and not to that of a central France or Normandy. A lovely ivory in the Victoria and Albert Museum, showing the adoration of the magi (see frontispiece and p. 171) is in the same Channel style, and, like the Clayton paintings and the Chichester panels, it also is to be assigned to a date shortly after the conquest. Somewhere around 1080 seems the most probable for the ivory, the paintings, and the carved slabs alike.

A fragmentary carving at Toller Fratrum in Dorset may also be noted here, for it is obviously to be assigned to the same school as the Chichester reliefs. The work is rather more primitive and the proportions and expressions are even more exaggerated than those of the coarser of the two Chichester slabs, namely, that bearing the raising of Lazarus, but the relationships are clear. Either a craftsman from Chichester or from wherever the slabs were carved must have gone to Toller Fratrum, or the stone must have been taken to that place in a finished state.

Another work which it is at first sight tempting to assign to this intermediary period is a relief at Barking in Essex, showing the crucifixion with the figure of Christ on the cross in the centre, St. John on one side, and the Virgin on the other. The arrangement is similar to that of the great roods at Breamore and Headbourne Worthy, and the sculpture has been similarly, though not quite so violently, cut away at a subsequent period; originally the figures were in fairly high relief. It was claimed as Saxon by Prior and Gardner, and there are certainly Saxon characteristics about it. The flat background is, however, covered with a diaper pattern in the manner of Gothic illuminations and the proportions of the figures are perhaps rather slighter than is usual in Saxon art. On the whole it would seem most likely that this is really a thirteenth-century work, and its Saxon appearance is due to the Byzantine basis of the iconography. There was, so far as miniatures are concerned, a second and very marked wave of Byzantine influence towards the end of the twelfth century, and the Barking slab may have been inspired by some Byzantine model, illumination, or, more probably, ivory, which came to this country at that time.

More definitely Norman in style are a number of slabs built into the west front of Lincoln cathedral. There are twenty of them in all and each bears a different scene; as they stand at present they are in disorder and have obviously been re-used. This resetting must have been done before the mid thirteenth century, for one of the slabs is partly obscured by a chapel which was built at that time; there is, however, no closer evidence to suggest when the resetting was done. The actual design of the front, as originally conceived, is eleventh century,[1] but as the slabs were reset they might equally well be of Saxon or of early Norman date. So great an authority as M. R. James considered them 'Saxon rather than Norman',[2] and others have assigned them to the Saxon period also. But our knowledge of early Norman sculpture, thanks to the work of Keyser and others, has become very much more extensive since James wrote about the Lincoln slabs, and in the light of present knowledge one is tempted to say 'Norman rather than Saxon'. The slabs are in fact to be assigned to that phase of stylistic overlap which in some areas carried on right into the twelfth century; we will have cause to say more of it when discussing the early Norman tympana. As regards actual date, the Lincoln slabs are no doubt to be assigned to the beginning of the twelfth century.

There remain to be considered a few pieces of sculpture which have variously been assigned to Saxon and Norman times on the basis of evidence which is well-nigh equally convincing in both cases; the most notable are the Christ at Barnack and the Virgin at York. The latter is a work of really outstanding quality, and before it was damaged it must have been of very great beauty. The Barnack Christ is more roughly handled, but is, none the less, by no means insignificant (Pl. 19 a). If the slab is compared with Byzantine renderings of the subject, such as the ivories in the Bodleian at Oxford, the Victoria and Albert Museum, or the Louvre,[3] its iconographical parentage is at once obvious, but the style is Romanesque, and the closest actual parallel is offered by a slab in the church of St. Radegonde at Poitiers, whereon Christ is depicted in a closely similar position (Pl. 19 b). It has been dated by Kingsley Porter on reliable external evidence to between 1083 and 1089.[4] The fact that in both sculptures the legs tend towards the position which was later to become a distinct manner-

---

[1] F. Saxl, 'Lincoln Cathedral: . . .', *Arch. Journ.* ciii (1946), 105.

[2] 'Sculptures at Lincoln Cathedral', *Proc. Camb. Ant. Soc.*, N.S. iv (1898–1903), 148.

[3] C. Diehl, *Manuel d'art byzantin*, ii, Fig. 328; O. M. Dalton, *Byzantine Art and Archaeology*, Fig. 141; G. Schlumberger, *L'Épopée byzantine*, i. 149. The ivory in the Victoria and Albert Museum is no. 272—1867.

[4] A. Kingsley Porter, *Romanesque Sculpture of the Pilgrimage Roads*, Boston (1923), text p. 304 and Pl. 909.

ism in southern French Romanesque sculpture is worthy of note;
they are set with feet close together and knees wide apart. The
arrangement of the folds of the costume as a linear, spiral pattern
is also a feature characteristic of Romanesque sculpture in France.
But still, the Barnack Christ does not bear any resemblance to
Norman works either in this country or in France; the relation-
ships are with the centre and south, and with work of a proto-
Romanesque rather than a truly Romanesque character. If it is of
Norman date, it must belong to the very beginning of the period.
But on balance a date within the Saxon period seems more likely.
The sculpture represents, in fact, that phase of art which Clapham,
when speaking of the architecture, has termed Saxon Romanesque.
A Saxon architect, Gautier Coorland, is known to have worked in
Poitiers on the church of St. Hilaire, where he was employed by
Emma, formerly queen of England—she had married Canute in
1017 and died in 1052; the church was finished in 1049. It is tempt-
ing to suggest that this link may have been in some way responsible for the close similarity between the sculptures at Barnack and
Poitiers. Could some sculptor who was employed by Gautier have
done one work in this country and the other, some years later, in
France? If he did, he probably went to France before 1049 when
Gautier's church at Poitiers was finished. A date towards the end
of the first half of the eleventh century may thus be suggested for
the Barnack slab.

   A battered figure of Christ in glory at Elstow in Cumberland
is probably of much the same date as the Barnack sculpture,
though it also has sometimes been regarded as a work of the
twelfth century. Christ's forked beard is a pre-Norman feature,
and the style of the work is early, though the iconography is rather
less near to the Byzantine than that of the Barnack Christ. The
sculpture was once probably part of a tympanum, and one which
depicted Christ between St. Peter and St. John is known to have
existed at Elstow in early times.

   The York Virgin (Pl. 22) belongs to a more highly accomplished
group of sculptures. No primitive features are present, and there
is no hint of naïveté as there is in the more provincial Saxon and
in much early Norman work. So marked, indeed, is this finish,

that it is tempting to suggest, not only that some model of the highest quality was available, but also that a craftsman who had learnt in a firmly established school had had a hand in its production. It is, in fact, not only to be attributed to what one would term a 'court school', but also to the hand of a sculptor who had learnt his craft in such workshops as those that flourished in the tenth century at Constantinople, or in the twelfth at Cluny.

From the point of view of its iconography the sculpture presents certain interesting problems. In Byzantine art the position of the figures in each composition was strictly laid down. The most usual type of Virgin was that known as the *Hodegetria* or Indicator of the Way, where the Virgin holds the Child on her left arm while she points to Him with her right hand; the Child's right hand is extended in blessing. In the York relief the Virgin's right arm passes under the Child's leg, and the left must have passed behind His back. This is in accordance with the position known as the *Eleousa* or Virgin of Tenderness, but in addition the face of the Child should, in this type, be pressed against that of His Mother in affection, while His right hand should grasp her cloak. One of the earliest, and certainly the most lovely, examples of this type is the eleventh-century painting now at Moscow, known as Our Lady of Vladimir; there is every reason to believe that it was painted at Constantinople.[1] The *Eleousa* type cannot have been completely followed in the case of the York sculpture, however, for the Child's head clearly did not reach high enough to touch that of the Virgin, and His hand still survives in the attitude of blessing. The position of the figures suggests, indeed, that we have to do with an intermediary iconographical type, due to a confusion between the two basic types. Though in general the east Christian artists followed the iconographical formulas very exactly, such confusion did sometimes arise; an ivory in the Walters Art Gallery at Baltimore and another in the Hermitage at Leningrad may be noted.[2] On both the Virgin holds the Child with her two hands;

[1] A. J. Anisimov, *Our Lady of Vladimir*, Prague (1928).
[2] For the former see the Walters Art Gallery, *Early Christian and Byzantine Art Exhibition* (1947), no. 129, Pl. XXIII; for the latter see A. Goldschmidt, *Die Byzantinische Elfenbeinskulpturen*, Berlin (1934), ii, no. 81, Pl. XXXII.

both are to be dated to the tenth century and are therefore earlier than the York Virgin, so that an imported model of the blended type could have been available. It is, however, equally possible that the confusion between the types arose in England, and that the English carver discovered for himself the arrangement that we see here; if so, models of both the *Hodegetria* and the *Eleousa* types must have been seen by him.

Another interesting feature is the actual position of the Virgin's right arm, which is one that is rare in east and west alike; it is to be found in Italy in certain thirteenth- and perhaps twelfth-century paintings;[1] it occurs in the Caucasus in thirteenth-century metal-work;[2] but the earliest rendering appears to be a Coptic ivory at Baltimore.[3] In these examples, however, the type is that of the Virgin of Tenderness. It may also be noted in passing that the York Madonna is shown with legs set parallel in the Byzantine manner and not with feet together and knees wide apart, as was usual in French work in the twelfth century. Nor do the proportions of the figure appear to be those usual in French Romanesque renderings of the subject, for there hardly seems to be room, so far as one can judge from what remains, for the long neck and large head that were usual there.

The date of this sculpture has given rise to very considerable discussion and controversy. A date in the eleventh century has been proposed by Clapham, Prior and Gardner, and Casson, and one in the twelfth by Maclagan, Saxl and Wittkower, Kendrick, and others. Both datings are supported by a considerable mass of evidence.

The eleventh-century date is, in the first place, borne out by the Byzantine affinities, for, if all that we have said above is accepted, it was in Saxon times that these elements were most to the fore in England. Clapham has called attention to the stylistic similarities between the York Virgin and a slab which bears the Virgin in the

---

[1] W. de Grüneisen, 'Madone du Triptyche inédit de Bonaventure Berlinghieri', in *Studien zur Kunst des Ostens, J. Strzygowski Festschrift*, Wien (1925), no. 206 and Pl. xxiv, Fig. 1.

[2] N. P. Kondakov, *Monuments of Antiquity of Georgia*, St. Petersburg (1890), Fig. 16 (in Russian).

[3] Walters Art Gallery, op. cit., no. 160, Pl. xx.

·Oran's position, from the Mangana area of Constantinople,[1] but an ivory formerly in the Stroganov collection of about 1000 affords an even closer comparison,[2] and numerous other stylistic parallels can be cited. Thus a small bronze triptych in the Victoria and Albert Museum which is to be dated to the eleventh century is obviously a child of the same parent.[3] Parallels with eleventh-century Byzantine works are far more convincing than one put forward by Saxl and Wittkower in favour of a twelfth-century date, namely, a relief in St. Zeno's chapel in St. Mark's at Venice. This they date to the thirteenth century,[4] but it is to be questioned seriously whether it is actually so late, and in any case the rendering of the theme might equally well be paralleled a century earlier. The parent of the group, in later Byzantine art, was no doubt closely akin to the great mosaic of the Virgin recently uncovered in St. Sophia at Constantinople, dating from about 1000,[5] and the York Madonna is far closer to it than to the thirteenth-century Byzantine variants.

In the second place we know that work of similarly high quality to that to be seen in the York Virgin was produced in England in Saxon times. A number of ivories on a small scale, and the lovely Romsey rood on a large one, may be compared. Technical parallels also exist and, as Casson has noted, they are especially clearly marked with regard to the carving of the draperies on an ivory known as the Godwin seal in the British Museum (Pl. 36 d).[6] Though not dated with absolute accuracy, there is very weighty evidence for associating the seal with a man of the name of Godwin; the name is mentioned between 967 and 1016 (see p. 165), and a date around the year 1000 appears to be likely. But it is perhaps in the direction of the negative evidence that the seal offers that it is most important, for the two figures that top it are just as 'Romanesque' as is the York Virgin; if the one work is to be

[1] *Romanesque Architecture in England before the Conquest*, 139.
[2] C. Diehl, *Manuel d'art byzantin* (1926), vol. ii, Fig. 327.
[3] H. Peirce and R. Tyler, *Byzantine Art* (1926), Pl. 72.
[4] F. Saxl and R. Wittkower, *British Art and the Mediterranean*, Pl. 27.
[5] T. Whittemore, *The Mosaics of St. Sophia, Istanbul,* Second Preliminary Report (1936), Pl. 1.
[6] *Burl. Mag.* lxii (1933), 31.

dated to about 1000, there is no reason why the other should not be assigned to the same period.

Further evidence favouring an early date is afforded by comparison with a number of German works of the first half of the eleventh century. A Madonna in the Lückger collection, which is to be dated to about 1050,[1] may be cited, and there is a similar but finer one at Paderborn.[2] Both are in wood, but the latter was originally covered with thin metal. It was presented to the cathedral between 1050 and 1060. Both suggest that the York Madonna would be in no way precocious were it assigned to a slightly earlier date. The rich series of metal sculptures associated with the name of Bishop Bernward of Hildesheim must also not be forgotten, and there were probably other sculptures of a type just as advanced in stucco, though none has survived. The style of these works is quite distinct from that of French sculpture of the twelfth century, yet the York Madonna is obviously quite clearly related to them.

Finally, to crown this considerable accumulation of external evidence, it has recently been pointed out by Clapham that the form of the letters A and C used in the inscription beside the head of the York Madonna also supports a Saxon date, for the square C, he thinks, went out of use about 1100, while the looped A disappeared before the conquest.[3] The form, it is true, might have been copied at a later date, and the square C was used in twelfth-century manuscripts; but it is on the whole most unlikely that an antiquated type of letter would have been used. In association with a primitive work an old form of letter might have been employed, but one would hardly expect to find it on an accomplished work savouring in every way of the most up-to-date 'court art' of its day.

In support of a twelfth-century date the most weighty evidence is stylistic. The markedly metallic character of the sculpture is thus suggestive of Romanesque parallels in France, and the linear pattern-like treatment of the folds again supports a comparison

[1] H. Picton, *Early German Art*, London (1939), 135 and Pl. xcvm. 3.
[2] *Burl. Mag.* xci (Nov. 1949), Fig. 1.
[3] 'The York Virgin and its Date', *Arch. Journ.* cv (1948), 6.

with similar work. Indeed, if France were the only part of the
continent that need be considered, the stylistic similarities would
be quite enough to support a date not before about 1140. Further,
the most striking parallels to the York Virgin on a large scale in
this country are almost certainly of Romanesque date. They are
the figures of St. John and a headless Christ at Lincoln, no doubt
part of a majesty. Both are larger than the York Madonna, but
show the same svelte sculptural treatment, especially in the carving
of the bird beside St. John's head. It has been held that the figures
show just the posture and expression usual in French Romanesque
work of the first quarter of the twelfth century, e.g. at Toulouse
or Santiago de Compostela. But they are surely also closely akin
to ivories of Saxon date like the St. John at St. Omer (Pl. 39), and
the folds of the costume of the stone sculpture, especially at the
ankles, are markedly suggestive of the characteristic Winchester
flutterings. In fact, ivories which are close in style to the Lincoln
St. John undoubtedly existed in England from the beginning of
the eleventh century, and there is no reason why they should not
have inspired work on a larger scale in stone, even if in France
similar results in major sculpture did not appear for a century or
more. It may also be noted that the handling of the York Virgin
is rather more finished and stylized—in fact, more Byzantine—
than that of the Lincoln figures.

It is thus extremely difficult to determine the date of the York
Madonna. It is really a question of balancing the weighty evidence
in favour of a Saxon date against the strong evidence in favour of
a Norman one. On the whole, however, in the author's view, the
former is preponderant, and it is suggested that the York Madonna
should be assigned to the first half of the eleventh century. It
represents in fact the culminating point of Anglo-Saxon sculpture
under the influence of that Byzantine trend of art which we first
noted in the slabs at Breedon, and which was exercised in this
country either independently or by way of the German part of the
continent all through the period with which we are dealing. It
ceased at or just before the conquest, though, as we have already
noted, there was a second and independent wave in the full
twelfth century, the effects of which were more limited, for they

are to be traced mainly in a distinct and fairly restricted group of manuscript-paintings. This second wave could hardly have been responsible for either the York Madonna or the Barnack Christ, for it affected the style of painting for a brief period rather than the basic essence of art as a whole. But if these works are not late Saxon, as we believe, they must have been done under French influence, exercised after the new art brought in by the Normans had reached full maturity in this country, so that in that case they would date from the second quarter of the twelfth century at the earliest.

3. ORNAMENTAL SCULPTURE

Apart from the examples of figure-sculpture described in the preceding section, all of which bear to greater or lesser degree the print of continental and, especially, Byzantine influence, and most of which are in the form of slabs for interior use, a very considerable quantity of sculpture was also produced all over the country, on which the ornament is of a non-figural or purely decorative character. In most cases the work was probably done by local craftsmen inspired either by models of earlier date in the Northumbrian or Celtic style or by subsequent influence from Scandinavia and the north. Interlacing ornament and knotwork, stylized animals or occasionally human beings, and especially the favourite northern dragon-like animals, constitute the usual motifs. Slabs intended for interior use are very much less numerous than the free-standing crosses intended for erection out of doors, though they do occur more often than would seem likely at a casual glance. Gabled stones, known as hog-backs, were also numerous in the north, and though the form was essentially a northern one, hog-backs are also sometimes found in the south; for instance, examples exist at Ramsbury in Wiltshire and at Bexhill in Sussex. The motifs of decoration and the style of work on these stones were often close to that on the crosses, but it will be best to deal with the slabs before considering the crosses, for the latter are not only more widely distributed over the country, but also show a greater diversity of styles, and are often harder to study owing to the very battered condition of their decorations.

Though the ornament of the non-figural slabs is invariably stylized, several marked types can be distinguished. The most obvious of them is that where the design is completely formal, consisting of plaitwork, geometrical interlace, or similar motifs; the geometrical interlace is probably the most important of them. In its purest form it consisted of a series of bands plaited together; in more complicated types knots were introduced and the bands were twisted and entwined in a surprising variety of ways; the following variants may be noted: (1) regular plaitwork, without any breaks; (2) broken plaitwork, with breaks made in an irregular way; (3) knotwork; (4) circular knotwork; (5) triangular knotwork; (6) ringwork or chainwork. In classical art the plait was the only form of interlace employed; by the eighth century in Italy (and not before) the plait had been broken and knotwork begun, as, for example, at Valpolicella (712), in the baptistry of Callixtus at Cividale (737), or on the jambs of the doorway of the chapel of St. Zeno in the church of St. Praxede at Rome (772–95). In the simplest form there was only one break; in complicated ones, a number. The development of knotwork in this way was perhaps the most important contribution of Lombardic craftsmanship to ornament. The art was brought by that people from hither Asia in the course of their wanderings, and the plaitwork and knotwork of a closely similar type that is also to be found in the Caucasus probably owes its origin to the same common source, and the popularity of the interlace in Coptic art is no doubt due to an early debt of Egypt to the same northern source.[1]

At the time that these developments were going forward in Italy, interlacing ornament and knotwork were being developed along similar lines in the north of Europe, especially in the British Isles. It is probable that very similar results were arrived at in these different areas without any very close contacts between them. All the stages in the development of knotwork that are found in Italy, for example, are also to be traced in the crosses of north Wales, though these are considerably later in date and there is every reason to believe that their decoration was evolved locally. Romilly

---

[1] The spread has been examined by Strzygowski in all his works. For a summary see *Early Church Art in Northern Europe*, ch. i, especially p. 41.

Allen has accorded a thorough analysis to the numerous twists and twinings,[1] but it is to be doubted if such analyses can ever produce results of great significance: it remains what is intrinsically a complicated mathematical problem; and it does not seem possible, in Britain at any rate, to correlate in any way the types of interlacing either with particular waves of cultural migration or with distinct periods. The most that can be said is that this non-representational art as a whole was in essence definitely northern, and wherever we find it in Britain influence from the north is to be postulated. Further, it followed the normal changes of any art; the finest work was usually fairly early, and the later manifestations tended to be over-stylized and often clumsy. The crosses of south Wales and Cornwall, most of which belong to the eleventh and twelfth centuries, are thus rather coarse and crude; that at Norbury in Derbyshire, where the decoration is particularly telling because of its simplicity, is to be dated early in our own period, that is to say, to the late ninth or tenth century.

A few particular forms also give hints for dating. What is usually termed the Scandinavian ring-knot, a knot with loose rings which have no organic connexion with the interlacement, is thus typical of the tenth century; it is especially common on the crosses of Cumberland and Derbyshire. Three-stranded cords are unusual in pre-conquest work, though they do appear occasionally, e.g. at Ashbourne in Derbyshire, at Tadcaster, and at Thorp Arch in the West Riding. A style of interlace proper to illumination was also often copied exactly in stonework, but such copyings usually belonged to the first period of Christian art in England; and though interlacing motifs had become an essential part of the stoneworker's repertory by the period with which we are dealing, they had well-nigh ceased to appear in the manuscripts. Only in Scotland did interlacings on the stones still continue to follow manuscript types quite closely.[2]

---

[1] *Celtic Art in Pagan and Christian Times*, 257 ff.

[2] The sculptured stones of Scotland fall outside the scope of this book, but they constitute an interesting series. The most recent study, where a full bibliography is included, is that of C. L. Curle, 'The Chronology of the Early Christian Monuments of Scotland', *Proc. Soc. Ant. of Scotland*, lxxiv (1939–40), 60.

The pure band interlace remained popular throughout the period with which we are dealing; indeed, it to a great extent supplanted the various elaborations which had been so popular in the seventh and eighth centuries where all sorts of plant, bird, and animal forms were treated as the elements of an interlace pattern. It was, however, not the only element that belonged to the first trend of northern non-representational art in Britain, for a number of geometric motifs, such as the spiral and double spiral, were also treated in a similar way for their pattern effect. These motifs belonged to a very old stream in art, for they are to be found at the basis of neolithic ornament in Britain many centuries before the period with which we are dealing: whether they survived in the country through the long intervening period, or were re-introduced from northern Europe at a subsequent date, it is hard to say. Perhaps one of the reasons why the art introduced by Norse invaders and conquerors was so readily accepted in Britain was because the elements of the same art were already known to the people whom the invaders subjected. Spiral motifs, which were extremely popular in pagan Saxon times, continued to be used in one form or another right down to the Norman conquest without any marked break, even if their popularity waned. The font at Deerhurst, usually dated to the early part of the tenth century, is an excellent example (Pl. 30 a), and numerous other instances could be cited. Spiral ornament was also important in the decoration of the metal-work. Spirals occur, for example, on many of the objects of the Trewhiddle hoard dating from c. 875, where we find them blended with stylized versions of the palmette or ivy scroll, both elements belonging to classic as opposed to northern art. But the Trewhiddle style was in fact actually neither purely northern nor purely southern; it constituted an essentially English development, and when once it had been evolved the style spread over a wider area. Its progress across the country was in a northerly rather than a southerly direction, and its influence was in the main exercised on metal—the Wallingford sword in the Ashmolean Museum may be cited as an example of the extension of the same style.

Apart from these motifs, there were several rather similar ones associated with Anglo-Saxon art of the later period. One of the most important was the stepped pattern, which was extremely common first on jewellery and later in architecture, for instance at the base of the pilaster strips which are usual on the exteriors of tenth- and eleventh-century churches. It also occurs occasionally in sculpture, e.g. on the border of the Deerhurst slab bearing the Virgin to which we have already called attention (p. 107). Zigzags were again typical of later Saxon work. The latter motif probably came from Merovingian sources, while the popular key pattern was perhaps suggested by surviving classical works. In Celtic art interlace, step patterns, key patterns, spirals, and zoomorphs were all common in the early Christian period: they were usually all employed together. As time went on some of them disappeared. Spirals went first, in the ninth and early tenth centuries, then key patterns, leaving only interlaced work and zoomorphs; these often survived into the Norman age. Though not an absolutely definite criterion, the presence or absence of these features offers a useful aid to dating. In Saxon art, on the other hand, it was the simpler, more geometric patterns, like the step pattern and the zigzag, that survived longest.

Another very important group of motifs were those where the understanding was purely decorative, but where animals or even human figures were included in a stylized pattern. Animals were, indeed, developed into a number of very distinctive decorations. The most usual of them was a spirited animal not unlike a lion, with its tail twisted beneath it; it is usually known as the Great Beast. Fundamentally of Scythian origin, these animal motifs spread westwards along both southerly and northerly routes, and, as far as central Europe was concerned, very profoundly affected what is known as the Migration Style. But from our point of view it is the examples of this art that penetrated to northern Europe and were adopted there that are most important, for they were used in Scandinavia, and from there came to this country along with one or another of the numerous waves of Norse invaders, each wave bringing with it an art of a slightly different type, though the basic elements of all of them were the same.

The first of these so far as our period is concerned is known as the Jellinge style. Animals of this style first appeared in Scandinavia in the middle of the ninth century; they reached Britain soon after, though usually they were modified by Irish influence on the way. Brønsted, indeed, even goes so far as to suggest that Irish influence was exercised in Scandinavia, but this seems hardly likely, and Shetelig's theory that the style was evolved locally in Scandinavia is more probable. The Jellinge animals were long and thin, with heads bent backwards; their joints were usually indicated by spiral

FIG. 12.   *Slab at Levisham, Yorkshire. After Clapham*

patterns. The outlines were double, and they were often accompanied by ribbon interlace patterns which by the mid tenth century began to overpower the animal patterns. Slabs at Levisham, Yorkshire (Fig. 12), and Plumbland, Cumberland, may be noted.

At the end of the tenth century the beasts began to become more naturalistic than the thin ones of the early Jellinge style, and a struggle for supremacy between the old and new types characterized the period around 1000. This struggle represents the interaction of the English and Scandinavian elements in art, the refusal completely to stylize the beast in the Scandinavian manner attesting the deep love of nature that has always constituted the hall-mark of truly English art. Indeed, the English style was actually so strong that it exercised a repercussion on Norway, as, for instance, in the decoration of the runestone of Harold Blue Tooth at Jellinge, which dates from about 980. Though fundamentally Norse, the style of the ornament of this stone represents to some extent a backwash of English influence on Scandinavia.

As would be expected, the majority of the examples of this style are to be found in the north and east of England, the areas which were most affected by the Norse invasion, but a few examples from the west country may be noted. Most important is a fragment of a cross at Colerne in Wiltshire, which is usually assigned to the reign of Alfred. Another at Ramsbury in the same county is of the same type; on external evidence it can be fairly exactly dated to c. 909.[1]

In Scandinavia the Jellinge style of beast ornament gave place to a new manner in the first half of the eleventh century. The new manner is known as the Ringerike style, and it is distinguished by the employment of a characteristic leaf ornament or of lanky beasts or birds in place of the lion-like animals of the Jellinge style. The leaf ornament is made up of scrolls or parts of them, treated as interlacings, or of very thin, long leaves, ultimately derived from the acanthus; the beasts are of serpentine form and long-necked birds are also sometimes present. The manner is better suited to manuscript-illumination or metal-work than to sculpture, and some quite important examples of the style are to be found on metal objects (see p. 228). When used for the decoration of stone the relief was usually very low, but the designs were made to stand out boldly from the background as if in silhouette. The style was developed in Britain from the end of the tenth century onwards, the most important examples belonging in the main to the first half of the eleventh; its greatest popularity is to be correlated with the age of Danish ascendancy during the reign of Canute (1016–1035). With Canute's death the style soon died in face of the growing love of naturalism, as exemplified in the Winchester school illuminations; in the same way the Danish character of the rulers gave way to the English character of the people. Thus by the end of his life Canute was more an English than a Danish king, and he allowed himself to be depicted in a purely English manner, together with his queen, at the commencement of the New Minster Register (c. 1020). (Pl. 81.)

The most important example of the Ringerike style in England is a slab from St. Paul's churchyard, now in the Guildhall Museum; it bears a vigorous beast upon it which Minns has described as

---

[1] J. Romilly Allen, 'Notes on the ornamentation of the early Christian monuments of Wilts.', *Wilts. Arch. and Nat. Hist. Mag.* xxvii (1894), 50 ff.

practically the last linear descendant of Scythian art (Pl. 23 a).[1]
Keyser has analysed the symbolism of the subject more imagina-
tively, for he describes it as a stag with a serpent coiled about it;
the serpent, he believes, indicates the constant difficulties with
which a virtuous man has to contend through the allurements and
entanglements of the vices inherent in our nature.[2] It is, however,
seriously to be doubted whether this esoteric significance is to be
read into the design, and whether it is not due to conservatism,
representing the copying of an old motif proper to the animal
art of Asia as seen through the eyes of one familiar with the
Scandinavian animal and the Celtic interlacing styles. Some smaller
fragments from the same place and of the same type are preserved
in the British Museum. One of them bears the runic inscription,
'Kona caused to erect this stone to Tuki'. Tuki was one of Canute's
ministers, who died in 1035; the group of stones may thus be
dated to about that date.

Less accomplished and less Scythian, but showing the Ringerike
style in a more developed form, are the well-known stones from
Bibury, now in the British Museum, which are to be dated to the
early eleventh century (Fig. 13). Other stones which show the
influence of the Ringerike style to a greater or lesser degree are
preserved at Somerford Keynes in Wiltshire, Dolton in Devonshire, Frome, Rowberrow, and West Camel in Somerset, Steven-
ton Manor in Hampshire, and Tenbury Wells, Cropthorne, and
Rous Lench (Pl. 23 b) in Worcestershire. There are a few rather
similar examples in the Isle of Man. All must date from the early
eleventh century.

It is surprising to find stones of this type so widely dispersed
over an area which was but little touched by the Danes, and F.
Cottrill attempted to explain this by assigning many of them to an
early date.[3] He regarded the stones at Colerne, Dolton, and Tenbury as eighth century, and compared them to the eighth-century
Tara brooch and to crosses of the same period at Hackness and
elsewhere. This can hardly be, for the Ringerike style was only

[1] E. H. Minns, The Art of the Northern Nomads (1942), 37.
[2] Norman Tympana and Lintels, p. xlii.
[3] 'Some pre-Conquest stone carvings in Wessex', Soc. Ant. Journ. xv (1935), 144 ff.

developed at a late date. But the decoration of the stones no doubt owed much of its character to metal-work prototypes, and it is probable that the presence of such stones in Wessex is due to a local copying of metal-work models; a bronze scabbard from York and a panel from Winchester in the same material, both to

FIG. 13. *Stone from Bibury, Gloucester-shire. After Clapham*

be dated to about the year 1000, give an idea of what these proto-types must have been like. Manuscript prototypes may also have had a role to play, and a few examples of the style in manuscript-illustration may be cited. The initials of a psalter of *c.* 1040 in the University Library at Cambridge (Ff. 1. 23) are thus definitely in the Ringerike style, while an interesting drawing in the Caedmon MS. in the Bodleian, which has been regarded as a sketch for the binding of the manuscript, shows a blend of Ringerike and purely Saxon elements. Ornament of the same type also appears on some objects of minor scale, such as a bone cylinder from St. Martin-le-Grand now in the Guildhall Museum.

In the eleventh century these slender beasts of the Ringerike
style were quite often used in tympana both before and, in out-of-
the-way districts, after the conquest. A tympanum at Southwell,
which is probably to be dated about 1030, may be noted; it has
been re-used in a twelfth-century building (Pl. 28 *b*). It bears a
typical Ringerike beast, interlaced with a plant, and a lion-like
animal more of the Jellinge type; between them is a figure with
spread wings, presumably the Archangel Michael. Similar beasts,
associated with primitive human figures, are fairly common; one,
which seems to represent a centaur, appears at Ault Hucknall in
Derbyshire, and a tympanum at Pitsford in Northamptonshire of
the mid twelfth century is similar. A slab in St. Nicholas' church at
Ipswich, bearing a winged angel, presumably St. Michael, and a
dragon-like beast, may also be compared, though the rendering is
more fully modelled and shows a distinct feeling for figural
sculpture. It belongs to the first half of the eleventh century.[1]
These Ringerike beasts seem to have done duty as symbols of evil
in the scene of the struggle between St. Michael and the devil
which was very popular in early Norman art.

Appearing simultaneously with the lion-like beasts of the
Jellinge style and the thin interlacing birds and serpents of the
Ringerike, a beast which is more like a deer is sometimes found.
These deer were never conventionalized as much as the Ringerike
animals, but their tails twist round their bodies in the same way
as do those of the Jellinge lions. A cross-shaft at Breedon of the
mid ninth century may be noted. Another at Melbury Bubb in
Dorset (Pl. 30*b*), probably of rather later date, now re-used upside
down as a font, bears a beast which is midway between this and the
usual Jellinge type. Later variants are to be seen at Gloucester and
in Derbyshire. This deer-like beast, though also probably derived
from the Scythian world, seems to have come to England not
from Scandinavia but from the Merovingian area of northern
France. It was conveyed no doubt by way of manuscript models.

In the northern world the Ringerike style gave place in the
eleventh century to a third Norse manner, which is known as the
Urnes style. It is characterized by subtle, flowing lines, a more

[1] These tympana are all illustrated by Keyser.

rounded rendering, and by an absence of violent stylization. Apart from the famous wood-carvings at Urnes itself, from which place the style takes its name, numerous stones may be cited in Norway and Sweden; it would, indeed, perhaps be better to call it the 'Runestone' style.[1] From east Sweden it was carried to Ireland while that country was still under the sway of Norwegian rulers, and it is to be seen there in such works as the cross of Cong (*c.* 1123) and the Clonmacnois crozier. But at the end of the century it began to be merged with local elements and so formed an Irish-Norse style. In England it was also assimilated, and though it is now best illustrated by a number of small objects, mostly of metal (see p. 230), it is probable that examples in sculpture were at one time more numerous than the surviving monuments suggest. The Southwell tympanum already hints at the new manner, and some capitals at Kirkburn church in the East Riding of Yorkshire are definitely in the Urnes style. The asp and basilisk below Christ's feet on the slab at Jevington in Sussex, already discussed (p. 95 and Pl. 10 *a*) are also of Urnes character.

4. THE CROSSES

During the age with which we are dealing a very secondary place must be accorded to the sculpture of the crosses from the artistic point of view. Three hundred years earlier, in Northumbria, the carving on the crosses was outstanding; in the period subsequent to the Danish conquest it was wellnigh universally poor and primitive, and the best work is found on the slabs and plaques intended to be set up inside the churches. It is not without interest to speculate on the causes of this change, which is to be explained, no doubt, by racial geography. The tradition of erecting single slabs on sacred sites was a very early one in Britain, going back to pre-Christian times; it was taken over, along with a good many other things, by the new faith, and from the seventh century onwards carved stones, which later took on a cruciform shape, began to be erected in most parts of the country. Their popularity from that time increased rapidly, and they soon became one of the

[1] For illustrations of Urnes itself and of examples of the Runestone style in Britain and Scandinavia see T. D. Kendrick, *Late Saxon and Viking Art*, Pls. LXXV–LXXIX.

most characteristic features of British art—on the continent such
things were practically unknown.

As the old Celtic inhabitants were driven westwards by successive waves of invaders, fresh ideas penetrated, together with
a new interest in church architecture which bears witness to
contacts with Rome and the Christian east. New subjects for
sculptured decoration also appeared, such as cornices, roods, slabs,
and, finally, tympana, and as these things became more usual in
the centres of culture, free-standing crosses tended to disappear or
to be relegated to out-of-the-way regions. This change was
naturally most rapid in the south, where contacts with the Mediterranean world were most to the fore. In the north of Britain and
in the Danelaw, where the crosses had been taken over as a favourite
art-form by the Danes, and in the Celtic region to the west, they
long remained popular, and even in the rest of England they
continued to crop up from time to time right down to the six-
teenth century, bearing witness to the strength of the older ideas
associated with elements of the population which had remained
unchanged in face of the numerous successive cultural waves that
had intruded between the ninth and the twelfth centuries. But in
the main the cross or menhir is a monument which must be associated with a racial stratum which was gradually eliminated by
subsequent invasions.

Each invasion, however, brought with it some new form of
ornament, and before the crosses were finally eclipsed as an art-
form, a very wide repertory of different types of decoration was
to appear on their shafts and heads. Thus figural work, stylized
animal motifs, acanthus and vine scrolls, geometric patterns, and
interlacings of various forms were all used.

The predominance of one type of ornament or another often
helps to throw light on the cultural history of the region to which
the sculptures belong. The formal beast ornament, for example,
nearly always betokens, as we have seen, the influence of the
Scandinavian world; it was concentrated in the north and east of
the country, but also penetrated at a late date far into Wessex.
Other types of stylized ornament, again, are to be associated with
Merovingian art and appear mainly in the south-east. Fine figural

work betokens the influence of Ottonian or Byzantine art, and is found mainly in the south, south-west, and centre of England. The crosses, indeed, tended to vary in style from region to region according to the basic character of the population in the different areas or the nature of the principal external influence to which each of them was subjected. Though they are, it is true, of less artistic merit, and are less interesting to the observer whose primary concern is artistic quality than are the sculptured slabs, they are more valuable to the historian in that they afford a key to the routes followed by invaders and traders during the period with which we are concerned. The actual presence or absence of crosses thus in itself serves as some indication of the racial and cultural affinities of the people who inhabited the different portions of the British Isles, and the character of their ornament helps to show in what direction their contacts lay, with what regions they traded, and what types of racial and cultural infiltration affected each region throughout the ages.

A few very marked types are to be associated with particular regions. In Scotland, for example, though Northumbrian and Irish influence was always important, a predilection for the slab with cross outlined upon it in shallow carving survived right down till the tenth century or later. In the north of England tall shafts and small heads were usual; in the centre the shafts were some-times inordinately long, and in Cheshire, Staffordshire, and parts of Derbyshire a clearly marked group predominated, distinguished by circular shafts obviously inspired by wooden prototypes. The fine tall cross at Gosforth, of late-ninth-century date, is the most important example of the group (Pl. 24 a). It is circular below and square above. Christian figure-subjects and scenes from the Scandi-navian Eddas are often found together on the shafts of these crosses, and Kendrick suggests that this was done because the carvers regarded the figures as part of an ornamental design rather than as subjects illustrating a theme; the innate conservatism of the primi-tive artist would seem a more likely explanation.

In the North Riding of Yorkshire another group, which may be termed the 'Round Shaft Derivative', has been distinguished by Kendrick. The shafts of these crosses are not necessarily round;

their prototype must have been a cross round below like a tree-trunk but chamfered off above to make it square, and the sloping rebate so formed was copied as part of the ornament on a square-shafted cross; this is clearly to be seen on a cross at Whalley in Lancashire (Pl. 25 a), which is to be dated to the eleventh century. Such crosses are all obviously of fairly late date. A group of rather solid, more squat crosses, usually with finely carved ornament, is to be associated with Derbyshire; a cross at Two Dales, Darley Dale, may be cited as a characteristic example (Pl. 25 b). In Lincolnshire the crosses follow the limestone ridge and are absent over the rest of the county, where their place was no doubt taken by wooden monuments which have long since vanished, though their legacy survives in the tall circular crosses of the Cheshire group, which still look like tree-trunks.

Perhaps the most markedly characteristic of all the groups, how-ever, is that distinguished by the wheel-shaped head. Crosses of this type are to be seen at their best in Ireland, and the rich series of monuments there has been admirably published by Miss Françoise Henry; they are mostly of tenth- and eleventh-century date, and some are even later, for the Celtic world was very con-servative. The form, however, probably originated not in Ireland but in the Isle of Man in the ninth century, whence it was dis-seminated on the one hand along the Viking sea routes to Ireland and on the other by Viking settlers in Yorkshire and Cheshire (see Fig. 1). The earliest examples in England probably date from about 900, but the type was only fully developed there by about 930. From Cheshire and south Yorkshire the form travelled south-wards to Wales; most of the examples there are of the eleventh century. It then penetrated by way of south Wales to Cornwall in the later eleventh century. The type also appeared in Scotland, where it was likewise intrusive, and is to be distinguished from the indigenous form, where the wheel pattern is no more than indicated in relief on a slab. There is room for extensive study in the development and distribution of the.variants of the wheel-cross form.

The distribution of the different motifs of decoration is again important in this context, but their study is intensely complicated and the conclusions that can be drawn are far from obvious; often, indeed, they are hardly apparent. The extent to which the motifs travelled is, however, indicated by a wooden gaming-board of the third quarter of the tenth century from Balinderry in Ireland. Its decoration is clearly related to that of the prevalent form of tenth-century Manx cross, where plaits and interlacings and occasional crude figures in low relief predominate; it is the type of decoration associated locally with the name of Gart Bjarnarson. It bears witness to the active role that the Vikings played at this time, and shows that their movements were not always of a purely predatory nature; they were also to some extent colonizers and traders, and they exercised a considerable influence on the formation of artistic taste and cultural outlook. O'Neill Hencken, indeed, in his publication of the gaming-board, describes it as a product of Celtic-Norse art.[1]

In addition to these differences which affect the actual forms of the crosses, a number of basic types of decoration may also be distinguished, all of which belong fundamentally to separate art streams, though by the period with which we are dealing they had already often become inextricably intermingled. First of these is the figural group, where our Lord, the Virgin, saints, and sometimes even scenes from the Bible story are shown. This trend was to be seen at its height in Northumbria in the seventh century, but the motifs continued to be used on the crosses from then onwards, though the general tendency was towards greater stylization and away from naturalism. Even here Collingwood sees two trends at work—the one, which he calls the Roman, which shows a greater degree of naturalism with full flowing lines, and the other, which he terms the Byzantine, which is more stylized, with flat, stiff figures; it easily degenerated into a clumsy, essentially primitive style. The distinctions he draws, however, are not always very clear; he does not necessarily use the term Byzantine in the same sense as other authorities, and the difference between the two influences was so quickly obscured by the development of native idioms or by progressive degeneration that it is only very occasionally that the two can be separated, in any case in the eleventh

[1] 'A gaming board of the Viking age', *Acta Archaeologica*, iv (1933), 85 ff.

century. There is, for instance, a clear distinction between monuments where the faces are fat, round, and well modelled, and those
where they are thin, narrow-cheeked, and hollow-faced, but these
differences are hardly to be ascribed to the working of two separate
streams of influence, but are rather to be accounted for by distinctions of date or quality; the round, full faces are thus early, and
come as the result of good and careful work; the thin faces are late
and illustrate a decadent phase.

In addition to the development or rather the gradual deterioration of the figural style of the north which went on continuously
from the seventh till the twelfth century, crosses in the south and
centre of the country were also sometimes affected by the new
figural style which came as the result of Byzantine or Carolingian
inspiration; we have already dealt with this when describing the
figured slabs. In considering the crosses it is necessary to remember
the existence of this style though its role was not very important.

The same continental influences that affected the purely figural
work in the south also exercised an influence on ornament, and
such German motifs as the caulicula and the Carolingian acanthus
were quite often present in the south and occasionally also in the
north. The former, for example, appears on a capital from Hexham,
now at Durham; the latter, predominant in illumination and used
frequently on the figured slabs, is also to be seen from time to
time on crosses; a shaft at Wolverhampton may be noted. Vine
scrolls, both alone and 'inhabited', are also usual, but it is extremely
hard to say whether individual examples were derived from old
Northumbrian prototypes or were the result of an independent
tenth-century influence from the continent.

Stylized animal ornament of Scandinavian type was also quite
frequently present on crosses, though the similar beast ornament
which we have ascribed to Merovingian influence was far less usual.
More important was the interlace, which is to be found on crosses
over the whole of Britain from the first simple renderings of the
seventh century onwards. Two strands, three strands, and occasionally even four-strand plaits all occurred; the patterns were varied
with great exuberance of invention, and their arrangement followed
a number of distinct rules. We have already called attention to

these when dealing with the slabs. In the case of the crosses it has so far proved impossible to associate one form of interlace with any particular area; nor are the various forms easily datable on the grounds of pattern alone; the degree of complication seems rather to depend on the capability of the craftsman, and in this direction one can do little more than assert that the very late work is in general rough and unelaborate.

The problems of dating are, as we have already noted, very complicated. Of the many hundreds of crosses which once existed all over the country, only very few are exactly dated either by inscriptions, records, or similar external evidence, and of the crosses that are mentioned in the records still fewer remain even in the form of fragments. Of these one of the most interesting was erected by Egbert at Kingston in Surrey to commemorate the holding of a great council there at the end of his reign; all that survive are some fragments built into the transept of All Saints' church which may or may not belong to it. They bear interlaced ornament in low relief of a rather conservative character. The same monarch also set up a cross at Caistor in Lincolnshire to commemorate his victory over Mercia in 927, but nothing seems to have survived.[1] Of crosses bearing inscriptions, a late shaft at Rolleston in Nottinghamshire may be noted. It bears on one face an Anglian beast and on the other an inscription which reads, 'Radulphus me fecit'; it has so far proved impossible to identify Radulphus, but the type of lettering suggests a date between 1050 and 1150.

A few other crosses can be dated on external evidence of an archaeological character. Most important among these are some shafts at Durham which were found under the Chapter house; it is almost certain that they belong to the period between 995 and 1050, for the see was only founded in the former year and the Chapter house was built shortly before 1110. The crosses would hardly have been broken up less than fifty years after their erection. They bear coarse, rather decadent figural work, which is typical of the survival of the Northumbrian style in the eleventh century. Crosses at Ramsbury in Wiltshire and at Shaftesbury belong almost

[1] W. E. St. Lawrence Finny, 'The Church of the Saxon coronation at Kingston', *Surrey Arch. Collns.* xlviii (1943), 3.

certainly to the early tenth century, for the abbey at the former place was founded in 909 and that at the latter under King Alfred (871–99), and the crosses were probably set up soon after these foundations were established.

Again, it is sometimes possible to indicate termini in one direction or another for larger groups of crosses. For example, in central England no crosses can antedate the conversion of Mercia about 700, nor are they likely to belong to the age of violent Danish invasions and ravaging between 865 and 917; thus the earlier types can with a considerable degree of certainty be assigned to the period between 700 and 865, and the later ones to that after 917; work of this age in the main shows marked Danish stylistic influence. In a careful study of the tall crosses of Cheshire and Staffordshire Pape has concluded on historical grounds that nearly all the examples we know in that area are to be assigned to the second half of the tenth century, and there seems every reason to accept this conclusion.[1]

Apart from these few instances, dates must be arrived at primarily on stylistic grounds, and although results which are comparatively accurate have been reached by authorities for different areas, little attempt has so far been made to devise a system of universal application. It is no easy matter, for one area was often in advance of another, and in out-of-the-way places old themes or systems lived on for a century or more after they had died out elsewhere.

Of the local systems the most complete is that worked out by Collingwood for Yorkshire. He distinguishes three main styles, with three sub-groups in the first, three in the second, and two in the third. The first falls outside our period. The three sub-groups of his second style, which he terms B, cover the later ninth (B 1), the early tenth (B 2), and the mid to later tenth centuries (B 3), and the two sub-groups of his third style, C, the first half of the eleventh (C 1), and the second half of the eleventh (C 2). These styles show quite close correlation with historical events. Thus Carlisle was sacked by the Danes in 876, and for the next fifty years or so Irish Vikings penetrated eastwards into Yorkshire. In 919

[1] 'The round shafted pre-Norman crosses of the north Staffordshire area', *Trans. North Staffs. Field Club*, lxxx (1945–6).

one of them, Ragnwald, who reigned till 927, brought an Irish Viking following with him. From 940 till 954 Irish control was once more imposed, and there was again ample opportunity for the penetration of Celtic influence. The period of these Irish contacts coincided with the production of the crosses classed by Collingwood in his group B. Chain patterns, ring patterns, and dragons were the most usual motifs at this time.

In the latter part of the tenth century, when English overlordship was once more established, southern influence began to penetrate and there was an improvement in technical skill. Interlace work tended to become more open, and the chiselling more clear-cut and precise. This new style was but little affected by the invasions of Swein and Canute between 1013 and 1016, and it is hard to say exactly when work of Collingwood's group C1 ended and that of his style C2 began. All that is clear is that crosses of the latter type continued to be erected in Yorkshire even after the Norman conquest, and some of the late examples are quite fine; the best is probably that at Nunburnholme, which Collingwood dates to the first quarter of the eleventh century. Its decoration shows a mixture of influences. That of the old eighth-century Anglian figural style is clear; Viking motifs and Celtic elements are apparent—the latter had disappeared from the area soon after 1000; and the excellence of the figures suggests that the sculptor had seen work of our 'court' group of sculpture from the south. Another fine work, though it is rather earlier in date as it must belong to the tenth century, is a large cross in Leeds parish church (Pl. 24 b). The style is, however, more conservative, and its sculptor was probably influenced by some old Northumbrian model rather than by contemporary work in the south.

Though wheel-headed crosses are occasionally to be found in Yorkshire as a legacy from the time of Irish overlordship when they were introduced from the Isle of Man, the spread of this form in an easterly direction was halted by the southern influence to which we have just alluded. Wheel-headed crosses did, however, become popular in other regions, and one of the characteristics of the tenth century was their adoption all along the western fringe of Britain. Examples are to be found in Lancashire and Cheshire,

and these counties are important as bridges or links. But it was to
the north, in Galloway, and to the south-west, in Wales, that the
type was most popular. The ornament that accompanied the wheel-
headed crosses was usually not very outstanding from the point of
view of quality; interlacings were done, but they were not properly
understood, and figural work was invariably of the poorest. The
best work was probably done in the Isle of Man itself, where an
interesting series of crosses was produced from the end of the tenth
century almost till the thirteenth. Subjects from the Norse sagas
were often included, along with Christian ones, in the decoration;
the Viking element in the population kept the old styles in fashion.
Work in the same style was done in Anglesey and north Wales,
and there are not a few crosses of the type in Anglesey; the
most important of them are two at Penmon. In north Wales the
cross at Maenachwyfan may be noted; it shows quite good work.

In Wales as a whole some 400 crosses have actually survived,
mostly in the west and along the coast, especially in Pembrokeshire. They are often of the wheel-head type and are almost
invariably decorated with interlace, plaitwork, or stylized acanthus
ornament; the absence of figure-sculpture is striking. Nash-Williams
distinguishes three groups, namely, rude pillarstones of natural or
near natural shape, unshaped or roughly shaped slabs, and shaped
crosses or slabs; it is only on the latter that ornament of any quality
is to be found, but even here the work is usually very rough, the
interlacing poorly conceived and incompetently executed, and the
proportions ungainly. From the artistic point of view they are of
no consequence, and they are very difficult to date with any degree
of exactitude. Most are to be assigned to the ninth or tenth century.
On the borders work is sometimes rather more accomplished: a
cross head of the tenth century at Llangan in Glamorgan thus has
a crucifixion upon it, though the relief is low and the sculpture
little more than mere engraving. Similar engraving is used on a
grave-slab at Llanvenoe in Herefordshire, where the crucifixion is
again shown. Christ appears to wear a robe coming to the knees
rather than a loincloth, but the work is so poor that it is impossible
to be sure. In the south of Wales the work is on the whole even
poorer; a tenth-century cross at Penally and one at Carew in

Pembrokeshire, which is dated by an inscription to between 1033 and 1035, may be noted.[1]

In Cornwall, crosses are very numerous indeed, but they stand mostly on bleak moors far from centres of habitation. Many are no more than upright stones with a simple ✝ carved on them, and even those that bear figures or interlacing show very primitive work of no particular interest. A few coped stones decorated with coarse plaited ornament also exist.

The rather more elegant and more elaborately decorated types of cross which we have noted in Yorkshire were closely related to those in the counties immediately to the south, notably Derbyshire. Sixty-five crosses or fragments of crosses have so far been recorded in this county, and many of them are really fine. Perhaps the best is a shaft from Ingleby, now at Repton. Two sides bear simple plaits, the third a tree, the leaves of which suggest foliage of the type usual in manuscripts of the Winchester school, and the fourth a man gathering fruit. Comparison with the work at Breedon has been suggested, but the cross is probably to be dated to the early eleventh century; indeed, this cross might almost be cited in support of a late date for the Breedon slabs.

In the rest of Mercia crosses are today less numerous than in Northumbria, but examples occur all over the area, even if in places they are few and far between. So far, for example, forty-nine have been recorded in Lincolnshire, seventeen in Northamptonshire, eight in Cambridgeshire, five in Huntingdonshire, twelve in Nottinghamshire, and ten in Norfolk. Most of the work in all these counties is post-Danish in date. In Lincolnshire most of the stones are to be assigned to the eleventh rather than to the tenth century, and there was a long overlap after the Norman conquest. In spite of the prolonged Danish domination, Scandinavian motifs are rare, and there is only one cross in the county of which the ornament is markedly Danish, namely, at Crowle. The usual ornament is made up of interlace patterns, but figural work is also present, and a few wheel-headed crosses also occur attesting contacts with the west. That at Conisholme bore a fine figure of Christ in high relief; the wheel is, however, broken. It

[1] E. Nash-Williams, *Early Christian Monuments of Wales*, 184.

is perhaps to be associated with the earlier figural work at Fletton, near Peterborough; if so, the cross must also be of comparatively early date and should be assigned to the ninth century. Another fine piece of figural work is to be found on a tenth-century shaft now at Digby; its original provenance is unknown. Clapham has suggested that it recalls Bewcastle,[1] but its marked Mediterranean style is more probably to be attributed to Carolingian influence, conveyed at a later date perhaps by means of an ivory.

In Cambridgeshire, grave-slabs with decoration in low relief are nearly as numerous as the crosses, and work on the two types of monument is akin. Sir Cyril Fox in fact distinguished a separate Cambridgeshire school which he thinks was situated at Cambridge. Examples of its work are to be found in neighbouring counties also, but they do not extend outside the area of the old Danelaw. The ornament is of old interlace type and shows no Danish elements, but the carvings are, on stylistic grounds, to be assigned to the tenth and eleventh centuries rather than to a pre-Danish date. More sculpturesque than most of this work is a small block at Kedington in Suffolk, about twenty-two miles south-west from Cambridge, which bears the crucified Christ in quite high relief; it is to be dated to the tenth century.

In Nottinghamshire, grave-slabs appear as well as crosses, and interlace, figural, and Norse ornament all occurs. A cross at Shelford may be cited as an illustration of figural work; it is poor and debased, and shows no signs of the new continental influence which is at the basis of most tenth-century figural work south of the Humber. The shaft has two broad and two narrow faces; one of the latter is plain; the other bears an interlace pattern, but the Virgin and Child appear on one of the wider faces and there is a four-winged seraphim on the other. Practically all the work in the county dates from after the accession of Canute in 1017, for until that time the area was dominated by pagans. What appears to be a slab bearing acanthus ornament in high relief, built into the south side of the tower at Barnack, may also be part of a cross shaft, for it stands on a large stone laid horizontally, which looks rather like

[1] Introduction to D. S. Davies, 'Pre-Conquest carved stones in Lincolnshire', *Arch. Journ.* lxxxiii (1926), 4.

the base of a cross. It has usually been dated to the tenth century, but might be earlier, and if a cross and not a slab, it almost certainly would be.

Though many more slabs than crosses have been preserved in Wessex, a few crosses do exist, and there is a good deal of work quite outside the accomplished continental figural style which we discussed at the outset. A fine cross at Colyton in Devon may, for example, be noted. In Sussex some ninth-century grave-slabs from Bexhill bear low relief interlacings akin to those of Yorkshire, and elaborate interlace work is to be found not only at various places in Wiltshire and Somerset, but also even at Winchester itself. Northern influence may also have been responsible for the ornament of a cross at Newent in Gloucestershire, though the carving is unusual and the technique would suggest that it was inspired by a metal-work prototype. A small slab, sculptured on both sides, at the same place is even closer to a metal-work prototype; it must belong to the early eleventh century.

Fragments of a cross shaft from All Hallows, Barkingside, which came to light as the result of bombing during the war, have also established the fact that there was a school of carvers working in London in the tenth and eleventh centuries which owed a great deal to the old Northumbrian style; the Barkingside fragments are in fact the last links in the line which started in the seventh century. They are to be dated between 1030 and 1050 and are important in that they show that work of a conservative character was done at the same time and in close association with that of the developing continental style.

5. ARCHITECTURAL SCULPTURE

In view of the profusion of the crosses and slabs in the later Saxon period and the richness of much of the architecture as attested by such buildings as those at Bradford-on-Avon, Barnack, or Earl's Barton, it is surprising that architectural features, notably cornices, capitals, window embrasures, or the voussoirs of arches, were not more frequently decorated. Normally, however, such features were extremely plain; the capitals were simple, either impost or cushion in type according to the shape of the columns below them, decorated cornices and corbels were rare, and arches were at most adorned with a simple dot motif. The only elaborate detail that survives, that at Breedon and Fletton, belongs stylistically to an earlier period. It may, however, be noted that some of the work is in that particular technique, 'slant carving', which is more usually known by its German name, *schrägschnit*. It is a technique which appears to have originated in the Scythian area, and was originally proper to wood rather than stone. It was, however, soon adapted to metal-working, and produced, when skilfully employed, a most delightful effect in light and shade. From the Scythian area it passed, along with numerous other elements, to the Germanic world and thence to Scandinavia, and when we see it in England its presence is to be attributed to influence from the north. It was well suited to architectural decoration, and one would expect to find it extensively employed in England though few sculptures are known. Decorative plaques which form part of the tympanum at Barton Seagrave in Northamptonshire and which may be late Saxon stones re-used show the technique.

Even if they are of early date the Breedon friezes must be noted, for, with actual examples so rare, they serve to give an idea of what might have been done in later times, and so help us to complete the picture. Of actual late Saxon works only very few can be mentioned. There are some lengths of frieze panel at Sompting in Sussex which must date from about 1000. A small head, built into the north wall of the church at Ampney St. Peter in Gloucestershire, was perhaps a corbel, but the sculpture is extremely crude, the work of some unskilled local craftsman, and it is very hard to date: the early tenth century seems most likely. To much the same period is to be assigned a fragmentary corbel and some plaitwork motifs that adorn the arch of a small doorway at Ashton Keynes in Wiltshire; the arch is cut out of a single block of stone, and this seems to have been a usual Saxon practice— a window formed in the same way at Coln Rogers may be compared.

The most important of all the architectural work of the period is, however, that at Barnack, where a number of pierced slabs intended to fill the lights of the tower windows are preserved

(Fig. 4). The piercings take the form of an interlaced design. Window-slabs of this type were probably more often of wood than of stone, and they no doubt existed in most churches. Fragments of one survive at Birstall in Leicestershire.

Capitals which attest continental influence, bearing as they do the Carolingian acanthus, survive in St. Augustine's at Canterbury, and at Langford. There are also rather crude capitals on the chancel arch at Bibury; they are of a basically classical type, and this is particularly interesting, for other Saxon work from the same place is completely northern in spirit. Fluting on a small pier which separates two triangular-headed arches on the interior of the west wall at Deerhurst is again classical, and might well have been inspired by a Roman altar that had been seen by the mason (Pl. 4 a). Some crudely carved capitals at Sompting (Pl. 26 b) in Sussex are also of Saxon date, but they herald the early Norman ones at such places as Durham castle chapel (Pl. 29), which belong to about 1070. They bear stylized plant motifs and curious grotesque human or animal figures crudely carved. There is nothing very Saxon about them, nor is it easy to find any parallels for them in France. In fact, they stand apart, and belong to no particular family; the most striking thing about them is the absolute lack of any feeling for sculpture. Of much the same date, but rather more proficient from the sculptural point of view, are capitals in St. Woollo's church at Newport, Monmouthshire, at Netheravon in Wiltshire, and at Bramber in Sussex. The fine series of capitals at Southwell Minster, which have sometimes been dated as early as 1090, are more probably early twelfth century. The capitals bear scenes from the life of Christ, and the work is of really high quality.[1]

A square stone presented to Grasmere church in 1913, which is sculptured on all four sides like a capital, may also be noted. It bears dragons' heads on two faces, a human figure with a sword on the third, and an acanthus motif on the fourth. All the compositions are enclosed in semicircular niches. The floral motif is Norman, of twelfth-century character, and heralds those on the

[1] J. Romilly Allen, 'Sculptured Norman capitals at Southwell Minster', *The Illustrated Archaeologist*, i (1894), 31 (with good plates); also W. J. Conybeare, 'The carved capitals of Southwell Minster', *Journ. Brit. Arch. Ass.* N.S., xxxix (1934), 176–80.

Bridekirk font. The dragons belong to the old Norse repertory, but are rendered with a real feeling for sculpture. The man might be described as Normano-Saxon. The stone is oolitic limestone, and must therefore have been brought from some distance; the work is not unlike some at Durham, and the stone may have been taken from there.[1] It is probably to be dated to the second half of the eleventh century.

Capitals of a more important group of early Norman date bear scenes from the Old and New Testaments sculptured in a silhouette technique; the most important examples are some detached ones in the Chapter house at Westminster and in Hereford cathedral; both series, however, are probably to be dated shortly after, rather than before the year 1100. The style is suggestive of painting, and it may be that the sculptor was copying an illumination. But there is no hint of the Winchester style here; it is rather, in embryo, the type of work which was to be developed so superbly in the Romanesque capitals of France during the next fifty years or so, and it may therefore be assumed that the work was done under close continental influence. Such influence would be natural at this date in both places, especially in Westminster, where a church in the Norman style had been begun by the Confessor even before the conquest.

No study of the sculpture of this transitional period would be complete without a brief reference to the decorative work which was to play so important a part in later Norman art in this country, both on capitals and, more especially, on the jambs and arches of the doorways. The Norman repertory was extremely rich, and comprised such motifs as the saw-tooth, the cheveron or its elaborations, the zigzag and the ribbon zigzag, the lozenge, the rosette, the billet, the dog-tooth, the key pattern, the battlement moulding, the cable moulding, the beak head, and the palmette.[2] With the exception of the cable moulding, which was known in Saxon art, they all belonged to post-conquest times, but they were

---

[1] A. G. Gilchrist, 'A sculptured stone in Grasmere church', *Trans. Cumb. and West Antiq. and Arch. Soc.* N.S., xxxv (1935), 73. He assigns it to the Saxon-Norman overlap period.

[2] For a useful study of these forms see P. M. Johnston, 'Romanesque ornament in England', *Journ. Brit. Arch. Ass.* xxx (1924), 91.

more elaborately developed in England than on the continent, and the brilliant quality of much of the work is one of the most distinguishing features of the Norman style in this country. In spite of this richness, however, motifs and styles of earlier type sometimes survive beside the Norman motifs; the series of late Norman capitals in St. Peter's church at Northampton may be noted, for their ornament is curiously similar to that of a panel in the Ringerike style in the same church; it is tempting to suggest that the Norman sculptor saw it, and copied it on his capitals.

6. FONTS

In early Christian times baptism was performed in a building specially constructed for the purpose, but the use of the font as we know it today had come in by the ninth century, as is attested by the fact that one is illustrated on the ivory cover of the Sacramentary of Drogo, bishop of Metz from 823 to 855, in the Bibliothèque Nationale.[1] Actual fonts of such early date are, however, practically unknown. Their employment was at first exceptional rather than normal, and wooden tubs were probably used more often than stone ones. When once the production of this piece of church furnishing had become a normal practice, it would seem that the old crude fonts were usually replaced by more elaborate ones, so that very few early examples have been preserved. They must have been of simple form, like the wooden tubs that they supplanted, and such examples as have survived are consequently hard to date on stylistic grounds. Indeed, the date is likely to vary according to the provenance, for in well-populated, accessible districts such things would certainly not have been made after the Saxon period, whereas in out-of-the-way places they might well have been done a century or so later.

Further, of the few surviving fonts that bear carved ornament in the Saxon style, not all are really to be counted as fonts, for it seems to have been quite a normal practice to re-use cross-shafts for this purpose. The so-called font at Bingley in Yorkshire,

[1] A. Goldschmidt, *Elfenbeinskulpturen*, i, Pl. xxx.

which bears a runic inscription of the eighth century, affords a case in point, and the fonts at Penmon in Anglesey, at Dalton in Devon, at Wilne in Derbyshire, and at Melbury Bubb in Dorset may also be noted. That at Melbury Bubb is a cross-shaft of the early tenth century which has been re-used upside down (Pl. 30 *b*). It is interesting as an illustration of the southward penetration of a style of ornament most familiar in Yorkshire, composed of plain and animal interlace. The interesting font at Deerhurst (Pl. 30 *a*) is also probably a very large cross-shaft re-used. The ornament is composed of two elements, a double spiral which is close to that on a pendant from the Trewhiddle hoard, and a vine scroll which is more akin to debased Northumbrian work. On the basis of the similarity to the Trewhiddle work a date around 910 seems most likely. A font at Morwenstow in Cornwall is rather similar; it stands in a Norman church and has been claimed as Norman, but the cable ornament that adorns it and the irregular form of the font are both characteristically Saxon. A few other fonts which are Saxon in date and which are not ornamented but bear inscriptions in Latin characters may also be mentioned, notably those at Patrishow in Brecon, at Little Billing in Northamptonshire, and at Potterne in Wiltshire. The last is of simple, tub-like shape, and, minus its inscription, is typical of what the majority of Saxon fonts were probably like. The tub-like font in St. Martin's church at Canterbury, which has sometimes been assigned to the eighth century or even earlier, was actually probably not made and certainly not decorated before the twelfth century.

A group of fonts which bear spirited sculptures of human and animal figures and which are regarded as Saxon by Bond[1] are on stylistic grounds more probably to be assigned to the post-conquest period. Such is the font at Curdworth in Warwickshire, which is decorated with grotesquely primitive figural carvings similar to those on the capitals in the Castle chapel at Durham; it is probably to be assigned to much the same date, that is, about 1070. There are rather similar fonts at South Milton in Devon, Ilam in Staffordshire, and Berrington in Shropshire, and on one at Alphing-

[1] *Fonts and Font Covers*, London, 1908.

ton in Devon there is an inhabited scroll border which suggests the influence of a manuscript of late-eleventh-century type; some of the initials of the Durham Bible may be compared.[1]

Very soon after the conquest, however, it must have become the rule to produce a new font not only for each new church, but also probably for many of the old Saxon churches which were not at once reconstructed. In the richer churches they were sometimes imports from the continent, where large workshops had grown up in close association with the quarries; the font at Winchester, which came from Tournai, is the most outstanding example. In the smaller churches, however, local craftsmen were employed from the first, and though the more accomplished examples are mostly of twelfth-century date, there are a number of fonts which, like the tympana, are to be assigned to the period of transition. Those of Gloucestershire, Northamptonshire, Sussex, Lancashire, and Derbyshire are particularly important in this connexion. The distribution of the fonts does not, therefore, correspond exactly with that of the tympana (see p. 153).

In Gloucestershire the majority of examples, even if conservative in style, are actually twelfth century in date.[2] In Sussex the font at Waldron may be noted. It is a simple stone basin, and might be assigned to any date were there not a number of others in the county which are probably early Norman.[3] Rather more elaborate is the font at Darenth in Kent; it is of simple cylindrical form, but is decorated with an elaborate series of figures in round arcades and low relief. It is obviously post-Saxon, but the ornament has something of the pre-Norman style about it, and gryphons and other animals which form part of the decoration show the survival of Scandinavian art. It is usually dated to the early twelfth century.

In Derbyshire and Northamptonshire there are a number of interesting fonts of cylindrical form, decorated with ornamental

[1] For a reproduction of the font see J. Romilly Allen, *The Illustrated Archaeologist*, i (1894), 252.

[2] A. C. Fryer, 'Gloucestershire fonts', *Trans. Bris. & Glos. Arch. Soc.* xxxii (1909), 301.

[3] The Sussex fonts have been fully published by J. L. André, 'Fonts in Sussex churches', *Sussex Arch. Collns.* xliv (1901), 28.

work in low relief and sometimes with figural ornament.[1] That at
Mellor may be noted; it bears a curious design, probably a horse
and rider. Like most of the others it is Norman rather than Saxon,
but might well belong to the eleventh rather than the twelfth
century.

In Lancashire, again, there are several fonts which are probably
eleventh century; that at Walton-on-the-Hill is of cylindrical form
with figural and floral ornament in low relief, comprising the
Virgin in a round niche, the flight into Egypt, and acanthus scrolls.
Ellis dates it to the time of Edward the Confessor on the grounds
that at that time a grant was made to the church of Walton.[2] On
the evidence of style this seems too early, but it might have been
made shortly after the conquest. The font at Kirkby has also been
described as Saxon, but it is certainly of post-conquest date, even
if it is eleventh century. There was, however, a Saxon church at
Kirby. The font at Huyton, which is of cylindrical form, bears very
primitive figure-subjects in low relief which are of an early type,
being almost like poor Roman work. This is due to incompetent
craftsmanship more than anything else, and a late Saxon or very
early Norman date is probable. The font at Wallasey, a cylindrical
bowl, with arcades but no figures or detailed ornament, is typical
of the simplest early Norman type, and is probably to be assigned
to the last quarter of the eleventh century.

Similar instances might be multiplied all over the country, but
all are primitive and they show nothing to warrant the distinction
of a separate eleventh-century Norman group except the well-
nigh universal cylindrical form and the general crudity of workmanship. One may assume rather that the fonts in the main
constitute a series, beginning about 1075, and continuing down
till the end of the twelfth century. As time went on shapes, designs,
and even material became more diversified. Thus in the full
twelfth century lead fonts became wellnigh as numerous as stone
ones, in any case in the south-west of England, and at the same

---

[1] See G. le Blanc Smith, 'Derbyshire fonts', in *Derbyshire Arch. Journ.* xxv. 217 ff.
and xxvii. 41.

[2] J. W. Ellis, 'The mediaeval fonts of the Hundreds of West Derby and Wirral',
Trans. Hist. Soc. of Lancs. and Cheshire, liii (1901), 61.

time fonts of bowl shape, supported on four columns, became
popular; previously, cylindrical and square ones were the only
shapes known, and even of these forms there are no square ones
that can definitely be dated before the conquest. Archaic features
did, however, survive till quite a late date, as, for example, on
the font at Bridekirk in Cumberland, where there is an inscription
in runic characters giving the name of its sculptor, Richard; he is
shown on one face carving a scroll. In spite of the runes, the font
is to be dated to the second half of the twelfth century.

7. SUNDIALS

A few sun-dials of Anglo-Saxon date exist, and there was originally probably at least one in every church; indeed they may have
been associated with other monuments also, for the earliest example
in this country appears on the Bewcastle cross. A. R. Green in his
paper on the subject was, however, only able to publish twenty-
four which are undoubtedly pre-conquest.[1] From the artistic
point of view the majority are of no importance, but they are
interesting for the light they throw on the Anglo-Saxon system of
time measurement. The form of dial seems to have been very
constant through later Saxon times; it consisted of a semicircular
plaque set vertically in a wall. The number of divisions on the
dials, however, varied, either because the requirements were
distinct in different regions or, more probably, because different
systems of time calculation were followed in different areas in
accordance with the dominating stratum of the population; the
system was thus distinct in regions where the people were of
Norse origin from that in which the people were English or had
been influenced from the continent. Usually the dials were divided into six compartments, sometimes there were eight, sometimes twelve. Portable sun-dials were also made and one of metal
which was dug up at Canterbury some years ago is now preserved
in the Cathedral library.[2]

The majority of examples that have survived are plain, except
perhaps for an inscription; of all of them the most complete is

[1] 'Anglo-Saxon sundials', *Soc. Ant. Journ.* viii (1928), 489.
[2] 'A Saxon pocket watch', *Country Life*, vol. cvii, no. 2788 (June 1950), p. 1890.

that at Kirkdale in Yorkshire, and the dial, which is divided into eight compartments, is accompanied by a long inscription; it is to be dated to between 1063 and 1065. Another example is more interesting from the artistic point of view, for it is accompanied by sculptural ornament, and suggests that other elaborate dials existed also. It is at Langford in Oxfordshire, and is semicircular in shape; it is upheld by two men who stand below it, their arms raised above their heads to support the dial. Little of it now remains, but the carving must have been very fine; it is perhaps to be attributed to the very hand that sculptured the superb rood at the same place, and may therefore be regarded as Saxon work of the early eleventh century. Another sun-dial, at North Stoke in Oxfordshire, is rather similar, but two hands hold the dial as if there was a figure behind instead of two distinct figures as at Langford. The head of the figure at North Stoke is visible above the dial, but there are no legs or lower extremities. It is probably early Norman rather than Saxon, but it is impossible to be sure.

8. THE EARLY NORMAN TYMPANA

The early Norman cathedrals, abbeys, and larger churches were characterized by their plainness, and it was only at a later date, primarily as the result of influence from central or south-western France and not from Normandy, that elaborate sculptures came to be associated with them. But the smaller churches of the late eleventh and early twelfth centuries were very often decorated with figure-sculptures either upon the tympana of their doors or upon their fonts. These sculptures were perhaps not always very accomplished, but they were often delightfully fresh and vigorous. They show in general no signs of the influence of the contemporary Romanesque art of France which soon after 1100 underwent such superb developments, but seem to have drawn rather upon the old styles that had been assimilated in the tenth century in England itself—Viking, local Saxon, or continental. Were it not for the fact that the buildings to which these tympana belong are definitely Norman, it would often, on stylistic grounds alone, be tempting to regard the carvings as Saxon.

The distribution of the tympana is very suggestive. Keyser, in his comprehensive work on them, has recorded some 200 examples, by far the greatest percentage of which is to be found in Dorset, Wiltshire, Gloucestershire, Worcestershire, and Herefordshire. This distribution, it is true, coincides with the limestone area, so that material for sculpture was readily available, but good stone existed in numerous other parts of southern, eastern, and central England also, where sculptures are very much rarer. It would therefore seem that the old Saxon craftsmen fled westwards from 1066 onwards in face of the new continental fashions, just as the old Celtic peoples had fled in face of Anglian and Saxon invaders, and that the old Saxon tastes and ideas were preserved in the same westerly areas. A few sculptors, faithful to the old traditions, continued to work in the south-eastern counties; but it was the west country, greater part of the old Wessex, that was the heart of the conservative Saxon figural art. There, for a century or so, the old styles were adapted to suit the new and better buildings erected under Norman inspiration. And even later, as Norman gave place to Early English, Early English to Decorated, it was in the same west country that much of the best fine sculpture was produced. Nor did sculpture ever become there quite so essentially architectural as it did in the east of England, or more still in France; the sculptures on the west front of Wells, for example, take the form of statues in niches; those of the choir of Lincoln are an intrinsic part of the building itself.

The problem of dating these tympana is extremely difficult. Occasionally external evidence comes to our aid. Thus architectural details at Knook in Wiltshire are of pre-conquest date, and serve to date the tympanum to the same period,[1] while on the other hand the church at Castor in Northamptonshire bears a dedication inscription containing the date 1124. A tympanum at Pennington, near Ulverston, with an angel with spread wings, is accompanied by a runic inscription which appears to read, 'Forbid into this church any trouble'. The inscription thus does not help much, but the presence of runes attests the survival of old ideas, even if the carving is post-Saxon. Such guides are, however, very rare, and in general the style of the actual sculpture or, more

[1] *Arch. Journ.* civ. 163.

definitely, the architecture of the building, are the only factors
that are there to help us, and even if an example in one place can
be firmly dated, a closely similar one elsewhere may be a generation
or more later purely because the area to which it belonged was a
very conservative one.

With regard to the nature of the designs, rather more definite
results are to be arrived at, and on this basis the tympana may be
classified under various groups. The first and most important of
these comprises work derived more or less directly from the 'court'
school of Anglo-Saxon sculpture. Scenes from the Bible form the
usual theme of the decoration. The majority of examples, however,
belong to the twelfth rather than to the eleventh century; two of
the finest are the tympana of the north and south doors at Quenington in Gloucestershire. They have sometimes been described
as Saxon, but more recently they have been assigned by Keyser,
with a high degree of probability, to the reign of King Stephen
(1135–54).[1] A stone showing Christ in glory above and the
harrowing of hell below at South Cerney, not far distant, is in a
very similar style and may be assigned to the same school, though
it is probably rather earlier in date.[2] Rather more Saxon in style is
a stone built in over the door of the north transept at Norwich; it
bears a standing figure in a semicircular niche with columns at
either side, and is to be dated to about 1110. From such works as
these a more or less unbroken chain of examples, by way of
Kirtling in Cambridgeshire, Pedmore in Worcestershire, or Rowlstone in Herefordshire to the essentially continentally inspired
work at Ely and Rochester, can be made out, and it is not easy to say
where in the chain the division between the Saxon, the Transitional, and the full Romanesque styles occurs. Perhaps the essential
aesthetic difference is that the early work is more spontaneous,
whereas the character of the later, inspired from France, was
determined according to fixed laws of geometric form and proportion.

---

[1] Josephine Knowles, 'Symbolism in Norman sculpture at Quenington, Gloucestershire', pp. 147–54; and C. E. Keyser, 'Supplementary notes on the Norman tympana
at Quenington', *Arch. Journ.* lxii (1905), 155–6.
[2] A plate and a short note on this appear in the *Soc. Ant. Journ.* xv (1935), 203.

A second group of tympana is characterized by the presence of animal motifs of Scandinavian type. They were in general more naturalistically rendered than in Saxon work of the Jellinge or Ringerike styles, but the old feeling for stylization remained—the tails of the beasts still twisted around their bodies, and they still tended to transform themselves into interlacings; patterns of an essentially northern character were also often included around the borders. The northern animals were also introduced into religious compositions such as St. Michael struggling with the devil in the form of a dragon or David struggling with the lion. A good example of the latter is to be found at Highworth in Wiltshire, where David stands behind a single lion, akin in appearance to the Anglian beast.[1] Examples of the former appear at Moreton Valance in Gloucestershire (Pl. 27 b), at Hoveringham in Nottinghamshire, and at Kingswinford in Staffordshire (Pl. 27 a); all these examples are probably to be assigned to the early twelfth century, though they are close to pre-conquest sculptures like the tympanum at Ault Hucknall in Derbyshire or the carvings in St. Nicholas's church at Ipswich, where there are two stones, one bearing St. Michael and the dragon and the other a wild boar; this is accompanied by an inscription in Latin which is certainly Saxon. A tympanum of the same type at St. Bees in Cumberland is also regarded by Keyser as of Saxon date.[2] St. Michael sometimes bears a sword, as at Kingswinford, sometimes a spear, and sometimes a cross; almost always he has large wings. It is, indeed, the presence of wings that distinguishes him from St. George, though it cannot be said for certain that every figure without them was intended to represent St. George and not St. Michael, for the iconography was very confused. St. Michael was also shown weighing souls, bearing a soul to heaven, or simply as an archangel, but these representations were less popular than that of the struggle with the devil, to some extent no doubt because the latter scene

---

[1] It might be Samson, but David seems the more likely, for he was a more popular figure.

[2] C. E. Keyser, 'Notes on a sculptured tympanum at Kingswinford church, Staffordshire, and other early representations in England of St. Michael the Archangel', *Arch. Journ.* lxii (1905), 139. He gives a most useful survey of the iconography of St. Michael.

afforded the artist an opportunity of introducing the northern beasts of which he was so fond; they appealed to him more than did the purely religious themes.

In another group of tympana of rather similar style the models must have been of near Eastern origin rather than Norse, for they show the characteristic confronting of identical motifs with a cross or single figure between them. The tympanum at Charney Basset near Wantage (Pl. 28 *a*) is typical and may be contrasted with that at Highworth. On the former, David is shown between two lions of heraldic type, standing upright on their hind legs. A very similar disposition is to be seen at Downe St. Mary in Devonshire. This arrangement was a very old one in the east, coming originally from Mesopotamia, where the figure represented the god Gilgemish. From there it travelled to Persia, and thence to Byzantium and to the Islamic world. It was probably by means of Islamic textiles that it reached England, for the Downe St. Mary tympanum also shows an acanthus border, so stylized that it looks like Kufic script. A similar disposition is to be found on tympana at Dinton in Buckinghamshire (Pl. 26 *a*) and at Fritwell in Oxfordshire; other examples are numerous. The arrangement of the design on these is completely near eastern, but the actual beasts were often anglicized, for their tails were made to curl up in the manner that we see on the British crosses; at Dinton a very northern beast was included below and the border made to take the form of a three-stranded plait. The English sculptor was responsible for adding such details and in doing so he was probably often influenced by manuscript models in the form of bestiaries, for a very rich source-book was available here which was certainly used by later sculptors.[1]

Sometimes the confronted animals would seem to be the result of the play of an older stream of influence on this country, for at times they are more similar to early Christian works at Ravenna and elsewhere in Italy than to prototypes in Islamic textiles or in the bestiaries. The tympanum at Beckford in Gloucestershire belongs to this class. It shows two hare-like animals on either side

[1] See G. C. Druce, 'The mediaeval bestiaries and their influence on ecclesiastical decorative art', *Journ. Brit. Arch. Ass.* xxv (1919), 41, and xxvi (1920), 35.

of a cross. Other tympana, akin stylistically to that at Beckford, suggest similar relationships with the early Christian art of Italy in that they make use of such motifs as the Greek or Maltese cross as the main subject of their decoration. It can hardly be that there was any direct influence from Ravenna, for their respective dates are too far separated. More probably manuscript models of early Christian type were used in such instances by the English sculptors. That these men were ready to seize on any model which attracted them is suggested by a small figure at Bredwardine in Hereford-shire which seems to represent the Egyptian god Bes; rosettes of definitely oriental character appear on the same slab. If the figure is indeed Bes, as G. T. Chester suggested,[1] it must have been copied from a small glazed figure brought home by a Crusader or trader who had visited Egypt. The occasional presence of the bird-beast of Sasanian art, progenitor of the wyvern of the medieval reper-tory, was, like the Gilgemish motif, most probably due to the influence of textiles, for though of Persian origin it was also a favourite motif with the weavers in the Byzantine and Islamic worlds. Capitals of very Islamic appearance at Devizes in Wilt-shire and Eaton in Hampshire may also have been inspired by textiles, for the traffic in eastern stuffs was very considerable.[2]

The next group of tympana is to be distinguished on the grounds of technique rather than motif, for the decorations follow a style and arrangement more proper to metal-work than to stone sculpture. The majority of the motifs, further, are of Celtic type, and are quite distinct from those we see on most of the other tympana. The earliest examples are the tympana at Fownhope in Herefordshire and Castor in Northamptonshire; in the full Norman period the same inspiration of metal-work prototypes is also to be seen, e.g. in the west door of Iffley church, near Oxford (*c.* 1160), and at Kilpeck in Herefordshire. The Castor tympanum bears the Madonna with Child on her knee; she has the same strangely exaggerated hands and proportions as the better-known rendering

---

[1] 'Notice on sculptures of oriental design at Bredwardine and Moccas, Hereford-shire', *Arch. Journ.* xlvii (1890), 140.

[2] See E. Sabbé, 'L'Importation des tissus orientaux', *Rev. belge de philol. et d'hist.* xiv. 1935.

at Fownhope, which dates from about 1150. This exaggeration may, indeed, be taken as a Norman feature and, together with the embroidery-like manner of the capital carving at Castor, distinguishes work of this period from the Saxon, which has far more feeling for figural sculpture and is much closer to the polished art of the Byzantine capital. Elements of Scandinavian, of Celtic, and of later Saxon figural art are all present. Yet the art is distinct; it shows not only the decadence of the old ideas, but also the play of a new aesthetic principle, introduced in this case probably through copying some piece of Norman metal-work. A tympanum at Buildwas in Shropshire is suggestive of an iron door-hinge rather than a piece of sculpture, and there is something of the flavour of metal-work about that showing Christ in glory supported by angels over the south door of St. Peter's church at Rowlstone in Herefordshire. The most striking effect of the use of metal-work prototypes is, however, to be seen at Kilpeck, and the sculptures there are particularly intriguing in the strangeness of their style. The heads of the corbels around the outside of the choir thus have the svelte outlines proper to that material, the ornament of the main arch is based on the loops of a gold necklace, and the individual figures of the door jambs are carved with the harsh, clear incisions characteristic of work in bronze; the figures that decorate the twelfth-century shrine of St. Manchan from Lemanaghan in Ireland may be compared. One might almost suggest that some metal-work hoard, comprising a casket, decorated with figure-work and formal ornament, and a rich necklace, had fallen into the sculptor's hand, and that he used the different pieces as models for the different parts of his work at Kilpeck. The style is thus very diverse; the profuse decorative ornament suggests later Scandinavian carving such as that at Urnes: the saints on the chancel arch are rather Ottonian in style, the heads of the corbel-table are more definitely Norman, yet at its ends there are large jaws with curved tongues clearly derived from the dragon heads of Viking art; parallels at Deerhurst and Leonard Stanley may serve to show how conservative the artists were. The date of Kilpeck is not easy to determine. On the one hand, Norman work such as that at Shobden is similar and supports a date between 1140 and 1150; on the other, parallels in other arts suggest the very beginning of the twelfth century. A comb from Wales, now in the British Museum, thus shows similar ornament; the famous Gloucester candlestick in the Victoria and Albert Museum is akin,[1] and work of much the same type appears on the Alcester Tau in the British Museum. The last of these is definitely Saxon (see p. 166), the candlestick is firmly dated between 1109 and 1112, and the comb is to be assigned to about 1110.[2] Some have thus regarded Kilpeck as early twelfth or even eleventh century; a date around 1120 was proposed by Cust.[3] On the whole, however, a later one, around 1140, seems most likely. The important thing, from our point of view, is the survival at Kilpeck of a number of pre-Norman elements, both stylistic and iconographic.

[1] W. R. Lethaby, *Mediaeval Art*, 1949, Pl. 31.
[2] E. S. Prior and A. Gardiner, *An Account of Mediaeval Figure Sculpture in England*, Fig. 148.
[3] 'Kilpeck', *Walpole Society*, v (1917), 87.

VI

IVORIES

THE stylistic influences that affected the development of the art of ivory-carving in England were basically the same as those which influenced sculpture, though on the whole continental elements, notably Carolingian and Ottonian, were rather more to the fore in the ivories, and it is often very hard to say whether a particular ivory was actually produced in England, northern France, or the area comprised by what is today Belgium. The ivory-carvers no doubt travelled themselves, and the actual works were also transported and copied locally, copies being naturally more exact when there was no problem of enlarging the model to great size, as for stone sculpture.

In addition to the Carolingian and Ottonian ivories which must have found their way to England, a few Byzantine ones were no doubt also imported, and their influence is sometimes clearly to be observed in local work. Scandinavian models, on the other hand, left practically no traces on art on a grand scale, though there are a few small objects, strap-ends, buttons, and the like, which are of Scandinavian character; most of them are to be assigned to the very beginning of our period. Many of them were probably imports, for such things were carried by the invading Norsemen as part of their personal equipment, but some were no doubt made by or for them in this country.

Such small things were usually made of bone, while the larger, figure-bearing plaques were of a more precious material, either actual ivory or walrus tusk (morse). Whalebone was employed for good work when more precious material was not available. On the whole the supply seems to have been fairly regular, and the various materials were used as they came to hand. It is not possible to draw any correlation between the nature of the material and the character of the carving upon it; one cannot, for example, say that work in morse tends to show more northern influence, or that in

ivory to be more Byzantine in style. At most it may be suggested
that bone tends in general to show the work of less accomplished,
and therefore presumably more provincial, carvers. Very hard
wood, such as boxwood, was also used for fine carving; a few
examples have survived and many more were doubtless known in
Saxon times.

So far as period is concerned, it seems likely that the age of
Alfred, which saw the production of work of the very highest
quality in enamel, metal, embroidery, and probably also stone
sculpture, was also responsible for fine work in ivory. Nothing
has, however, survived which can be assigned to that date, for the
earliest later Saxon ivories that we know are to be attributed to
the latter part of the tenth century, and are products of that great
period of brilliance which was exemplified above all in the manuscript paintings of the Winchester school. The importance of
ivories is attested by inventories and records. Thus bishop Leofric
(1050–73) gave to Exeter two great crosses of bone or ivory, two
large gospel books bound in bone or ivory, three shrines, a portable
altar, and two large and six smaller candlesticks apparently in the
same material.[1] Treasures, which were almost certainly of ivory,
are mentioned at earlier dates at Salisbury, at Ely, and at Canterbury, and others probably also existed elsewhere. Only a very
small percentage of these have, however, survived to this day.
The records attest their quantity; as to their quality, the modicum
that we do know affords admirable evidence.

One of the most beautiful of all the ivories—it must have been
among the finest ever carved in Saxon times—is the superb piece in
the Victoria and Albert Museum (No. 7943—1862) consisting of
an ivory figure of the crucified Christ mounted on a gold filigree
cross, with small enamel plaques representing an evangelical symbol on each arm (Pl. 31). The gold and enamel are sumptuous in
themselves, but this richness is surpassed by the sheer excellence of
the ivory-carving. The gentle tenderness of the face and the simple
lines of the body show great mastery, and the folds of the loin-
cloth are delicate and subtle. Stylistically the carving falls into place
alongside some of the best painting of the earliest days of the

[1] See Max Foerster, *The Exeter Book of Old English Poetry*, London, 1933, p. 10.

Winchester school, and such a manuscript as the Benedictional of
St. Æthelwold (975–80) may be compared. Iconographically an
even closer parallel has been put forward by Miss Longhurst in
the form of a lovely drawing in a psalter in the British Museum
(Harley 2904, f. 3v), which is typically Winchester work (Pl. 74 a).
The miniatures of the Sherborne Pontifical in the Bibliothèque
Nationale (Lat. 943) are of the same style though much less subtle.
The carver of the ivory had a far more developed feeling for
plasticity and a greater sense of quality. Yet in spite of these
parallels with Winchester work, the grandeur and dignity of the
Carolingian world are not far distant in the ivory, and it would
appear to be rather earlier in date than the manuscript illustrations.
The Benedictional is dated to 975 or after, so that the ivory is
probably to be assigned to a date around 950. The metal setting
may be a little later; in any case it is Ottonian rather than English,
and the ivory must have been attached to it subsequently, so that
it is not of value for dating purposes.

The same majestic feeling may be seen in one or two other
ivories which seem to be closer to Carolingian than to developed
Winchester art. Foremost of these is one bearing the nativity in
the Liverpool Museum (Pl. 37). Stylistically it is close to a late
Carolingian casket of the Metz school in the Brunswick Museum,[1]
though there is a marked iconographical difference in that the crib
with the Child is, on the Liverpool ivory, in the foreground,
while on the Brunswick ivory it is behind. The latter position is
in accordance with the Byzantine tradition, the former, as Miss
Longhurst points out, is an English feature, and a rendering of the
scene, which is iconographically closely parallel, appears in the
famous Benedictional of St. Æthelwold (975–80) (Pl. 51 a). The
style is, however, distinct, for the miniature shows the typical
excited movement of the Winchester work, the ivory the static
grandeur of the Carolingian. The ivory is presumably of earlier
date than the miniature—the middle of the tenth century seems
probable. Little black pearls had been added for the eyes, and this
seems to have been done quite often in English ivory-carving.

---

[1] M. H. Longhurst, *English Ivories*, Fig. 4, p. 14; O. Homburger; *Die Anfänge der
Malerschule von Winchester*, Pl. v.

Again of early date is a rectangular plaque in the Archaeological Museum at Cambridge, from Elmham in Norfolk (Pl. 32). It is in two registers, bearing in the upper Christ enthroned and surrounded by a mandorla between the Virgin and St. Peter, and in the lower a cross in the centre with two flying angels above and four saints on either side below. The carving is very much worn, but it is still well-enough preserved for its English stylistic character to be apparent, and the iconography again shows that originality of arrangement which characterizes so much English work of this period. The ivory is to be dated to soon after the middle of the tenth century. Though Goldschmidt assigns it to the twelfth century,[1] a book cover in the Metropolitan Museum at New York is also perhaps to be included in this group. It bears a figure of Christ, His right hand outstretched and His left holding a Bible; the disposition is that usual in Byzantine art, but the Christ is beardless and suggestive of a Carolingian model. It is possibly to be dated around 1000.

More definitely Byzantine in inspiration is a pectoral cross in the Victoria and Albert Museum (No. A 10—1921). It is oval in shape and bears Christ on the cross in the centre and at each corner the symbols of the evangelists, each in a medallion; above is the Dextera Dei (Pl. 36 a). The medallions are similar to those made of enamel which often appear attached to metal-work crosses or plaques in the Byzantine world, and the body of Christ, which is treated with great delicacy and feeling, is close to a Byzantine model. A continental provenance has been suggested by some authorities, but there is every reason to regard the cross as English; Miss Longhurst has called attention to the similarity it shows to the stone slab at Stepney (Pl. 9 a); the two are clearly akin, and there seem to be no real grounds for following Goldschmidt in dating the ivory to the twelfth century. It might indeed be even earlier than the slab, for its style is not far removed from that of the Liverpool Nativity and the Cambridge Majesty. The slab has been dated here to about 1020, and a date around 1000, or perhaps even in the tenth century, seems most probable for the ivory.

Far more primitive in character and akin to the provincial as

[1] *Elfenbeinskulpturen*, vol. iv, no. 270, p 55, and Pl. LXXIII.

opposed to the 'court' group of stone sculptures is a plaque, or rather another pectoral cross, bearing the crucifixion, also in the Victoria and Albert Museum (A 80—1923). The Christ is of a more primitive, oriental type (Pl. 36 b), and the figures of Longinus and Stephaton, with spear and reed, which are shown on either side belong to the eastern iconographical tradition which we see in Cappadocia, and not to the central Byzantine or Constantinopolitan one, where the Virgin and St. John take their places. Parallels exist in Ireland, as well as in some of the more crude sculptures of England like those at Daglingworth, but this iconographical system is not followed in the stone sculptures which we have attributed to the 'court' school. The Dextera Dei, a non-Celtic feature, appears at the top, and both Longinus and Stephaton have nimbi; this must be due to the carelessness of the artist, who failed to understand his theme properly, for they were, of course, not saintly. Two angels, bearing wreaths, are included above the arms of the cross; they are of most primitive, clumsy proportions. Goldschmidt assigns this ivory to the twelfth century, but the early eleventh or even later tenth would again seem more probable.

Two more small ivories, bearing rather similar crucifixions, are preserved in the British Museum (Pl. 36 c) and the National Museum at Copenhagen. They must both belong to the end of the tenth or the first half of the eleventh century. The former, though very primitive, is characterized by a number of features which are typically English, such as the Dextera Dei and the thin slender body. It has been suggested that the latter, which was found at a place called Herlufsholm, may be Scandinavian, for work which was closely akin was produced in Denmark at this time.[1] It has the extended, emaciated proportions proper to Celtic art. But it must be remembered that a good deal of loot from England was taken back by the Danes, and this cross may well have reached Denmark in this way. It serves to illustrate that at this time the influences were from the south northwards rather than in the reverse direction, and shows that England was by now a source of inspiration rather than a recipient. Contacts with Denmark are further attested by one of the few

[1] M. H. Longhurst, English Ivories, 8, and Pl. on 133.

dated ivories that have survived, namely, a cross in the National Museum at Copenhagen made for Gunnhild, the niece of Canute, in 1076 by a certain Liutger.[1] It has been suggested that Liutger was an Englishman, and there are English features about the work, though the generally rather crowded composition and the arrangement of the central medallion as a quatrefoil enclosing a circle are un-English. On the whole it is more satisfactory to regard this as a Danish and not an English piece of work.

A much more important ivory, and one which is unquestionably English, is the Godwin seal in the British Museum (Pl. 36 *d*). It bears an inscription reading 'Sigillum Godwini Ministri' with a B, perhaps for 'Beati', between the first two words. On its handle are two figures, representing our Lord and God the Father; a third one, which originally existed above them, portraying the Holy Spirit, has been broken off. Below, a prostrate figure depicting the devil can just be distinguished. At first glance one would tend to compare these figures with a piece of Toulousan sculpture of the early twelfth century. But there is reason to identify the seal with one Godwin, a minister of King Edgar who witnessed charters dated 967 and 972, or with a man of the same name known in the time of King Æthelred, and mentioned in 980 and 1016; he may or may not be the same person as the former. Though the seal is small, the style of the carving is more monumental than that of normal Winchester work. It may be compared with the miniatures of Cotton, Titus, D. XXVII, in the British Museum (Pl. 82 *b*), which is dated to between 1012 and 1020, but is perhaps slightly earlier; a date round about 1000 seems most probable on stylistic grounds, and this conclusion is supported by the inscription.

Of similar date, though rather less 'Romanesque' in style, is a particularly lovely ivory at Winchester in the shape of an inverted triangle bearing two angels back to back, swinging censers (Pl. 33); they herald the superb stone angels at Westminster some two centuries later in date in the elegant sway of their movements, but at the same time they recall the Saxon angels at Bradford-on-Avon (Pl. 7). In this Winchester ivory the style is much closer to that of

[1] M. H. Longhurst, op. cit., Pl. I, p. 8.

the manuscripts than it was with regard to any of the ivories previously mentioned, and King Edgar's Charter may be compared. The charter is dated to 966 (Pl. 46), and the ivory must be of very much the same date.

The style of the carving on the Godwin seal and the Winchester plaque is closely paralleled on a superb ivory in the British Museum known as the Alcester Tau (Pl. 40). It bears, amongst elaborate ornamental work, two figures of Christ; on one side He is shown on the cross, on the other in glory, treading on the asp and basilisk. The ornamental work is of very delicate quality. The Alcester Tau is to be regarded as the earliest surviving example of a type of ivory, of which there are a number of examples, to be dated immediately after the Norman conquest, though the form is early rather than late eleventh century. A similar cross is, for instance, shown sculptured on the tomb of abbot Morard of St. Germain, Paris, who died in 1014, and another appears on that of abbot Isarn of St. Victor's, Marseilles, who died in 1048.[1] The Alcester Tau was, so far as we can tell, part of the furniture of Evesham Abbey, which was a foundation of Saxon times, and it is probably to be dated to the early years of the eleventh century. It shows also some resemblance to the plaque with Christ and other figures in the Archaeological Museum at Cambridge which we have already noted, but the carver of the Alcester Tau was a far greater artist, and displayed a vivid interest in foliage, which is absent in both the other ivories. A few other tau crosses which are also probably to be assigned to the eleventh rather than the twelfth century may be noted, though they show much less accomplished work. One, in the Victoria and Albert Museum (A 1—1914), is thus very rough and provincial; it is probably to be dated to the period of overlap between the conquest and the beginning of the twelfth century to which we have assigned a number of the tympana.[2] Another ivory, in the Pfarrkirche at Deutz, shows a mixture of styles, but England seems to be the most probable country to which to assign it, though it might have been made locally; it is reputed to have been presented by archbishop Heribert

---

[1] C. Cahier and A. Martin, *Mélanges d'archéologie*, Paris (1856), iv. 174.
[2] M. H. Longhurst, *English Ivories*, No. xxvi, Pl. 27.

of Cologne (992–1021). A third ivory, in the Victoria and Albert Museum (372—1871),[1] is almost certainly to be assigned to the twelfth century, for the style of the figures is that of fully developed Romanesque art, and the elaborate scrolls they inhabit are also late; they are similar to those in the twelfth-century manuscripts. A fragmentary ivory in the British Museum, bearing a figure of the Virgin and Child, may also be part of a cross head.[2] It was discovered in Chelsea. The figures are confused with a scroll pattern which must originally have constituted the principal part of the decoration. The work is rather suggestive of that on the Alcester Tau, and the fragment may well have formed a part of such a cross; it is probably to be assigned to about 1050.

All these ivories approach more or less closely to the Winchester style of manuscript work, but another group is to be distinguished in which the Winchester characteristics are very marked indeed. Most striking are two free-standing figures at St. Omer (Pl. 39 a and b). Their costumes show the fluttering, agitated movements which belong to the more extreme examples of the school, though with it all the feeling for plasticity and modelling which was so much to the fore in Saxon sculpture has not disappeared. The ivories represent the Virgin and St. John, and must undoubtedly have formed part of a crucifixion group; the arrangement would have been that normal in Byzantine iconography, with Christ on the cross in the centre, with the Virgin on His right and St. John on His left side. Whether the figures were actually attached to a solid background of some other material and employed as a book cover, as Miss Longhurst suggests, is very uncertain; such book covers were known, but the relief is here so considerable that a cover made from it would have been most impracticable; nor are the ivories worn in the way that one would expect from such a usage. On the whole it seems more likely that three separate figures, the Virgin, Christ on the cross, and St. John, formed a free-standing group, perhaps used on an altar or kept as a treasure. The ivories are probably to be dated to the early part of the eleventh century; a date about 1010 may be suggested.

[1] Ibid., No. xxvii, Pl. 28.
[2] Ibid., No. xx, Pl. 21.

Rather more harsh in treatment, but nevertheless akin, is a fragmentary ivory bearing the baptism in the Marquet de Vasselot collection (Pl. 35 a). The faces are perhaps not quite as accomplished as in some of the other ivories, but the draperies are subtle and delicate and show considerable sculpturesque feeling. The work, which is again to be assigned to the early years of the eleventh century, seems to herald the full accomplishment of French Romanesque.

Closely akin to these is an ivory of the Virgin and Child in the ownership of Mr. W. Wyatt, which was shown at the exhibition of English art in 1934 (No. 1159). It is perhaps a little later in date, and is possibly to be assigned to around the year 1040 (Pl. 35 b). The Virgin bears the Child on her knee, and the serpent, symbol of evil, is shown beneath her feet. The figures are enclosed in a quatrefoil mandorla, supported below by angels, the angularity of whose attitudes recalls many an example in Byzantine art as well as—more nearly at hand—those sculptured in stone at Bradford-on-Avon. The Virgin is far more florid in style, and is close to the later Winchester work. The flowing rhythms are very lovely, and it is sad that the faces and other more prominent portions of the ivory have been so sadly worn by abrasion.

A tendency towards greater harshness in the faces which is apparent in some of these ivories, especially that in the Marquet de Vasselot collection, is carried farther in an ivory now in the Victoria and Albert Museum (No. A 5—1935) bearing the Virgin and Child, seated on the arc of Heaven and enclosed in an oval mandorla (Pl. 34 a). It was published for the first time by Miss Longhurst.[1] It is to be dated about 1000. The faces are severe, the folds of the costumes hard and angular, and the tender delicacy of line and suavity of expression of the typical Winchester work are absent. The ivory is no doubt English and the style is not unlike that of the Prudentius in the British Museum (Add. 24199). It is, however, probably to be assigned to some local school, perhaps in the south midlands, Another ivory in the Victoria and Albert Museum (No. A 32—1928) is of exactly the same shape and size, but bears Christ in place of the Virgin. The iconography is

[1] Op. cit., No. xviii, Pl. 20.

Byzantine, the detail, and especially the features of the face, are quite English.

The realist characteristics to be seen in both these works are carried rather farther in the carving of a boxwood casket, formerly in the possession of Mr. P. Nelson and once on loan to the Victoria and Albert Museum (Pl. 38 *b*). The style and technique are those of ivory-carving and, as was often the case with the ivories, the eyes of the figures were originally inlaid with little beads. The casket is rectangular in shape, with a lid pointed like the roof of a house. It bears in high relief a number of subjects from the life of Christ, namely, the nativity, the baptism, the entry into Jerusalem, the communion of the apostles, the crucifixion, and the last judgement. The iconography is basically of the Syrian type, but the carving is akin to that of Anglo-Saxon stone sculpture of the provincial areas and lacks the grace of the best Winchester work. Nelson suggests that it was done at Lichfield, near which place it was found, and this seems very probable.[1] The ivory previously discussed might well have been carved in the same locality. The casket, like the ivory, is to be dated to the early eleventh century.

A few carvings in bone, which are to be assigned to the eleventh century, also exist; most important is one which is presumably a knife-handle, in the British Museum; it takes the form of two lions standing face to face (No. 33). It was found at Bildeston in Suffolk. A comb, from Outwell in Cambridgeshire, at one time in the possession of M. Alphonse Kahn in Paris, may also be noted. It has a sunken panel on either side with a coiled serpent in one and two crouching monkeys in the other. The serpent is essentially northern in feeling; indeed, it almost takes on the form of an inter-lace pattern. The work is probably to be assigned to a local school, strongly affected by Scandinavian influence. More markedly Scandinavian is a button or toggle, in the British Museum, of the late tenth century, showing a man in chain-mail bound by serpents; it is closely related to Scandinavian work of the Jellinge style. A pin from the Thames, also in the British Museum, bears orna-ment of the Ringerike type. All these works attest the Scandinavian influence with regard to minor works. But there are a few bone

[1] 'An ancient box-wood casket', *Archaeol.* lxxxvi. 91.

objects which are of continental type, notably a bone plaque in
the British Museum bearing two gryphons confronted (Pl. 38 *a*).
It came from Old Sarum. The work is rather rough, and the carving
has certain elements in common with some of the more primitive ivories of the early eleventh century, but the motif is of
a type which was very common for the decoration of tympana
in the smaller churches of the early Norman period; it was
originally imported from the east, probably by way of a textile,
but similar ivories may also have been used by the stone
sculptors as models. It is to be dated to the third quarter of the
eleventh century.

The ivories that we have discussed so far, whether purely
English in style or showing continental influences, have had one
thing in common, namely, that the iconography has followed
some traditional system, either Constantinopolitan or Syrian, fairly
closely. But as well as being artists of great power, the English
carvers seem also to have been iconographical originators, and, if
it is indeed to be assigned to the eleventh century as is generally
supposed, this is nowhere more apparent than in the superb staff or
crozier head in the Victoria and Albert Museum (218—1865),
where a number of scenes from the nativity and passion are shown
most cunningly disposed around the crook (Pl. 41). Not only is
the arrangement imaginative and original, but the work itself is
of extremely high quality, the faces are expressive, and the attitudes
are subtle and effective. Throughout there is a supreme feeling for
the possibilities of the material, which is apparent not only in the
attitudes but also in every line of figure and costume. The extremes
of agitation which sometimes appear in the garments under
Winchester influence, though well enough in drawing, are out of
place in sculpture and are here avoided, and a more plastic com-
prehension reigns supreme. The carver of the crozier was no doubt
an individual genius—but his work marks a stage. It sees the culmination of the Saxon plastic style on the one hand, but looks forward to a freer, one might almost say more humanist art, on
the other. Comparisons have been drawn between this ivory
and a MS. in the British Museum (Cotton, Caligula, A. XV,
especially f. 122*v*), on the grounds of which the ivory has

usually been dated soon after 1050.[1] It is also close to a penner in the British Museum of the early eleventh century. It has, however, also been claimed for the second quarter of the twelfth century.[2] The Saxon date is borne out by the style of many of the figures, especially the man on the side of the stem, who looks upward with his head bent back in exactly the same attitude as that of the figure on the Codford St. Peter stone (Pl. 6). The shape of the crozier, the billet ornament, and some of the draperies are, on the other hand, more Norman, and the carving of the figure at the extremity of the loop is suggestive of that of the Dorchester and Guildhall Museum ivories.[3] On the whole a date in the later eleventh century seems most likely in spite of the later Norman elements.

Finally, two ivories of a very distinct type must be noted; one of them, in the Louvre, bears the Virgin and Child (Pl. 34 b), the other, in the Victoria and Albert Museum (142—1866), shows the adoration of the magi (frontispiece). The former is more rugged and is closer to normal Saxon work than the latter; the crucifixes in the British and the Victoria and Albert Museums reproduced on Pl. 36 may be compared. The adoration is not only more delicate in expression and detail, but also far more elaborate in iconography and composition, numerous subsidiary figures being included. The two are obviously by different hands, but both equally obviously belong to the same school, and the style of this school was both unusual and at the same time very distinctive. Goldschmidt assigns both the ivories to north France or Belgium and to a date around 1100. Miss Longhurst, on the other hand, thinks they are English, and has compared the Victoria and Albert Museum ivory to the Vita Edmundi, executed at Bury in the second quarter of the twelfth century,[4] and to a psalter in the British Museum (Cotton, Nero, C. IV), probably done at Winchester. She notes, however, that the ivory shows a certain Spanish quality in the decorative portion of the work.[5] Spanish influence

---

[1] M. H. Longhurst, *English Ivories*, 18. H. P. Mitchell also regards it as Anglo-Saxon, *Burl. Mag.* xlii. 168.

[2] The case for a twelfth-century date will be argued by Mr. Boase in the next volume of this History.   [3] M. H. Longhurst, op. cit., Pls. 5 and 26.

[4] The MS. was formerly in the Holford Collection and is now in the Pierpont Morgan Library. Miss Longhurst illustrates one page, ibid., p. 11.   [5] Ibid., 23.

is conceivable, for similar hints of Spanish art have been noted in other English work of this time by W. S. Cook.[1] Miss Longhurst dates the ivory to the beginning of the twelfth century. Prior and Gardner, on the other hand, compare it to the Chichester reliefs, and date both to c. 1000. It is hard to agree with Miss Longhurst when she denies any similarity between the two; relationships are in fact quite marked, so much so indeed that it is tempting to assign the ivory not only to the same date but also to the same locality as the Chichester reliefs. It is also akin to the Clayton wall-paintings. We have already called attention to the difficulty of dating the Chichester reliefs, and the date of the ivory is no easier to establish. But the lace-like folds of the Virgin's costume, the character of the beasts down below, the proportions and outline of the figures of the kings, and indeed the whole style are all factors which suggest that it is later than the stone sculpture. As independent evidence suggests that both the Clayton paintings and the Chichester reliefs are to be assigned to about 1080, a date shortly before 1100 would therefore seem the most likely for the London ivory. That in the Louvre is rather less similar to the Chichester work, but stylistic factors would seem to support an earlier date; around 1070 may be suggested. Both are perhaps to be regarded as works of that Channel school to which we call attention in connexion with the Chichester reliefs and the Clayton paintings (p. 215).

[1] 'The earliest painted panels of Catalonia', *Art Bulletin*, 1923, 85.

VII

MANUSCRIPT PAINTING

THE outsides of Saxon churches strike the beholder at first
sight by their richness. Pilaster strips, criss-cross strap-work,
arcades, and so forth run riot over the façades of the more
important and elaborate buildings, such as the tower at Earl's
Barton, and even the poorer village churches, like that of Coln
Rogers in Gloucestershire, were adorned with simple pilaster
strips or long-and-short work. The interiors as we know them
today are, on the other hand, plain, at times even rough, and the
masonry is usually so poor that it would seem that the wall faces
must originally in many cases have been plastered. And when the
outsides were so ornate there are reasonable grounds for con-
cluding that the insides were decorated also. Stone sculptures must
have formed a part of this decoration, and stucco panels which
have since perished may also have been set up, as on the continent,
but the walls themselves were doubtless also covered with paintings. The smallness of the windows left considerable areas available for such decoration, yet their comparative number in most
churches admitted enough light to permit of paintings being seen.
Occasional references in the texts attest the existence of such paintings in some of the churches, and their presence in the majority
may be accepted on circumstantial evidence. No wall-paintings of
the Saxon period have, however, survived, and contemporary
examples are almost equally rare on the continent, though there
again there is ample evidence to prove that they existed. It is,
therefore, impossible to do more than call attention to the fact that
wall-paintings must once have been important, for it is hardly
possible to reconstruct what they were like in the mind's eye on the
basis of the illuminations in the manuscripts.

With regard to painting on a small scale, on the other hand, the
case is very different; indeed, an almost unequalled wealth of miniature paintings in books has come down to us. These miniatures

are not of a character which would permit of satisfactory enlargement to a great size as would, for example, those in Byzantine manuscripts. They are too delicate and too decorative, and are not sufficiently monumental in character. But they are, in spite of that, none the less significant as works of art in themselves, and they afford a wellnigh unlimited source of delight and beauty. The line drawings which appear in many of the volumes are as fine and as enchanting as are the paintings.

The history of manuscript-painting in the British Isles is a long one, for the illustration and decoration of books was an important art—one might almost say the most important art—in the Northumbrian period. Yet the brilliant tradition of the Northumbrian and Hibernian schools, which produced such glories as the book of Lindisfarne or the book of Kells, was completely interrupted by the Danish invasion, and in this art much more than in any other the age with which we are dealing is marked by the opening of a new and completely distinct chapter. As far as the full-page paintings are concerned there is practically nothing of that continuity, marked by progressive decadence, which we see in the crosses of northern Britain; rather do we find a period of almost complete barrenness succeeded by one of brilliant renaissance, when work attained to an amazingly high standard of artistic excellence, partly under continental influence but more as the result of the growth of a new and strongly marked national idiom.

The reason for the break is not far to seek; the old manuscript art was at basis essentially decorative and non-representational; the new, however decorative, was primarily a figural art. Owing to the absence of local models for figural work this new art was more actively inspired by what was being done on the continent at the time (or, rather, by what had been done there a century or so before) than were the essentially insular schools of the seventh and eighth centuries. In its development, however, the art soon took on a particularly English character, and before long this character became a south English—one might almost say a Wessex—one, for the sterner, more rugged features that are to be found in so much of Northumbrian art are absent, and instead a gracious, gentle manner was developed, which tells through charm rather than force; much the same characteristics distinguish the manners of the men of Wessex today as compared to those of their northern brothers. In its fruition the Wessex style became not only one of the most important but also one of the most original phases in the whole story of English painting, and however prominent the continental features may have been as regards iconography or design, there was always a marked English character about the work when once developed. Indeed, these English elements eventually made their way to the continent and in turn influenced the painting of the Netherlands and northern France in the second half of the eleventh century and the sculpture of central France at the very beginning of the twelfth.

It is, however, far from easy to define these Anglian features in concrete terms. Close familiarity with the material, supplemented by vision and deep perception, are the factors requisite for its understanding, and no better approach to the study of the illuminations of this age is possible than to look long and carefully at one of the illuminated pages that illustrate the Benedictional of St. Æthelwold in the duke of Devonshire's collection at Chatsworth, for it is perhaps the most complete and perfect example of the so-called Winchester school that has come down to us, though there are happily a number of other manuscripts of little less excellence and richness in many other great libraries, most notably the British Museum.[1] The basically interpretational approach in the figural work, the exquisite delicacy of line and proportion in the decorative detail, the graceful fluttering of the draperies and the foliage, and the charming, slightly fantastic imagination at the back of the artists' minds, all alike strike the observer. The whole approach is delightfully fresh and vivid, and there is something particularly charming about the subtle blend of naturalism and stylization that characterizes the work. The same outlook is apparent in the choice of subject, for the large, rather grandiose figure compositions which were so popular in Carolingian art, where the emperor rather than the divine theme occupied the principal place, were

[1] There are good coloured reproductions in G. F. Warner, *Illuminated Manuscripts in the British Museum* (1903), or G. F. Warner and H. A. Wilson, *The Benedictional of St. Æthelwold*, Roxburgh Club (1910).

avoided, while the purely religious scenes were handled in a more truly spiritual manner. In the Saxon work that survives royal portraits are rare; that at the commencement of King Edgar's Charter (Pl. 46), where the king is humble and reverent in his attitude, may be cited. It contrasts strongly with the royal portraits of so many Carolingian manuscripts, where pompous imperialism is the dominating theme.

Something of the same simple taste, the same delicacy of treatment, the same freshness of outlook, is to be observed on a smaller scale in the initials, even though the majority of these are made up of leaves or animal patterns and are only occasionally figural. Indeed, it is by way of the initials that the new art must be approached, for full-page illuminations only appear well on in the tenth century, whereas manuscripts containing decorative initials in line, if not in colour, are to be found as early as the very beginning of our period. These initials are often of very great beauty. In some of the earliest, motifs which are ultimately of northern inspiration, such as interlacings, birds, dragons' heads, and so on, predominate. Sometimes the heads had complete bodies; later, they often terminated in scrolls. As continental influence penetrated, scroll-work and floral designs became more usual, and the zoomorphic motifs tended to disappear, till finally, around the time of the conquest, 'inhabited' scrolls supplanted the more purely decorative ones wellnigh completely.

The immediate prototypes of the interlacing or stylized zoomorphic initials are to be found in south English works of the ninth century, such as the book of Cerne in Cambridge University Library (Ll. 1. 10), where the full-page work is in the Hiberno-Northumbrian manner, but where there are also a number of initials terminating in dragons' heads which herald those that became usual in the ninth and tenth centuries, though they are rather heavier and fuller than many of the later ones where thin line work replaces the more masterful type of draughtsmanship. The difference is apparent if these initials are compared with those in Alfred's translation of the Cura Pastoralis in the Bodleian (Hatton 20), dating from between 890 and 899, where thin lines dominate (Pl. 42 a). The motifs are, however, the same in the two, namely,

twirls terminating in animals' or serpents' heads, and in both manuscripts colours have been added to give greater effect; in that in
the Bodleian pale green, buff, and pale red are used, in the book
of Cerne they are yellow, dark green, black, and pale purple.
In addition to the initials the former manuscript also contains a
drawing of a fantastic animal's head, unfinished and crudely
done.

The initials of an Ovid in the Bodleian (Auct. F. IV. 32), which is
to be dated to about 900, are in monochrome line, and consist of
gripping heads forming a continuous pattern. But the real glory
of the manuscript is a full-page illustration in black and red line,
showing a figure kneeling at the feet of Christ. The kneeling figure
represents St. Dunstan (Pl. 43). The manuscript was at Glastonbury
in St. Dunstan's time, and the smaller figure, if not the whole
picture, is traditionally believed to have been drawn by him. As
we know from the records that St. Dunstan was proficient in the
arts, there seems no reason to dispute this; he may even have been
responsible for the whole picture. If so it must date from round
about 960. It would thus be a later addition to the rest of the book.
In any case Glastonbury would seem a likely home.

Further development of the initials is to be seen in those of an
Aldhelm in the British Museum (Roy. 5 F. III). They are primitive
and unaccomplished and in monochrome, yet the executor had
probably been influenced by the sight of the naturalistic Carolingian style, and his work reflects something of the spirit behind the
literary and cultural reforms on which Alfred was engaged at
about the time that he was working. The same tendency is apparent
in the Durham Ritual (A. IV. 19), done in southern England in the
early tenth century. It contains dragons' heads akin to those on the
Ramsbury cross, which is of the same date. Each leaf has one curl
longer than the other two, and this type of long and short leaf
is very characteristic of English manuscripts, not only of these
early ones, but also of those containing more elaborate and more
skilful work which date from the eleventh century. The form of
leaf is based on the Carolingian acanthus, but is developed in an
essentially English way. We see it, for example, on the stole of St.
Cuthbert (916), on an early-tenth-century copy of Aldhelm's De

Virginitate in the British Museum (Roy. 7. D. XXIV), and in the first few pages of the Æthelstan Psalter (B.M. Cotton, Galba, A. XVIII) which were done in England in the tenth century. In both instances initials of the same type are found drawn in thin outline and lightly coloured in red, yellow, green, and blue.

A distinct type of initial, where the leaves are very emaciated and where heads are combined with interlacings and scroll-work, seems to have been commonest about 1000, though it first appeared rather earlier. Two subdivisions of the group are to be distinguished, the first where the ornament is thin and wiry, and the second where it is thicker but only drawn in outline. Typical of the former is an Amalarius at Trinity College, Cambridge (B. II. 2), dating from about 975, where the initials are strong and powerful, in thin black line, and elaborately coloured in bright blue, green, yellow, and red (Pl. 42 b). To the second manner are to be assigned quite a number of manuscripts, most important of which are probably a Boethius (Auct. F. 1. 15) and an Arator (Rawlinson, C 570), both in the Bodleian. The latter contains two very fine initials on folios 2 and 3 and a few others which are rather less fine, at the ends; that on folio 2 is especially elaborate and shows a really masterly command of delicate line (Pl. 42 c). But the motifs are archaic and are quite distinct from those which were used in the ordinary Winchester work of the later tenth century. The Boethius contains four very fine initials, a C on folio 5 (Pl. 44 a), a P on folio 16 (Pl. 44 b), an H on folio 48v, and a D on folio 65. All are in thin black line, tinted in pale red, and made up of acanthus scrolls, birds' heads, and interlacings. They are thinner and rather more florid than those of the Arator, but the style of both is closely similar. Both manuscripts are usually dated to the late tenth century, but it is tempting to regard the Arator as earlier than the Boethius, and dates around 970 and 1000 respectively would seem most likely. The Arator has sometimes been assigned to Canterbury; wherever it was done, it shows very fine, delicate work. A few even more delicate, but perhaps less spirited initials are to be found in the Penitential of archbishop Egbert in the Bodleian (Bodley 718), which is again to be dated late in the tenth century. It is possible that this copy was written at

Abingdon; if so it is one of the very few books that can be assigned to that very important centre.

At first glance there is not a great deal about the majority of these initials that suggests continental influence, but if we compare them to the ornamentation of works in metal that were produced in England at the same time, the greater degree of continental influence in the manuscripts becomes at once apparent. In metal-work of secular, even more in that of military character, ornament derived from the Trewhiddle and Wallingford styles was developed along quite independent and essentially insular lines, and such fundamentally continental motifs as the Carolingian acanthus were hardly used at all; in the manuscripts continental motifs became more and more popular as time proceeded. It seems, indeed, at first surprising how very distinct the ornamental styles of the manuscripts and the metal-work are at this time. Yet the reason is not far to seek: the writing and illustration of the manuscripts were essentially ecclesiastical arts; they were executed in the monasteries for and by monks. The metal-work on the other hand was mostly secular, and even when it was intended for church usage the craftsmen responsible for it were no doubt in many cases laymen who probably had little to do with the monastic centres. And in the tenth century it was through the monasteries that the links with the continent were maintained rather than through purely secular contacts.

As the tenth century proceeded it seems that coloured initials gradually replaced those in line. The earliest of them, however, made use of similar motifs, and showed the same rather heavy treatment, quite distinct from the more metallic, linear style of the later eleventh century. The colours, too, seem to have been just as distinct as the drawing, and the rather muddy tones—grey-blues, dirty yellows, or purplish-reds—that appear in the Heliand MS. in the British Museum (Cotton, Caligula, A. VII) are typical. This MS. is to be dated to the second half of the tenth century, but should probably be assigned to nearer its middle than its end. Priebsch regards it as close to a continental original, and draws attention to the links binding England and France at this time. The style of drawing is, however, essentially English, though it is hardly as close to that of the Caedmon MS. as some authorities have maintained. It is not easy to suggest in what place it may have been done, but the west country is not unlikely, for the style is too heavy for Winchester, and the same would apply to Canterbury. Priebsch has, however, assigned it to Canterbury on the basis of the ligatures in the text, though he adds that Winchester would also be possible.[1] Wormald favours the south of England, but not Winchester or Canterbury.[2] The similarity of the style of the initials to those in the Bodleian Ovid (Auct. F. IV. 32) suggests Glastonbury as a possible home, but it must be remembered that the copying in the case of these initials was often very faithful, and it is not easy to suggest localities on the basis of them alone.

In view of the importance of the continental influence behind many of the motifs, it has been suggested that the interlace ornament which appears so frequently in the initials was in some cases due to the influence of continental models and not to any direct legacy from the old Hibernian or Northumbrian art. The suggestion is a possible one, for the old interlacing style was preserved on the continent after it had almost died out in Britain, and in late Carolingian and early Ottonian art it was combined in a most subtle manner with such classical motifs as the acanthus. One of the most striking examples of this blending is to be found in the Lothair Gospels in the Bibliothèque Nationale (Lat. 266), a volume which dates from between 840 and 843. Yet even if the interlace was combined with the acanthus on the continent in the ninth century, and then found its way back to Britain in the tenth, it is not essential to assume, as some authorities tend to do, that the interlace is necessarily a sign of continental influence whenever we see it in later Anglo-Saxon manuscripts. The old Northumbrian-Hibernian school might well have exercised a direct role, even though the chain between that area in the eighth and Wessex in the tenth and eleventh centuries was a broken one. Art historians in the past have as a whole tended to stress the importance of an uninterrupted tradition at the cost of a broken one. But recently a new school of thought, led by Focillon, has called attention to

---

[1] R. Priebsch, *The Heliand Manuscript*, 41.
[2] F. Wormald, 'Decorative initials in English manuscripts', *Archaeol.* xci. 120, No. 2.

the amazing way in which a style, tradition, or a series of motifs may lie dormant over long periods, only to flourish anew with spontaneous vigour at a given moment.[1] And this may well have happened with regard to the interlace in Britain.

Even during the third quarter of the tenth century, however, the initials of linear type in monochrome or in one or two primary colours, taking the form of stylized animals, acanthus, or interlace, had begun to give place to more elaborate and ornate ones of a type closely allied to that of the full-page illuminations, and from that time on the stylistic developments of the full-page illustrations and of the initials can best be studied together, the initials being a reflection on a smaller scale of what was being done on a larger one on the full page. The manner of the colouring and drawing of both is equally distinctive, and from soon after 960 a universal style predominated which, for the sake of convenience, has usually been termed that of Winchester. It is, however, nowadays far from generally admitted that all the manuscripts in which Winchester characteristics are present were actually produced at that place.

How and where this new style was born has been much debated; but though the full glory of the work is undoubtedly to be attributed to the English spirit behind it, the first movements towards the new manner were made on the continent at quite an early date, and these new ideas were seized upon by the English artists for fuller and more complete development. The peculiar fluttering style which characterizes the draperies in the coloured illuminations of this country was, for example, heralded by a curious, almost palsied manner of drawing, which appeared on the continent in the early ninth century in such a manuscript as the Ebbo Gospels at Épernay (816–35) (Pl. 45 a). The framework borders which are developed so elaborately in Winchester art were probably derived from the more formal borders usual in the Carolingian world, as, for example, those in a ninth-century manuscript from Tours, now at Laon (No. 63) (Pl. 45 b),[2] and the particularly

---

[1] *Moyen Âge—Survivances et Réveils*, Montréal (1945), 106, and elsewhere.

[2] E. Fleury, *Les Manuscrits à miniatures de la Bibl. de Laon*, Laon (1863), 38. The figures are, however, practically useless. Similar borders appear in other manuscripts; see A. Boinet, *La miniature carolingienne*, Paris (1913), Pls. cIII, cIV, and cV.

characteristic, gracious line-drawings of such a manuscript as the Canterbury Psalter (B.M. Harley 603) were direct copies of the Utrecht Psalter, which was done at Reims in the ninth century. Yet the final result, the Winchester style as it may be called, was so essentially English that these questions of origin fade almost into insignificance beside those concerned with the qualities and aesthetic significance of the various works.

The earliest manuscript of later Saxon art in which the Winchester style is to be at all discerned is a small psalter in the British Museum (Cotton, Galba, A. XVIII) which is associated with the name of King Æthelstan; in any case it is to be dated quite early in the tenth century. Most of it is actually of continental workmanship and some of the text is even in Greek, but it now contains three full-page illuminations which must have been added in England between about 925 and 940; a fourth page which also belongs to it is now bound up in a later manuscript in the Bodleian (Rawlinson B. 484, f. 85). The first of the miniatures (f. 2) is in four horizontal bands, and represents Christ in majesty within a mandorla with a chorus of angels and prophets; the second (f. 20) bears Him enthroned within a mandorla; the third (f. 120) depicts the ascension. The miniature in the Bodleian is in two registers, and shows the washing of the Child below and the nativity above. Christ is in all cases long-haired and beardless, in the Carolingian manner, and except for the ascension the style is completely continental. That scene, however, is more subtle, and though the work is far from polished, it shows hints of the delicate handling so typical of the next generation. It must have been by a different hand from that responsible for the other three pictures. The very dark faces, especially in the page in the Bodleian, are quite un-English. The ascension may thus be described as precocious, but as we have already suggested such precocity is not surprising, for in our view the lovely sculpture at Codford St. Peter in Wiltshire (Pl. 6) already contains hints of the Winchester style, though, of course, the detailed characteristics of the school are not to be found there in anything like a developed form.

Of much the same date as the psalter is Bede's Life of St. Cuthbert at Corpus Christi College, Cambridge (No. 183), which was given to Durham by Æthelstan. It must have been written between 935 and 939, for it mentions a bishop of Winchester who was only appointed in 934, and does not refer to a successor of Ælfheah of Wells who died in 939. It is more ambitious than Æthelstan's Psalter, and heralds, in any case in its initials, the glory of the fully developed Winchester style, though continental influence is still prominent and the colours are rather heavy. The frontispiece shows a king, presumably Æthelstan himself, offering a book to a saint (Pl. 47). Robinson suggests that the book may have been done at Glastonbury,[1] but others have proposed Winchester. Glastonbury was certainly one of the most important monasteries in the country at the time, and though we know nothing of it as a centre of illumination, it is very probable that good work was done there. We have already alluded to St. Dunstan's interest in art, and he was, more than anyone else, responsible for Glastonbury's prosperity. The style of the painting and drawing is also quite distinct from what was to become characteristic of Winchester, for the line is hard, solid, and angular, the forms are full and cylindrical, and the colours—silver and deep red—are equally individual. The whole style, in fact, savours of the continent much more than of subsequent developments in England.

No other manuscripts now exist that can be attributed to the years between about 940 and 960, but after that time the new style burst into full flower with surprising vigour and richness. What exactly it was that brought about this flowering can hardly be stated in definite terms. The ground was no doubt ready, thanks to the period of preparation that had followed upon the reforms of Alfred. The seed was fertile, thanks to contacts with the continent and the role played by the great church reformers. The atmosphere was clement, thanks to the developed culture and progressive artistic tastes of many of the later Anglo-Saxon rulers, notably Edgar, who came to the throne in 959. And finally, a number of particularly enlightened husbandmen appeared on the scene, most important of whom were St. Dunstan, St. Æthelwold, and St. Oswald.

The influence of these men on religious thought, on art, and

[1] *The Times of St. Dunstan*, 54, and *The Saxon Bishop of Wells*, 13 f.

indeed on culture as a whole, must have been considerable. Dunstan was born near Glastonbury about 909, Æthewold near Winchester; both were educated at Æthelstan's court; they were then together at Glastonbury, where Dunstan was abbot. Dunstan was banished, but returned to England in 957 to become archbishop of Canterbury; soon after Æthelwold was made bishop of Winchester (963–84). We have already suggested that Dunstan may have actually done paintings himself, and we know that he was a craftsman, but Æthelwold seems to have been even more important as a patron. In 954 he left Glastonbury to found a monastery of his own at Abingdon, and this monastery played an important role in the subsequent growth of English manuscript-illumination, for it was there that the new school first crystallized into tangible form, and when Æthelwold moved to Winchester in 963, he took a good many of the monks with him. It was one of them, no doubt already expert under his direction, who produced the superb Foundation Charter given by King Edgar for the New Minster at Winchester in 966. While at Abingdon it is recorded that Æthelwold presented certain books to the monastery: what exactly they were we do not know; but that some at least of them were continental volumes containing illuminations akin to those in the Ebbo Gospels at Épernay is highly probable. Others no doubt were illustrated in a more narrative style, with the sketchy line-drawings which we associate with the Utrecht Psalter and which exercised so important an influence on the development of illumination at Canterbury.

The Foundation Charter is actually the first surviving manuscript which shows the characteristics of the new style in a fully developed form. It is now in the British Museum (Cotton, Vespasian, A VIII). Its text is in gold; there are three ornamental pages at the beginning and there is a beautiful full-page miniature showing the king between the Virgin and St. Peter offering the Charter to our Lord who is shown before an oval mandorla upheld by angels (Pl. 46). The whole is surrounded by a foliate border. The script displays clear continental affinities, and the colouring of the costumes is fairly close to that of Carolingian miniatures. The iconography on the other hand is derived directly from some Byzantine prototype, and is distinct from the system usual in

Carolingian art. This Byzantine system was sometimes followed on the western part of the continent, notably in work of the Metz school, and it was important in Ottonian art, so that direct Byzantine influence need not necessarily be postulated to explain the Charter. A book-cover in St. Paul's at Kärnten has, for instance, been cited by Homburger not only as a parallel to King Edgar's Charter, but also as an instance of Byzantine iconography in work of the Metz school.[1] But these extraneous elements in iconography only become apparent as the result of study. It is the excellence and the high artistic competence of the work itself that first strikes the observer, and whatever sources of inspiration may be cited, whatever parallels drawn, there is already to be observed here a distinctive quality which marks the painting not only as an outstanding work of art, but also as something undoubtedly and unquestionably English. This Englishness is primarily a question of style, but it is attested also by the presence of certain more concrete elements. Most striking of them is the development of the frame-like borders, which are in all the earlier works composed of firmly drawn acanthus plants. In this case they are in blue, green, red, and purple, and in pale shades of the same tones, intertwining around a double framework of coloured gold. In later examples these borders usually terminate at the corners in large, extremely decorative rosettes. Almost equally distinctive is the colouring of the faces in heavy flake-white; only that of the king is more brightly finished off with pink on the cheeks. This predilection for white is to be seen again in the Benedictional of St. Æthelwold and in many of the subsequent Anglo-Saxon manuscripts. English, again, is the dislike of grandiose imperial portraits; in a purely Carolingian version of such a subject one would have expected a far more pompous and enlarged rendering of the monarch.

The peak of excellence in manuscript production was reached some ten years after the production of the Foundation Charter, when the superb Benedictional of St. Æthelwold, now in the duke of Devonshire's collection at Chatsworth, was illustrated. It is to be dated between 975 and 980, and is certainly the most glorious

[1] *Die Anfänge der Malerschule von Winchester*, 43. For the book-cover see F. X. Krauss, *Kirchenschatz von St. Blasien*, Taf. ii.

product of the school both in respect of the quantity and of the quality of its illustrations. There are forty-nine decorated pages, twenty-eight of them with large-scale illuminations. Here again there are obvious links with the continent, and this is not surprising, for the long-established contacts with such monasteries as Corbie and Fleury had been strengthened by the importation of monks to England as well as by visits of leading English ecclesiastics to the monasteries abroad, and manuscripts like the Sacramentary of Drogo, bishop of Metz from 826 to 855, may well have been seen by the painters of the Benedictional. The text of the Benedictional shows this contact most clearly, for it is in Carolingian minuscule, but the composition of many of the scenes bears out the evidence of the script. The closest parallels are afforded by works of the Metz school, and the scenes of the baptism, crucifixion, and transfiguration may be compared to an ivory casket at Brunswick; the baptism is especially close. The personification of the Jordan here is of the usual Byzantine type, as is the whole disposition of the scene. The iconography must have been derived in both cases from Byzantine prototypes, in the case of the Benedictional probably indirectly by way of Metz. The iconography of the second coming of Christ (f. 9v) in the Benedictional is again strikingly Byzantine, and there is also something that suggests the influence of Byzantine art in the conception of the individual figures, though the technique of painting is distinct. In the English work the faces were first coloured pink, the features were then outlined in a darker shade of the same colour, and streaks and patches of chalky white were finally added, thickly and heavily. In Byzantine painting the high-lights were also added last, but they are of quite different character, taking the form of thin, delicate streaks of white, pink, pale violet, or pale green, put on very dexterously. It was also usual in Byzantine painting for a darker tone to underlie a lighter in the faces, and a dark yellow, reddish, or sometimes green undercoat was there the normal preparation for the face. In the Benedictional the contrary is the case, and a light tone underlies a darker one.

The extensive use of gold and the brilliance of the colouring have again both been cited to support the Byzantine affinities of the manuscript, and the conventionalized buildings that appear in many of the scenes must also clearly have been derived from eastern rather than western prototypes; their history is a long one which begins in such manuscripts as the Vienna Genesis. Such buildings are used with striking effect in the annunciation (f. 5*v*, Pl. 50 *a*), and they occur again in the scene of the three Marys at the tomb, (Pl. 51 *b*), which is the best known of all the illustrations in the Benedictional, as it has been frequently reproduced. But there are a number of others that are as fine from the artistic point of view, notably the entry into Jerusalem (f. 46*v*) and the ascension (f. 64*v*). In the former (Pl. 49) the town of Jerusalem obviously follows a Byzantine model, as do the elements of the scene, such as the followers, the cloak laid in the asses' path, and the figures cutting branches. But our Lord sits astride on the ass in the western manner, whereas in Byzantium and the east He sits sideways. The artist shows a new interest in nature; the branches that are being cut to strew in our Lord's path have blooms on them; some are perhaps pussy-willows, and others look more like bunches of flowers—one might almost say tulips, though the flower was not known in the west till many centuries later. The ascension (Pl. 50 *b*) shows the same vitality of handling and the composition is even more dynamic. The way that movement is given to our Lord's figure by a variation in form of the back and front of the mandorla against which He is silhouetted is especially striking, and the amazement of the spectators below is clearly apparent. Another similar scene is the pentecost (f. 67*v*); it is especially interesting, for the legs of the figures appear at first sight to be crossed, and are suggestive of a mannerism particularly popular in twelfth-century Toulousan sculpture. The effect is no doubt fortuitous, being due to the confined space rather than to any actual crossing of the legs, yet the Romanesque character of the picture is striking, and is worthy of note in view of the fact that it is just such 'Romanesque' features as this that have been cited in support of a twelfth-century date for some of the stone sculpture that we here claim as Anglo-Saxon.

More than one hand must have worked on these illustrations, for not all the paintings are as vivacious and full of movement as the entry and the ascension. This is especially true of the presentation of our Lord in the temple (f. 34*v*, Pl. 48). The border here is in the form of an arch on columns and is not a decorative fantasy; the figures are solid and dumpy, the attitudes are static rather than dynamic. As an illustration the picture is effective; as an artistic creation it falls short of some of the others. Nor is the iconography invariably Byzantine. The symbol of St. John on folio 19 thus follows the type adopted in the book of Lindisfarne; the fact that the magi on folio 24· wear crowns and not turbans is obviously western; and the whole conception of the paintings as elaborate pieces of coloured pattern rather than religious pictures of esoteric significance is again an important distinction. This is especially obvious in the great role played by the borders as essential parts of the pictures; in some of the scenes like the nativity on folio 15*v* it is hard to tell where border ends and picture begins (Pl. 51 *a*).

In more than one instance, indeed, the borders tend to obscure the illustrative material, and the enormous corner-pieces in the form of exaggerated acanthus-leaf rosettes are retained in the mind's eye far more clearly than are the figural subjects. It is in this, perhaps more than anything else, that the originality of the school consists, and when once seen these heavy yet vivid borders are not readily forgotten. Never were such things dreamt of in the Byzantine world; in Islamic art, where leaves and plant motifs had a vital role to play, this particular conception of pattern was never attempted; in Carolingian and Ottonian painting the treatment of ornament was in general quite different, even if prototypes can be cited. Herein lies the Englishness of these paintings; a hint of the old Northumbrian feeling for formal stylization has survived, but there is added to it something new, something more alive. Such a fine sense of pure decoration combined with a basic naturalism has but seldom been achieved in the story of art. The world of these illustrations seems to live the more vividly, thanks to the very fact that photographic or imitative naturalism was carefully avoided.

It has been generally assumed that the Benedictional of St. Æthelwold was produced at Winchester; it is in fact to be regarded almost as the 'type example' of the work of the Winchester school.

A monk by the name of Godeman is mentioned in the text, and he has usually been identified with a Winchester monk of that name who became abbot of Thorney about 973.[1] More recently, however, Tolhurst has proposed that this Godeman was really a monk of Ely.[2] The attribution to Ely is further supported by the prominence given in the dedication to certain saints connected with Ely. Tolhurst's arguments are put forward in a very convincing manner, but they fail to take into account sufficiently the importance of stylistic considerations, and it must be remembered that his evidence, though of great importance in determining the monastery for which a manuscript was written, is not necessarily valid in respect of that at which the work was done. The manner of painting in this case derives directly from that of the Foundation Charter of Edgar, and at so early a stage after the revival of painting it is hardly likely that there would have been two or more flourishing centres where books almost identical in appearance were produced. One might expect such divergence of effort when a new generation of painters had been taught by the earliest masters, but hardly at the very outset. Edgar's Charter is dated 966; it is the first truly distinctive production of the new school, and one would not expect to see artists breaking off and founding subsidiary schools till, say, about 980. The evidence of tradition which assigns the Benedictional to Winchester should also be taken into account, for tradition has in the long run turned out to be correct more often than not. Thus until more complete evidence than that put forward by Tolhurst is forthcoming, it will be best to regard the Benedictional of St. Æthelwold as a product of Winchester.

The next manuscript of this group, so far as date is concerned, is the Benedictional of Archbishop Robert, now at Rouen (Y 7), which was probably written for Æthelgar, bishop of Selsey from 980 and successor to Dunstan as archbishop of Canterbury in 988. It must have been executed about 980, and, though rather less sumptuous, is close in style to St. Æthelwold's Benedictional. It, too, was probably done at the New Minster. It contains only

---

[1] This identification of Godeman was first suggested by J. Gage, *Archaeol.* xxiv (1832), 22.　　[2] Ibid. lxxxiii (1933), 44.

three figural miniatures; they represent the nativity, the pentecost (Pl. 52 *a*), and the Marys at the tomb (Pl. 52 *b*). The figures of the last are enclosed in a rich foliated border of the same type as those of St. Æthelwold's Benedictional (Pl. 51 *b*); the other two compositions are framed in semicircular arches, supported on capitals; arches, columns, and capitals alike are enriched with foliate motifs. Behind and above the arch enclosing the pentecost scene (Pl. 52 *a*) are two little buildings which must ultimately have been derived from some classical prototype. Though in such details these miniatures are closer to the antique than those of St. Æthelwold's Benedictional, the manuscript marks, nevertheless, something of an advance, especially with regard to the drawing of the faces. In addition to these three miniatures there are five other pages enriched with foliate borders which enclose short portions of text in fine, plain capitals. Two of them have arched tops, three are of the more usual rectangular type; all are equally rich and decorative.

Also at Rouen is another important manuscript of this group, the Missal or, rather, the Sacramentary of Robert of Jumièges[1] (Rouen Y 6). It is very rich, containing thirteen figures or scenes in elaborate borders, and twelve pages where similar borders enclose capital letters or short portions of the text. Three distinct types of border are present; firstly, rectangular ones of the usual shape, which appear on eleven of the lettered pages and around six of the figural subjects; secondly, architectural ones like those of the other Rouen MS. which are to be found on one lettered page and around six more figural ones; and, finally, a particularly elaborate rectangular border round the remaining figural subject, namely, the pentecost (Pl. 54 *b*). This is the most imaginative of all the compositions in the Missal. The extremely ornate border and the theme of the picture itself are in astonishingly close accord, and the agitation of the former reflects the whole emotion of the latter. It is very excited—and exciting—work.

The other figured pages include, in addition to the pentecost

---

[1] Robert, abbot of Jumièges, was made bishop of London by Edward in 1044 and archbishop of Canterbury in 1051; the next year he was driven out of England. He is variously alluded to by different writers as Robert of Jumièges or archbishop Robert.

(f. 84*v*), St. Peter (f. 131*v*) and St. Andrew (f. 164*v*) enthroned (the former beardless, the latter bearded) and a full cycle of New Testament scenes, namely, the nativity (f. 32*v*), the announcement of good tidings to the shepherds and the flight into Egypt (f. 33), the journey of the wise men and their arrival before Herod (f. 36*v*), the waking of the wise men and, above it, the adoration (f. 37), the arrest of our Lord (f. 71), the crucifixion (f. 71*v*), the deposition (f. 72), the angel and the three Marys at the sepulchre (f. 72*v*), the ascension (f. 81*v*), and an elaborate composition for All Saints (f. 158*v*). All are interesting, several of the scenes especially so. The adoration may be noted partly for its spirited border and partly because of the Phrygian caps worn by the magi (Pl. 53 *a*); they wear them again in the scene where they appear before Herod. The figure of Christ of the crucifixion is worthy of note (Pl. 53 *b*), for He is quite close to the rendering on the very fine ivory in the Victoria and Albert Museum shown on Plate 31. The two cannot be very far apart in date, though the ivory is certainly the earlier. The agitated 'cloud' motif below the figures and the medallions of the border, which herald those of a late manuscript in the British Museum (Arundel 60) are striking. Similar medallions are present in the next composition, the deposition (Pl. 54 *a*). Finally, the ascension (Pl. 55 *a*) and the three Marys (Pl. 55 *b*) are also interesting, the former because a closely similar rendering of Christ's legs is to be found on folio 61 of the Caedmon MS. and also in Harley 603, though both are in line and not in colour, and the latter because it is interesting to contrast it with the earlier rendering of the same scene in St. Æthelwold's Benedictional which we illustrate on Plate 51 *b*.

Even if on the whole these pictures are less polished than those of St. Æthelwold's Benedictional, they show great imagination and mastery, and they are certainly not to be dismissed in scathing terms as inferior, as Saunders seeks to do. The manuscript is indeed extremely important both on artistic grounds and because there are only two other more or less complete early English missals that survive, namely, the Red Book of Darley (Corpus Christi College, Cambridge, No. 422) and the Leofric Missal in the Bodleian (Bodley 579). The latter was perhaps done at

Glastonbury; its calendar dates from about 970, though other parts of the manuscript are earlier. The former was probably done at Winchester, though its calendar refers to Sherborne. It was dated by M. R. James to the tenth or early eleventh century, but the mid eleventh is more likely; it is anyhow after the tenth, for St. Alphege is mentioned in the calendar. It contains a fine P, on folio 51, done in red, green, and pink, as well as a figure of Christ in glory supported by two angels, on folio 52, and a crucifixion, on folio 53. The drawing, in thin dark brown line, is of the usual type, but the mandorla, haloes, cross, and other details are filled in in heavy green in a way that is not paralleled in any other manuscript. The proportions of the figures are rather clumsy, and the general effect is primitive; the work has a Celtic flavour.

Stylistically it is clear that the Sacramentary of Robert of Jumièges is later than St. Æthelwold's Benedictional, though the two are also clearly closely related. One might, indeed, say that the two manuscripts represent respectively the fully classical and the more Baroque phases in the evolution of this art. The folds of the costumes are in general more agitated in the Rouen MS., the composition of the scenes is more uneasy, and the backgrounds more full of detail—there is even a distinct 'horror vacui' about the pictures of this book which was not present in the Benedictional. Kendrick goes so far as to suggest that its illuminator must have been a Celt, primarily on the grounds of the face of St. Peter (f. 131v), which shows a distinct resemblance to the faces in some of the early Hibernian manuscripts.[1] Perhaps the Celticness of the painter was also responsible for the rather barbaric spirit of the work as shown in the abhorrence of open spaces. The borders of the miniatures, however, reveal real mastery, and their fine, full acanthus scrolls are things of rare beauty.

In addition to the stylistic factors there are also some concrete historical facts which help to date this manuscript. It was presented to the abbey of Jumièges by Robert whilst he was bishop of London, that is, between 1044 and 1051. It was, however, executed at an earlier date. The Paschal tables begin at 1000, which sets a limit in one direction; there is no mention of St. Alphege, who

[1] *Anglo-Saxon and Viking Art*, 14.

was martyred in 1012, and as he would almost certainly have been included in any work written more than a few years after his death, around the year 1015 may be regarded as a terminus in the other. About 1008 seems the most probable date for the main portion of the manuscript. It thus belongs to the second generation, when a dispersion of painters might well have taken place, and when work of the Winchester type was being executed at other centres by craftsmen who had actually been trained at Winchester in the early days of the school there. There are thus on purely stylistic grounds no arguments against the possibility that the Missal was produced elsewhere. Peterborough and Ely have in fact been suggested as well as Winchester, and convincing arguments have been put forward in favour of all three, while even at Winchester there were by about the year 1000 two distinct centres where work was being done, those of the New Minster or St. Peter's, and the Old Minster or St. Swithin's. The large proportion of Winchester feasts that are mentioned in the calendar favours Winchester, but would apply to the New and the Old Minsters equally; it is, however, unlikely that there would be much difference in the illuminations executed in foundations so closely associated. Much of the textual evidence, on the other hand, militates against Winchester itself, but favours a centre in close touch with it. Peterborough and Ely are in this respect both possible. The names of four saints who were especially venerated at Peterborough occur in the Litany, and this supports the assignation to that place, while the inclusion of St. Etheldrida in the canons of the Mass and the mention of other saints peculiar to Ely suggest the monastery there. This monastery was refounded by St. Æthelwold in 970, and monks were in all probability taken from Winchester for the purpose, so that the essentially Winchester character of the work could easily be accounted for. An attribution to Ely is on the whole more likely in this case than in that of the Benedictional; but Peterborough is just as likely as Ely, and the evidence against assigning the Missal to Winchester is far from complete. For the time being the case must in fact be left open. The one thing that is definite is that the style of the illuminations is essentially that of the Winchester school.

Closely akin to the Sacramentary is a Benedictional in the Bibliothèque Nationale (Lat. 987). It contains no full-page illustrations, but there are some lovely coloured borders, some simple, in the form of rounded arches with little buildings above at each side, and some of the usual rosette type (ff. 31 and 41). The manuscript also contains on folio 111 an unfinished drawing in dark brown line, showing Christ enthroned. It is in a rather decadent Winchester manner, and is probably a later addition. It has been suggested that this manuscript was finished off at Canterbury, but there is reason to suppose that it was at least begun at Winchester, probably about 1020.

Other manuscripts which are related are preserved in a number of collections. A gospel book at Besançon (No. 14) is interesting, for it is early, perhaps even earlier than the Sacramentary of Robert of Jumièges.[1] One in the Landesmuseum at Hanover, known as the Eadui Gospels, is perhaps to be dated to around 1020.[2] A psalter in the Bodleian (Junius 27), with fine initials (it is to be dated to the tenth century), and two portraits of evangelists and the corresponding initials at the commencement of their Gospels, which were added in the late tenth century to an earlier Irish manuscript, in the British Museum (Add. 40618), may also be noted. The designs of the latter are original and the faces are quite expressive, but the work is not of the very first class. There are also some fragments of a Missal at Worcester which was probably done at the New Minster in the early eleventh century.

More important than any of these, however, is a manuscript in the British Museum (Add. 34890), known as the New Minster Gospels, which contains some fine and very elaborate work; three portraits of evangelists and three superb opening pages survive. In the rendering there are a number of notable innovations which may have been due to the influence of some new centre. First, outline drawing was used for the features in the portraits of the evangelists and the subsidiary figures; secondly, silver pigment was employed as well as gold in the borders; thirdly,

[1] O. Homburger, Die Anfänge der Malerschule von Winchester, 60, 65, Pl. x.
[2] One portrait of an evangelist is figured in Burl. Mag. xcii (1950), Fig. 22, p. 81.

figures in square frames or circular medallions were included in the borders of the portraits and opening page of St. John's Gospel in place of the usual foliage; fourthly, the colouring is heavier in tone than that of much of the Winchester work. The circular medallions look as though they had been inspired by plaques of cloisonné enamel (Pl. 56). These innovations may be no more than the outcome of a natural stylistic evolution such as one would expect to find in a workshop as active as that of Winchester, where numerous craftsmen were no doubt employed. But on the whole they would seem to be extensive enough to indicate a new school, though one undoubtedly closely allied to that established by Æthelwold. The work is in any case very fine, and shows a fresh elegance which is just as apparent in the initials as in the figural subjects; the L of 'Liber Generationis' (f. iiv) or the I of 'In principio' (f. 115; Pl. 56 b) may be noted. The interlacing patterns in gold which play so prominent a part in these initials are conservative, but the acanthus leaves are typical of the fully fledged Winchester style. The manuscript is probably to be dated to the early years of the eleventh century.

With the beginning of the eleventh century the colourful Winchester style began to be diffused throughout southern England, and of the schools that we actually know which were dependent in the main on Winchester, but boasted at the same time a distinctive manner of their own, the most important was no doubt Canterbury. The city had possessed two very considerable libraries from early times, associated respectively with the cathedral priory of Christ Church and the abbey of St. Augustine. Continental manuscripts had been collected there, and by the end of the tenth century both foreign and English manuscripts were being copied and probably also illuminated at both of them. Quite a number of them happily survive, notably at Trinity College, Cambridge.

The earliest of the manuscripts that are undoubtedly to be assigned to Canterbury is a copy of the Gospels in the British Museum (Roy. 1. D. IX). It has a charter for Christ Church, Canterbury, at the end, which determines its provenance, and contains a fine opening page to each of the Gospels, though there are no portraits; that of St. Matthew's Gospel (f. 6) is illustrated (Pl. 58); it is interesting to compare them with those of the New Minster Gospels (B.M. Add. 34890). The stylistic differences are marked, for in the Canterbury book the borders are especially heavy and strong and the drawing is unusually solid. The colours too are distinct, darkish-red, olive green, and greyish-blue predominating; a rather redder tone also distinguishes the gold. Without the evidence of the text these factors would alone have suggested a different school, but it would not have been possible to establish the locality. The manuscript is to be dated between 1013 and 1020, and it has been suggested that it was presented to Canterbury by King Canute.

Among the numerous books at Trinity College, Cambridge, many of which came from Canterbury, a copy of Boethius (No. O. 3. 7), of fairly late tenth-century date, may be mentioned here, for though there is no decoration in the text it contains at the beginning a full-page portrait of a female figure, the personification of philosophy, done in dark-brown line, picked out here and there in red (Pl. 59). The usual Winchester flutterings are present, but the work still has a touch of the style of St. Dunstan's portrait of Christ in the Bodleian (Pl. 43) and it may be assigned to about 990. Most other Canterbury books have initials only, like the Bosworth Psalter in the British Museum (Add. 37517). Here each verse of the psalms begins with an initial in red, and each first verse with a more elaborate one, usually in different colours. Four of them are particularly outstanding; a large Q on folio 33 is illustrated here (Pl. 57 b). It is done in red, yellow, brown, pale purple, blue, and two shades of green. Foliage of Winchester type is combined with interlacing pattern and a decoration of animals' heads bent round. The interlace is a heritage from the old Northumbrian-Hibernian schools, though it is hard to say whether it passed directly or reached Canterbury by way of the continent. It has been suggested that this manuscript was done during St. Dunstan's archbishopric, but it is hardly likely that it can be so early; a date towards the end of the tenth century seems more probable. The manuscript contains a calendar which is later still, but even this must have been done before about 1012, and on its evidence Wormald has assigned the calendar to St. Augustine's.[1] On folio 128v there is an unfinished drawing in outline of the Saviour, which must have been added in the twelfth century.

Simple capitals in red, green, and blue, like those of the Bosworth Psalter, were very popular for the next century or more. They appear, for example, in a copy of the Lives of the Saints in the British Museum (Cotton, Vespasian, B. XX), which was also done at Canterbury, though after the conquest. A few of them are worthy of note, especially a P on folio 95v. A curious little drawing of a monk's head on the margin of folio 192 is a later addition. Initials of a similar type are also present in an Arator MS. at Trinity College, Cambridge (No. B. 14. 3). The manuscript is to be dated to the end of the tenth century, and is again probably to be assigned to Canterbury. On the evidence of its initials another volume at Trinity College, Cambridge (No. O. 2. 31), as well as bishop Aldhelm's de Virginitate at Lambeth (No. 200) and the Sherborne Pontifical in the Bibliothèque Nationale (Lat. 943), would seem to have come from the same scriptorium. In all of them the line-drawing of the initials is very delicate, and consists of interlaced acanthus scrolls ending in animals' heads; an A from the Sherborne Pontifical is illustrated (Pl. 42 d). The influence of earlier manuscripts which were associated with Canterbury, notably the Codex Aureus at Stockholm, is apparent, and some of the interlaced work is reminiscent of the ninth-century book of Cerne or of the early pages of books in the Bodleian illustrated on Plate 42. The Sherborne Pontifical—which is to be dated between 992 and 995— also contains some very fine line-drawings; one of them, showing the crucifixion, is illustrated on Plate 64 b. Though polished and delicate it is rather hard. The work is in outline, in dark brown and red. On folios 5v, 6, and 6v there are also full-page drawings of Christ in different aspects, delicately drawn in dark brown.

Another work which has by some been attributed to Canterbury is folio 8 of a collection of privileges in the British Museum (Cotton, Claudius, A. III). It is probably to be assigned to the eleventh century, though there are already hints of the twelfth. The picture shows St. Gregory enthroned in a church-like structure

[1] *English Calendars before* 1000, Henry Bradshaw Society, 1933.

of very Byzantine appearance, with three figures kneeling before
him; the whole is enclosed in an elaborate scroll border. Both
must have been inspired by Byzantine or Italian prototypes, and
though the ornament of the St. Gregory is essentially Romanesque,
the architecture of the building and the pose of the figures
are Byzantine. It was probably produced across the Channel
rather than this side of it, in spite of the English elements in the
work. Another late volume which was more probably done at
Canterbury, though continental influence is to the fore, is a
Passionale in the British Museum (Arundel 91). It is to be dated to
the late eleventh century.

Wormald has associated another psalter in the British Museum
(Arundel 155) with Canterbury on the basis of its calendar, but this
time it was done at Christ Church and not at St. Augustine's. The
manuscript is to be dated around 1025 and contains, in addition
to capitals in gold or colours, a lovely B on folio 12. The B is
inside a frame and foliage border of Winchester type (Pl. 57 a).
The canon tables are framed by neatly drawn architectural
compositions, and at the top of those on folios 9v and 10v are
figures, the latter plain, the former partly tinted green. The
work is far less agitated than is so often the case in line-drawings,
but neither here nor in the coloured work of the B is there enough
stylistic peculiarity to suggest a distinction between the school of
St. Augustine's and that of Christ Church. But certain features
may perhaps be regarded as the hall-marks of Canterbury in
general, notably a rather deep colour scheme, a very colouristic
treatment, where heavy, strong tones are used, a great feeling for
impressive ornament, and a rather solid, firm system of arrangement. These features appear in the B of Arundel 155 and are to be
seen to a more marked extent in a copy of the Gospels at Trinity
College, Cambridge (B. 10. 4).

This manuscript was given to Trinity College by Thomas
Nevill, dean of Canterbury from 1597 to 1615, and as most of
his other books were by Canterbury scribes, the attribution of the
manuscript to Canterbury is supported by external as well as by
stylistic evidence. The book was probably finished about 1020,
though James suggests that some of the work may have been done

at the end of the preceding century. It must have been among the richest Gospel books of its age, for it contains fifteen very elaborately decorated pages of canon tables, a great figure of the Almighty enclosed in a particularly ornate border, a portrait of each of the evangelists, and an opening initial to each Gospel, again enclosed in an elaborate rosette border. Medallions containing busts of saints and prophets are included in the borders in the cases of St. Matthew's, St. Mark's, and St. John's Gospels (Pl. 60). Gold is profusely used, and the colours are unusually rich and lavish, including deep purple, purple-red, violet, pink, grey-green, grey-blue, and grey-pink. The depiction of the Majesty on the verso of the last of the pages of canon tables (f. 16v) is especially striking (Pl. 62). It is in better condition than the evangelist portraits, some of which have been damaged by damp, but tells also because of the richness of the work. The border is especially effective and the figure itself majestic and imposing, and the grandeur of its pose is enhanced by the glory of the colouring, for the garment is pink, the cloak gold, lined in black; the background is pale brick, the mandorla bright blue, the halo grey-green, and the hair grey-blue. Altogether the work is of outstanding richness and brilliance.

Two Gospels, formerly at Holkham Hall (Nos. 15 and 16), and now in the Pierpont Morgan collection (Nos. 708 and 709), are again, on stylistic grounds, perhaps to be assigned to Canterbury rather than to Winchester, but the figures are much slighter than those in the Trinity Gospels, and their whole character inclines to decadence. One of the manuscripts contains four miniatures of the evangelists within very beautiful Winchester borders. The other has nine painted pages, the most important of which shows the crucifixion.[1] An additional figure is included in the foreground of this scene, and it has been suggested that it represents Judith, widow of Harold's brother Tostig, who was killed at Stamford Bridge in 1066. Judith subsequently married duke Guelph IV of Suabia, and the two of them presented the manuscripts to the abbey of Weingarten. They were no doubt done for Judith before she left England in or soon after 1066. St. Luke, from MS. No. 709,

[1] T. D. Kendrick, *Late Saxon and Viking Art*, Pl. XII.

is illustrated (Pl. 63). The style of the drawing of the figures of
these manuscripts is akin to that of a figure of Christ, King of
Kings, which appears as the title-page of a volume of Homilies at
Trinity College, Cambridge (No. B. 15. 34). Christ is in a sitting
position though there is no throne beneath, and the figure is
enclosed in a mandorla (Pl. 61 b). The drawing is delicate, in
brown ink, tinted in brown and darkish-green. Unfortunately
this manuscript is not from the same source as the majority of those
at Trinity, which all came from Canterbury, so that nothing can be
said as to its provenance. Indeed, on stylistic grounds East Anglia
would seem as likely as Canterbury, for a drawing in a manuscript
in the Bodleian (Douce No. 296) is akin, and this has been assigned
to Croyland (Pl. 75 a and p. 210). Another drawing which may
also be compared is on folio 1v of a psalter in the library of Corpus
Christi College at Cambridge (No. 411). It shows a bearded man
full length, holding a book, within a border of interlacing patterns
of archaic type (Pl. 61 a). The drawing constitutes an eleventh-
century English addition to the manuscript, which is otherwise
older, and a product of Tours.

Another important manuscript which is in the Canterbury style,
though there is no evidence to prove that it was actually done
there, is a copy of the Gospels at Wadham College, Oxford (A. 10.
22). It is beautifully written and in first-class condition, and is
interesting in that it contains a number of drawings in black and
red line which have the appearance of sketches intended to be
coloured rather than of pure drawings like those of the Utrecht
Psalter; one, on folio 42, consists of a border of Winchester foliage
only; the main subject on the centre of the page was never even
drawn. The finest, however, is an elaborate rendering of the three
Marys at the sepulchre on folio 108v (Pl. 64 a). The border is
typically Winchester, and the figures are not unlike those of the
same subject in the Benedictional of St. Æthelwold (Pl. 51 b),
though the line is harder and more metallic. This might just as well
be due to date, however, as to locality, for the book is considerably
later than the Benedictional. One other portrait (f. 10v) and some
initials are of the same unfinished type, but the B of the Beatus
page is fully coloured in brilliant tones of red, blue, and pale pink

(Pl. 73 b). An L on folio 11 and its Winchester border are also coloured in the same brilliant tones of red, green, gold, and blue. Both the initials are obviously late; the shades of the colouring, indeed, already hint at those of such early post-conquest manuscripts as Durham ones (see p. 221), but the drawing is purely Saxon. A date around 1040 seems most likely.

In addition to the manuscripts which may on stylistic or other grounds be assigned to Canterbury, M. R. James notes a considerable number which were at one time in the libraries of St. Augustine's or Christ Church, and which we know from the early catalogues. But though these were all at one time housed at Canterbury they were not all necessarily produced there, so that the lists do not help greatly in the problem of establishing the characteristics of the different schools. Of these books the most important from the artistic point of view is the lovely Caedmon MS. in the Bodleian, which is illustrated with line-drawings in place of the coloured miniatures which have characterized all the manuscripts we have examined so far. But it is not the earliest of the Canterbury MSS. illustrated in line, for a very high standard of drawing seems to have been maintained there from the end of the tenth century as a result of the presence in Canterbury of a psalter which was used as a model both at Christ Church and at St. Augustine's. The model, which is now preserved at Utrecht, was written and illustrated at Reims about the year 840.[1] Subsequently it was taken to England and deposited at St. Augustine's, Canterbury, where it was copied almost line for line about the year 1000. A second copy, now at Trinity College, Cambridge (No. R. 17. 1) and known as the Eadwine Psalter, was done about the middle of the twelfth century,[2] and a third, now in the Bibliothèque Nationale (Lat. 8846), was made at the end of that century or the beginning of the thirteenth.

The first English copy of the psalter is now preserved in the

---

[1] It was reproduced in facsimile by the Paleographical Society in 1874. More recently it has been republished with a critical and descriptive text by E. T. de Wald: *The Illustrations of the Utrecht Psalter*, Princeton (c. 1940).

[2] See M. R. James, *The Canterbury Psalter*, facsimile edition done for the Friends of Canterbury Cathedral (1935).

British Museum (Harley 603). Its text follows the Roman version, which was usual in England, whereas that of the original is the Gallican, which was in favour on the continent. But throughout, in both of them, the scenes are interspersed in the text in exactly the same way. They serve to interpret the sense of the narrative and not merely to illustrate one or two selected events as do the coloured illuminations which have been discussed above. The scenes are shown against landscape backgrounds, and often two or three incidents are grouped together before the same background, subsidiary figures being added to express the development of the story. Greater variation is probably to be seen in the backgrounds than in the actual scenes themselves, so that we are in the presence of what is really an early essay in the art of landscape painting.

The miniatures of the first part of Harley 603 follow those of the Utrecht Psalter closely; those in the latter part, which are by a different hand, are more original but not always quite so accomplished. There are a good many pages left blank in the middle. The same technique was followed by both hands, for the drawings were first done in outline and then tinted; in some cases the tints have never been added. The second painter preferred brighter colours and a particularly vivid blue distinguishes much of his work, whereas the first used a lovely fresh green. The works of both hands show the same defects natural to a copyist, and this can be clearly seen if a page of Harley 603 is compared with one from the original; that illustrating Psalms xv and xvi affords a typical instance (Pl. 65). It shows, in the upper register, a man being invited to enter the tabernacle, while on the right he rests on the holy hill. In the lower register the three Marys are shown at the sepulchre, illustrating verse 10, 'neither wilt thou suffer thine Holy One to see corruption'. In the original the drawings are well placed in the available space; the edges of the mountains are clearly defined and are made true to nature; the figures are stronger; the line is more determined. In the copy the artist has misjudged the space at his disposal, so that his drawings overlap the text or have to be distorted, as in the case of the tree on the holy hill which is bent almost double; the shading at the edges of the mountains has been replaced by a rather pointless jagged edge; the figures are over-fussy; in general the work displays a certain lack of definition and decision.

In spite of these deficiencies in copying, however, Harley 603 shows certain improvements. The drawings are thus very fresh and alive and have great charm and delicacy, and coloured tinting is used with very great effect, whereas the original was in monochrome. Fol. 51v is full of strength and force in spite of the delicate line (Pl. 66 a). It illustrates Psalm civ, and shows, above, God on the wings of the wind, with ministering angels around, while at the foot are ranged the creations of the Lord, valleys, mountains, springs, the wild asses, the beasts of the field, and the cedars of Lebanon. Man is shown in the centre, at his labour, eating, and in the process of having his beard anointed with oil. Below is the great wide sea, the ships and 'that Leviathan'; to the right are the mountains, refuge for the goats, and to the left the young lions go after their prey. Folio 6v (Psalm xi) is more gentle and delicate (Pl. 66 b). It depicts the psalmist holding a pair of scales, standing before God's holy temple. In the middle the wicked bend their bows and men tear down a temple, while on the right the wicked are destroyed by fire and brimstone.

The Caedmon MS. in the Bodleian (Junius 11) has already been mentioned; it, too, is to be ascribed to Canterbury, and dates from about 1000. Its drawings are in brown line with additions in red, green, and black; they present a most enchanting effect. Three artists are to be distinguished: two, who did the majority of the work, and a third, working in the twelfth century, who left unfinished a drawing on f. 96. A great many pages which were left blank or partly blank for drawings to be added remain blank to this day. The first two artists both worked in the style of the Utrecht Psalter, but one of them, the first, had a much firmer and more determined hand; the other, the second, produced more feathery, blurred outlines. The efforts of the first at the nude are not very convincing except for Satan on folio 20, but his work has considerable strength and impressiveness. The fall of the rebel angels on folio 3 is especially striking (Pl. 68). The manner is not far distant from that of the New Minster Register (B.M. Stowe 944), though the arrangement of the scene in four tiers perhaps accentuates the resemblance fortuitously. Christ among the Cherubim on the title-page is also a fine piece of composition in spite of the rather hard rendering of the features. But the way in which a celestial atmosphere is suggested by the wavy lines of the clouds is most subtle; they have something of the same ethereal significance that is to be seen in such Persian miniatures as those of the History of the World, which is now in part in the University library at Edinburgh and in part in the collection of the Royal Asiatic Society.[1]

The lighter touch of the second hand is, however, perhaps rather pleasanter. His work is well illustrated by folio 49, where the story of Cain and Abel is portrayed. The style here is much closer to that of the first English version of the Utrecht Psalter than it is in the earlier pictures in the Caedmon. Homburger would identify this artist with the man who illustrated a copy of Prudentius in the library of Corpus Christi College at Cambridge,[2] but this suggestion is unlikely, for the Cambridge MS. is probably a good deal later in date, and stylistic evidence suggests that it is to be assigned to the west country (p. 213).

Other scenes are particularly interesting in view of their subject-matter, notably, that showing Adam and Eve clothing themselves on folio 34 (Pl. 69 a) and that of the Ark on folio 66 (Pl. 69 b). The line and style of the former are markedly Saxon—the sculpture at Codford St. Peter may be compared—and the ark on the latter is strikingly suggestive of a Viking vessel such as the Oseberg ship. A medallion on folio 2 is also important, for it bears the name of Ælfwine; Gollancz has suggested that this was the Ælfwine who became abbot of New Minster in 1035,[3] but this cannot, of course, be proved.

An unfinished drawing by the third artist is to be regarded as of later date than the rest of the manuscript. It is certainly much more classical in feeling and was no doubt inspired by a manuscript from the east Christian area. Another hand again must have been

---

[1] A. U. Pope, *A Survey of Persian Art*, Oxford, (1936) Pls. 827 and 828. It was written in 1307.   [2] *Die Anfänge der Malerschule von Winchester*, 5.

[3] *The Caedmon Manuscript*, xxxv.

responsible for a drawing on folio 225, representing an interlaced design of Scandinavian type. There is another sketch in the same manner on the last page. The latter seems to have no connexion with the manuscript but to represent a design for a bracelet. Gollancz has, however, suggested that the drawing on folio 225 was a sketch for the binding of the book; the present binding is an addition dating from about 1460. This surmise is possible, but little more; the illustration might equally be a careless sketch like that on the last folio; indeed, the fact that it is not finished makes this the more probable.

A Pontifical now at Rouen (Bibl. de la Ville A 27) is also probably to be included in this group, for though on the basis of the text it can be assigned to Wessex, perhaps even to Wells, the two drawings which it contains are on separate leaves and may have been incorporated into the manuscript; even the text is by several distinct hands. These drawings show respectively a bishop and a priest holding a book (f. 1*v*) and the consecration of a church (f. 2*v*); both are in black and red line. The handling is strong, even hard, but it is fairly close to that of the first hand in the Caedmon MS.; the secular figures in the foreground of the consecration scene are particularly alike (Pl. 70 *a*). The manuscript must be later than 1030 on textual evidence; the illustrations would, on stylistic grounds, appear to be of the first half of the eleventh century.

To Canterbury again, and this time to St. Augustine's abbey and not to Christ Church, is probably to be assigned, on the basis of its text, a manuscript in the British Museum which contains a series of tables for finding Easter Day (Cotton, Caligula, A. XV). Several hands worked on the text and it is bound up with an earlier manuscript which is probably French, but the two very lovely line-drawings, tinted in green and red, which appear at the top of folios 122*v* and 123*v*, are both by the same hand and are to be dated around 1065. The draughtsmanship is very light and fluttering and the style essentially Winchester; the artist, however, must have followed a model of the Reims school fairly closely. At times his line becomes particularly agitated, and the clouds on folio 122*v* are almost Chinese (Pl. 67 *a*).

The Gospels of St. Vaast from Arras and an Amalarius from St. Omer, both now at Boulogne (Nos. 10 and 82) are, on grounds of their initials, to be assigned to the same group, as are two books in the British Museum, a Rule of St. Benedict from St. Augustine's at Canterbury (B.M. Harley 5431), and a grammatical collection (Cotton, Cleopatra, A. VI), which contain a few simple initials. The one is to be assigned to about the year 1000 and the other is perhaps slightly later, though the work is more conservative. The ornament of the initials is of a distinct type, composed of creatures with complete heads and bodies, as opposed to the more usual ones where the heads only are shown, divorced from their bodies. These initials are, especially in Harley 5431, still quite close to Hiberno-Saxon prototypes, but none of them is very elaborate and colours were not used.

Ælfric's paraphrase of the Pentateuch and the book of Joshua in the British Museum (Cotton, Claudius, B. IV), is again probably to be assigned to Canterbury and to be dated about 1050. It contains a very large number of pictures both fully coloured and in tinted line-work, and several hands are to be distinguished. All the pictures, however, are essentially illustrative, and are not of outstanding artistic importance. Some of them herald those of the Bayeux tapestry in their narrative content; two scenes from Genesis are shown on Plate 72. A figure on folio 6v is interesting, for it suggests the angular style of those so frequently seen in Romanesque wall paintings in France, like those of St. Savin. Many of the illustrations towards the end are unfinished, and show the progress of the work at a number of different stages. The colours of the dresses were in some cases first applied with a brush, in patches, without previous outlining. Then the heads, limbs, and hands, and the details of the dresses were drawn in outline, and then, finally, the features were added. The visual imagination of the artist must thus have been very sure, though the splodges of colour, without the outlines and details, look most odd. The fluttering type of garment so characteristic of Anglo-Saxon art both in the linear and the colouristic work was thus in this case a superficial addition to the main design. A striking feature of these illustrations is the non-naturalistic nature of the colouring, such curious tones as blue for the hair being used. This is in keeping with the aesthetic approach of the period, and similar non-naturalistic tones are to be seen in other Saxon manuscripts. In this volume the choice of colours was not very subtle. A history of Alexander in the British Museum (Roy. 13. A. 1) is perhaps also to be assigned to Canterbury.

Another important centre, though we know less about it than we do about Canterbury, was Bury St. Edmunds. It seems to have maintained similar close contacts with Winchester. A psalter in the Vatican (Reg. 12) would, indeed, be assigned to Winchester on stylistic grounds alone were it not for the text, which establishes the Bury provenance. It is to be dated somewhere around 1040, and is certainly not earlier than 1032. In addition to some very fine initials in the colouristic manner[1] it contains a number of delicate drawings in the margins, over which the text is in part written (Pl. 71 a). The Bury Gospels in the British Museum (Harley 76), on the other hand, shows a distinct style, for broad bands of colour replace the foliations typical of the Winchester work, the acanthus leaves are stylized almost to a marbled pattern, and there is in general a greater heaviness of touch; the costumes of the figures are, indeed, over-rigid, and the faces unduly lugubrious. But as yet we do not know enough to claim that these were characteristics of the Bury school alone. The manuscript contains fourteen pages of ornately decorated canon tables at the beginning and an elaborate I enclosed in a heavy frame on folio 45. It is probably to be assigned to the late tenth century. Work of a similar type appears in a portrait of the apostle Matthew in a copy of the Gospels at Copenhagen, though its iconography is based on that of the Lindisfarne Gospels. It was perhaps the work of a monk from Bury who visited or was transferred to Durham and who saw the Lindisfarne MS. while he was there. Another important manuscript of the colourful style is a copy of the Gospels at Pembroke College, Cambridge (No. 301); it is not unlike the York Gospels in style (see p. 210), but is later in date, for it must belong to the eleventh rather than the tenth century.

A copy of the Psychomachia of Prudentius in the British Museum

---

[1] The B of the Beatus page is reproduced in *New Palaeog. Soc.*, second series (1913–30), vol. ii, Pl. 167.

(Add. 24199), which dates from the late tenth century and contains fine line-drawings, presents certain problems.[1] The text is in Caroline minuscule, but the illustrations are essentially English, and show all the characteristics of light, delicate line-work and fluttering—but not jittery—drapery that characterizes this country. They are, however, more florid than is usual, and this feature is perhaps to be associated with East Anglia. Except for folio 2v, where the Phrygian caps of seven mounted figures are coloured in, the work is all in thin black line; towards the end of the volume, spaces for drawings have been left blank or the drawings have been only half finished; a few additions, in a much coarser hand, must have been done later. It has been suggested that another but smaller copy of the same book also in the British Museum (Cotton, Cleopatra, C. VIII) is to be assigned to Bury. The hand is quite distinct from that working on Add. 24199, and on stylistic grounds alone the book cannot be assigned to Bury rather than elsewhere in East Anglia or even to Canterbury. It is to be dated towards the middle of the eleventh century: its drawings, which are in black and red line, combined occasionally with additional tintings in green, are of rather finer quality than those in the former manuscript. Though interspersed in the text the illustrations are enclosed in frames which the artist seems to have been at considerable pains to ignore (Pl. 71 b). A single leaf from a rather similar manuscript is preserved at Munich. The Psychomachia, or Battle of the Soul, describes the struggle between the Virtues and Vices, and offers a series of inspiring subjects for illustration. But on the whole the quality of the pictures in both these books is rather hard and unsympathetic. It is not as good as that in the service books.

It is probable that manuscripts were executed at another abbey not far from Bury, namely, Ramsey. The most important of the surviving examples is a psalter in the British Museum (Harley 2904), which is probably to be dated between 974 and 986. It contains a number of elaborate initials in gold and other colours,

---

[1] This and other copies of the Psychomachia are fully illustrated by R. Stettiner, *Die illustrierten Prudentius Handschriften*, Berlin (1905). See also H. Woodruff, 'Illustrated MSS. of Prudentius', *Art Studies*, Harvard (1929), 33.

all of which are of surprisingly high quality; the B of the 'Beatus vir qui non abiit' is one of the most lovely initials ever produced in the whole story of English illumination (Pl. 73 *a*). It may be contrasted with the much more pedestrian B in the Wadham College Gospels that is illustrated beside it. The main body of the letter is gold, the dragons' heads are grey-green, and they spurt out blue and white-ochre leaves; the remaining leaves are blue, red, pale purple, and deep green. The ornament is rich and leafy, and the leaves spring from stout stems and turn over at the ends; at a later date they tend to become thinner and more emaciated with long wiry stalks. Wormald has divided the initials of this period into two main groups,[1] and those of Harley 2904 are typical of the first of them, the grandest type, in which continental influence is to the fore. Opposed to this style are the less complicated, monochrome letters of the humbler manuscripts. The atmosphere in Harley 2904 is one of pure delight; abstract though the motifs may be, it is essentially a living art of this world. The B has an intense brilliance about it which savours of a summer day in England notwithstanding its entirely non-naturalistic colouring. The severe expressionism and harsh line that characterizes so much of the tenth-century German work, the exaggerated preoccupation with the glories of the infinite that is the hall-mark of the Byzantine, have here been left far behind, and joy of life is the dominant theme.

In addition to the initials the manuscript contains a particularly fine line-drawing of the crucifixion (Pl. 74 *a*). It is in brownish-red line, with the costumes of the Virgin and St. John, as well as the bracket below our Lord's feet, tinted in royal blue. In spite of the awkward attitude of St. John and the almost hunch-backed figure of the Virgin, this drawing is of rare beauty, more monumental and at the same time more full of feeling than the drawings of the Utrecht Psalter family, yet more subtle than the rendering of the same scene in the Sherborne Pontifical in the Bibliothèque Nationale (Lat. 943, Pl. 64 *b*). It seems to show all the grandeur and all the subtlety of the Saxon school at its height, and the result is full of vitality in spite of the strict adherence to the old iconography. Another crucifixion in a manuscript done at Winchester

---

[1] *Archaeol.* xci (1945), 107.

about the time of the conquest (B.M. Arundel 60) may also be compared (Pl. 74 *b*). This is a far weaker work than either of the above; it has indeed the appearance of an outline that was intended to be coloured rather than a finished drawing.

Harley 2904 is probably to be dated between 974 and 986, and it has been assigned to East Anglia on the basis of the saints mentioned in the Litany. Niver goes so far as to identify it with a psalter which was executed at Ramsey for St. Oswald and which is referred to in a fourteenth-century catalogue of the library.[1] Ramsey was an important centre of manuscript production and this attribution is quite probable.

To Croyland, on the basis of its calendar, is to be assigned a manuscript of the psalms in the Bodleian (Douce 296) which is to be dated to the earlier eleventh century. It contains a fine B on the Beatus page, richly coloured capitals throughout, and one other elaborate initial, a Q in the form of a man of rather Norman appearance slaying a dragon, may be noted. There is also one full-page illumination showing our Lord treading on asp and basilisk (Pl. 75 *a*). The border is in the typical Winchester manner, but the figure is perhaps taller and slimmer than usual and the colours are rather paler. The same tall figures appear in the two Pierpont Morgan MSS. (708 and 709) (see p. 199) which seem to have been done at Canterbury, so it is impossible to say that this was a characteristic peculiar to Croyland. All that is clear is that the proportions of the figures are different from those of the purest Winchester work, and quite clearly distinct from the much heavier manner of such manuscripts as the York Gospels or Queen Margaret Gospels in the Bodleian (Lat. Liturg. 5).

The York Gospels originally contained portraits of the four evangelists; St. John is now missing. The style here is very different from that of the East Anglian manuscripts, for the figures are much more classical, the acanthus borders are absent, and the draperies are heavier; they are of a rather continental as opposed to Winchester type (Pl. 76 *a*). An initial at the beginning of St. Matthew's Gospel is, however, of a southern English character, as is the hand of the first page of the text. It is thus possible that the book was

---

[1] 'The Psalter in the British Museum, Harley 2904', *Kingsley Porter Studies*, 606 f.

begun in the south, perhaps at Winchester itself, and was then finished off elsewhere, perhaps at York, under the patronage of St. Oswald. The manuscript has been assigned to very diverse dates, but it is most probable that it was done during St. Oswald's archbishopric (972–92).

The same deep colouring and rather ponderous manner characterizes a very interesting little Gospel book in the Bodleian (Lat. Liturg. f. 5), but the continental affinities are here even more marked. It is usually known as the Gospel Book of Queen Margaret. It contains one illuminated initial on the Incipit page of St. Matthew's Gospel, which is rather Celtic in appearance, as well as portraits of each of the four evangelists (Pl. 76 b). The iconography is closer to that of some continental prototype than is usual, and the style of the work is almost as Carolingian as it is English. St. Matthew, for example, wears a heavy olive-green over-mantle and grey-blue robe; his hair is brick-red, as is the seat, and the rest of the throne is blue, gold, and red, as is the border. All these are deeper tones than were usual in England. His face is uncoloured, but the features are drawn in reddish-black. His attitude is severe and rigid, and there are no hints of the Winchester lightness. St. Mark shows rather more movement, and this characteristic is carried farther in the portrait of St. Luke, which almost approaches to the 'jittery' manner of the Ebbo Gospels (Pl. 45 a). Queen Margaret died in 1093, and she no doubt took the manuscript with her to Scotland when she married King Malcolm Canmore in 1067. It is safe to say that the book was executed before about 1060; on stylistic grounds alone it might be considerably earlier. Where it was done is more difficult to establish, but it can hardly have been in East Anglia or Canterbury, for the style is so very distinct. It may perhaps have been done in the west country. In any case, its continental affinities are to be attributed to conservatism rather than to contemporary contacts with France or Germany.

The Hereford Gospel Book at Pembroke College, Cambridge (No. 302), is akin to it and shows the same deep colouring. It is possible that both of them are to be assigned to the same centre. This book contains full-page illustrations of the evangelists seated before curtained backgrounds (Pl. 77 a). Their angular attitudes and the crumpled folds of their costumes are clearly of Winchester type, but there is a much greater heaviness; the folds of the curtains almost look as though they were carved out of wood by means of the method known as chip carving. Gold is used very profusely and the palette is a rich one, blues, greens, violets, pink, and bright red all appearing. The book is to be dated to the second quarter of the eleventh century.

A few other books can be associated with the west country on external rather than stylistic evidence. Most important of them is a Troper in the British Museum (Cotton, Caligula, A. XIV). Two hands are to be distinguished, the one producing what are really coloured drawings in a manner close to that of the Winchester school, the other doing heavy coloured work rather like that of the Reichenau school in Germany; throughout his drawing is harsh and his colours are heavy and glaring; gold or yellow and an unpleasant brownish-red predominate. The former was responsible for the pentecost scene on folio 31v shown on Plate 67 b. The harsh line and rather 'Romanesque' attitudes are worthy of note, but it is the heavy coloured work of the other hand that is most typical of the west country. The volume has been attributed to Hereford, and this attribution seems quite probable; anyhow the style is distinctive and obviously provincial. The book must date from the second quarter of the eleventh century.

Though the work is more linear and closer to that of such manuscripts as those at Rouen, a psalter at Salisbury (No. 150) has also been assigned to the west country on the evidence of its text. There is only one fully decorated page, which bears a fine A topped by a figure of Christ, the whole enclosed in a foliate border (Pl. 78). This border has the same architectural form as those on some of the pages of the Rouen MSS., but is more clumsily done; a curious feature, which is quite original, is the addition of four little legs and feet at the bottom of each column. The Christ above the A is close to a Byzantine or similar model and shows little of the fluttering lightness of Winchester work. Other initials in the book are on a small scale, akin to those of Winchester or Canterbury; the Sherborne Pontifical, in the Bibliothèque Nationale (Lat. 943) may be compared. The Salisbury MS. is probably to be dated between 969 and 978.[1]

Another west-country manuscript is a copy of the Psychomachia of Prudentius, now at Corpus Christi College, Cambridge (No. 23), which came originally from Malmesbury. It was probably produced there, for the colours are of the same rather deep tones as those of the British Museum Troper. Scenes from the life of Abraham are included as well as the conflicts of the Virtues and Vices. M. R. James suggests that the manuscript is a twelfth-century copy,[2] but the style is so completely Anglo-Saxon that a date around 1000 seems more probable. The work is imaginative and of high quality though rather harsher and more brilliant than that of the Caedmon or other related manuscripts. This is especially apparent in the illustration on folio 36 (Pl. 80 *b*). The figures and undergarments of the women are in red line, the robe of one is bright green, of the other bright blue, and the curtain is emerald green. The rest is in brown or red line, except for the details of the battlements and the hair of the two little men at the top, which is heavily coloured in deep emerald green. The imagination of the artist is clearly to be seen in his rendering of the animals on folio 3 (Pl. 80 *a*).

A more reliable classification of manuscripts than that based on stylistic features, however, is that suggested by the calendars, though, of course, it can only be applied to such manuscripts as contain them. Such manuscripts have been listed and carefully examined by Wormald, and in addition to the Canterbury, Bury St. Edmunds, and Croyland books that have been mentioned above, he makes a number of other attributions, but as most of the volumes are not illustrated, they hardly concern us.[3] A copy of

[1] The initials are reproduced and there is a short account in the *Eighteenth Annual Report of the Friends of Salisbury Cathedral*, Salisbury, 1948.

[2] *Catalogue of Manuscripts at Corpus Christi College, Cambridge*, i. 44.

[3] Wormald's assignations are as follows: see his *English Calendars before 1000*, Henry Bradshaw Soc., lxxii (1933). To Exeter a very simple MS. with practically no decoration in the British Museum (Cotton, Vitellius, A. xii); to Glastonbury Bodleian 579; to the north country Bodleian Digby 63; to Wells Cotton, Vitellius, A. XVIII; to Winchester Cotton, Titus, D. XXVII, Trinity College, Cambridge, R. 15. 32, B.M. Arundel 60, and Cotton, Vitellius, E. XVIII; to Worcester Corpus Christi College, Cambridge, Nos. 9 and 391; to the west country Salisbury 150 and

St. Gregory's Dialogues at Clare College, Cambridge (Kk. 5. 6), which has been assigned to Worcester, on the grounds of its text, by M. R. James, may, however, be noted, for it contains several fine initials, though they are of the bright-coloured type of those in the later Carilef MSS. at Durham, and are to be dated to the very end of the eleventh, if not to the early twelfth century.

Though in early days the continent had been essentially an area of inspiration so far as England was concerned, the role seems in the eleventh century to have been at times reversed, and quite a number of manuscripts which are broadly speaking of Winchester type were produced in northern France at that time. It is, indeed, even possible that the Winchester style was copied overseas at an earlier date, for the miniatures of the Wittekind Codex, written at Fulda between 970 and 980, already hint at the typical flutterings.[1] Later work which shows a rather continental handling of the typical Winchester folds seems to have been produced in north France and Flanders. It would seem, indeed, that there was actually a 'Channel' school in being, and the work must have been done by Frenchmen who had seen Winchester books or by Englishmen who had settled abroad. The most important of the examples of this group is a copy of the Gospels in the British Museum (Add. 11850) containing elaborately decorated canon tables, portraits of the four evangelists, and a lovely opening page to each Gospel (Pl. 77 b). The motifs of the decoration, and especially the rosette borders, are close to those of the work done at Winchester, but the emaciated figures, and, above all, the colouring, are different, and it is on the basis of these factors that the attribution to France must depend. The manuscript may be dated to the end of the eleventh century; its importance for us lies in the evidence it affords of the spread of the Winchester style overseas. Even so, one may say that Winchester elements are only superficial, whereas Ottonian ones are fundamental. A rather similar manuscript, perhaps done at Fleury, is preserved at Orleans (No. 175).

Closely allied to this 'Channel' school on the continent was one

Cambridge University Library Kk. 5. 32; and perhaps to Evesham an Homelarium of St. Wulfstan in the Bodleian, Hatton 113.

[1] Amadeo Tarouca, *Stilgesetze des Frühen Abendlandes*, Mainz, 1943, Pl. xviii.

in England, which we know best from a few wall-paintings now preserved in central Sussex; it is usually known as the Lewes Priory school. The most important examples of the work of this school are a series of scenes at Hardham which are to be dated to about 1125; they are comparatively well preserved. Others at Clayton, not far distant, are in less good condition, but they must have been rather more polished, and they show more marked continental influence. Though they, too, have usually been assigned to the twelfth century, the case for dating them to the end of the eleventh has recently been very ably argued by Miss Audrey Baker.[1] Her analysis is particularly thorough and scholarly, and unless further evidence comes to light it seems reasonable to accept the Clayton paintings as works of the Anglo-Norman transition. But old Ottonian elements seem to be just as much to the fore as the new French Romanesque ones.

A few manuscripts seem to belong to the same group; some of them may actually have been done on the continent. A psalter from St. Omer, and now at Boulogne(No. 20), was certainly produced at St. Omer; it is dated 999. A Latin Gospels, also at Boulogne (No. 11), is more continental in style, but both show clearly the effect of Winchester influence on the continent. A copy of St. Augustine's De Civitate Dei in the Laurentian Library at Florence (Pluto, XII. 17) must have been done either by an English artist working abroad or by a continental artist who had been trained in England. It shows a good deal of Saxon influence, but is probably to be dated in the twelfth rather than the eleventh century. A Gospel book at Monte Cassino (No. 437), with portraits of the evangelists and fine initials at the opening of each Gospel, was unquestionably done in England and exported. It dates from about the middle of the century; St. John is illustrated on Plate 75 *b*.

The fullest development of the colourful work of the Winchester

---

[1] 'Lewes Priory', *Walpole Soc.* xxxi (1946), 26. She points out that the closest similarities of style are to be found in wall-paintings at Burgfelden in Swabia, which are usually dated to the late tenth century. The case for the twelfth century has been put by E. Tristram and T. Borenius, *English Mediaeval Painting*, 15. See also Tristram, *English Medieval Wall Paintings*, i, Oxford (1944), 115.

school is to be seen in a psalter in the British Museum (Arundel 60), which must have been written about 1060. It contains a Beatus page and two other initial pages in colour, with elaborate borders, and a well-known page showing the crucifixion. The borders are basically of the conventional Winchester type, but display considerable variations, especially on folio 53, where there is a curious sort of wicker-work design (Pl. 79 b). The B of the Beatus page is in keeping with late Saxon developments, for in addition to the usual scroll-work, a number of little figures appear clambering amongst the stems; Wormald has aptly termed this the 'gymnastic' style. The colour scheme is also fairly typical of the period. Tomato-red, strong blue and green, pale yellow, of the tones usual in early Norman work, occur in addition to the grey-blues and grey-purples of Saxon art. All the colours are applied with a greater feeling for pure decoration than was usual in earlier Saxon work and there is perhaps rather less subtlety even if there is greater brilliance.

The most distinctive page is, however, that showing the crucifixion (f. 52v, Pl. 79 a). The border is made up of rather solid scrolls, with a medallion at each corner containing the symbols of the evangelists; they seem to follow some sort of metal-work prototype. The crucifixion itself is less Saxon, and the emaciated proportions of the figure are very suggestive of Ottonian work of fifty years earlier. Even the mushroom-like trees are paralleled in Ottonian art, though they only reached full popularity in the twelfth century.[1] The whole composition, excluding the border, is indeed Ottonian and would seem to have been directly inspired by such miniatures as those in the Gospels of Otto III (996–1002) at Munich.[2] Kendrick compares the border to Hildesheim work inspired by Bishop Bernward's revival, and German influence was certainly to the fore in the crucifixion page. The rest of the work is, however, English in the main, and it must have been done in

[1] For an Ottonian parallel see the Egbert Codex, done about 980, or the Gospels of Otto III (996–1002), H. Jantzen, Ottonische Kunst, Pl. 38, and Georg Leidinger, Miniaturen aus Handschriften der Kgl. Hof- und Staatsbibliothek in München, Munich, i, Pl. 46, &c. In Norman times trees of this type are quite usual; see, for example, those in the psalter in the British Museum (Cotton, Nero, C. IV).

[2] See especially the entry into Jerusalem, Leidinger, loc. cit.

this country, though it is not easy to say where. On the evidence of a litany which is included in the text, Winchester has been suggested by Wormald, and the Cathedral is more likely than the New Minster.[1] As there is no reason to suppose that the book was executed in more than one place the evidence of the litany may be accepted.

In addition to the coloured pages Arundel 60 also contains at the beginning some marginal line-drawing in reddish-brown showing the signs of the zodiac, and on folio 12*v* there is an elaborate full-page drawing of the crucifixion tinted in green, blue, red, and yellow (Pl. 74 *b*). The line is rather hard and expressionless and the drawing is certainly nothing like so fine as that in Harley 2904 which is to be associated with Ramsey, nor is it nearly as subtle as are the lovely line-drawings of the New Minster Liber Vitae (Stowe 944) or those of a book of church offices done for the New Minster between about 1012 and 1020, now in the British Museum (Cotton, Titus, D. XXVI and XXVII). No. XXVII contains two miniatures, a crucifixion on folio 65*v* (Pl. 82 *a*), and a drawing showing a curious medley of figures on folio 75*v*, which Kantorowitz has called the Quinity;[2] it is derived from a composition of the Trinity such as we see on the Godwin seal (Pl. 36, *d*). The crucifixion lacks any hint of that harsher touch to be seen in that in Arundel 60. It is pleasantly tinted in pale green, while in the Quinity a touch of blue also appears in the haloes. No. XXVI contains one miniature, St. Peter (fol. 19*v*), in rather firmer line.

The Liber Vitae is more important. It was done at the New Minster between 1016 and 1020, and is now in the British Museum (Stowe 944). On the title-page is a line-drawing showing Canute and his wife Ælfgifu, placing a cross on the altar of New Minster; above is the Almighty before a mandorla between the Virgin and St. Peter (Pl. 81). Certain details, notably the cross, the mandorla, and the bibles are coloured pale blue, pale yellow, brick-red, and dark emerald-green. The style of the drawing is in every way typical of Winchester in the narrowest sense of the term. But of finer quality is the well-known line-drawing of the last judgement

---

[1] 'The English saints in the Litany in Arundel 60', *Analecta Bollondia*, lxiv (1946), 73.

[2] 'The Quinity of Winchester', *Art Bulletin*, xxix (1947).

on folio 3, shown in three registers, above St. Peter at the gate of heaven, in the middle the judgement, and below the archangel Michael shutting the damned into purgatory (Pl. 84). Opposite to it, on folio 2, is a similar drawing of part of the last judgement, but it is unfinished, and in dark brown line only, whereas that on folio 3 has details filled in in bright pale blue, bright pale green, and red. It is no hieratic rendering, but a fresh and peculiarly vivid interpretation. The soul of the dead man is shown in the middle register as a strange, pathetic little figure anxiously awaiting St. Peter's final decision as to his fate, but St. Peter already repulses the devil with his immense key. Nothing could be more expressive, more pathetic, more enchanting; it is one of the most exquisite and most moving pieces of English line-drawing that has come down to us.

Though not quite so delicate, a manuscript in the Bodleian (Bodley 155) may be compared. It contains two full-page line-drawings, one at the beginning which is a later addition and one on folio 3v of an angel (Pl. 70 b). Red and black are both used and the line is very hard and severe, so that the folds are more like crumpled wire than the usual flutterings. This harshness is probably due to the date; the style is close enough to such an example of the Winchester manner as the Liber Vitae to suggest that the two were done in the same place, though the angel must be a good deal later in date.

A hymnal in the British Museum (Cotton, Julius, A. VI) is another similar book with illustrations of Winchester type though it found its way at an early date to Durham. It is important for it contains the first calendar pictures that are known in Saxon art. These take the form of very delicate drawings at the foot of each page of the calendar and show the labours of the months. They are all small—none is more than 2 inches high—but all are spirited and lively, and indicate the Saxon artists' keen love of the open air and his great capacity for seizing the essential of each scene and movement. The scenes of ploughing (f. 3), the shepherds with their flocks (f. 5), and reaping (f. 6) are especially vivid (Pl. 85 a). A closely similar model must have been followed by one of the artists working on the calendar preceding the British Museum copy of the Marvels of the East (Cotton, Tiberius, B. V, see p. 224), but these are heavy and in colour and are to be compared only iconographically (Pl. 85 b). Vivid line-drawings rather similar to those in the hymnal also occur at intervals throughout the text of the first few pages of a manuscript in the Bibliothèque Nationale (Lat. 8824); on the later folios spaces were left, but the drawings were never done. They are in thin black line and recall the work in the first Canterbury copy of the Utrecht Psalter. The same arrangement is to be found in a copy of Aldhelm's De Virginitate at Lambeth (No. 200), which is to be dated to the end of the tenth century.

Another very fine series of line-drawings appears in a psalter in the British Museum (Cotton, Tiberius, C. VI) which must have been executed between 1041 and 1066. It is indeed one of the richest manuscripts that have come down to us, for it contains in addition to a number of fine coloured initials of rather conservative type, four pages with initials in foliate borders and two elaborate paintings, one of David seated, playing his harp (f. 30v) and the other (f. 18v) of our Lord in glory with saints below. In addition there are in the text three fine, tinted drawings, and after the canon tables there are nineteen full-page illustrations, in addition to some smaller drawings. These nineteen drawings, which are tinted in blue, green, pale red, and yellow, are all delightfully free and vigorous, and all are interesting. On folio 7v is the Ancient of Days, a peculiar Blake-like conception; on folio 8 are David and the lion with some mushroom-like trees similar to those in Arundel 60 (Pl. 83 b); on folio 8v are David and Goliath; on folio 9 Saul; on folio 9v David being anointed by Samuel; on folio 10 David enthroned, playing the harp; on folio 10v our Lord defying the devil; on folio 11 the entry into Jerusalem; on folio 11v the washing of the feet; on folio 12 the betrayal; on folio 12v our Lord before Pilate; on folio 13 the crucifixion with Longinus and Stephaton; on folio 13v the resurrection; on folio 14 our Lord at the mouth of hell (Pl. 83 a); on folio 14v the doubting Thomas; on folio 15 the ascension; on folio 15v pentecost; and on folio 16 the archangel Michael defying the devil. The iconographical importance of all these compositions is considerable; but they are in

most cases of great artistic quality also. The finest is perhaps that
showing Christ at the mouth of hell. He bends down to rescue the
blessed whilst monsters disport themselves below. Contorted
though the figure is, it is tremendously expressive and sensitive,
and the emotional handling of the scene is close to that of the
Liber Vitae. The entry is somewhat harsher and stiffer, but, nevertheless, has great beauty, especially when seen in the original,
where the tinting is particularly effective. David and the lion is
a more spirited scene, and the strange contortions of David are
striking and expressive. The manuscript is really outstanding. It
must have been done shortly before the conquest and serves to
show the excellence of the best work at that time. So good is it,
indeed, that it is tempting to assign it to the very centre of Anglo-
Saxon painting, namely, Winchester itself.

There are a few other manuscripts which must be only slightly
later in date and in which Saxon elements are equally to the fore.
As Wormald has shown, the old manner continued to survive for
a considerable period,[1] and in the other direction new elements had
begun to be developed even before the middle of the century,
especially in the initials.[2] It is, indeed, the inclusion of human
figures in the initials that more than anything else marks the new
age, and the large historiated initial is perhaps the most characteristic art form of early Norman times. Yet we see it heralded in
such manuscripts as the psalter in the Cambridge University
Library (Ff. 1. 23), which is to be dated between 1030 and 1050.
The title-page is rather unusual; the draperies are of normal type
and the B of the Beatus page and the rosette borders follow conventional models, but though the conception is colouristic, only
brown, red, and occasional yellow tints are used, so that the effect is
that of monochrome work and much of the beauty of the coloured
Winchester pages is absent. It has been usually held that this is a
Winchester book, but the style of the first two pages does not support such an attribution and some provincial centre seems more
likely. The saints mentioned in the Litany suggest Winchcombe.

---

[1] 'The survival of Anglo-Saxon illumination after the Norman conquest', *Proc.
Brit. Acad.* xxx (1944), *passim.*
[2] See, for instance, E. Maunde Thompson, *English Illuminated Manuscripts* (1895), 28.

Apart from the new importance of the historiated initial, developed Norman painting is to be distinguished from the Saxon by certain other features both in the colouring and in the drawing. In the Norman the whole style is much heavier, and hard, clinging contours which follow the line of the figure exactly replace the delicate, free Saxon outlines; the manner is to be seen fully developed in the elaborate St. Albans Psalter, done between 1119 and 1146.[1] Changes are equally distinct with regard to the colouring, where brighter shades of a more primary character were substituted for the delicate, gentle, blended tones so dear to the Saxon artists; brilliant reds, greens, and blues were thus in particular favour in place of the pinks, greyish-greens, or violet-blues so often found in Saxon work. At the same time the initials were distinguished by the introduction of a number of new motifs such as monsters, dragons with wide-open jaws and tails ending in scroll-work of Winchester type, human figures clambering over the framework of the letters, and so on. Wormald suggests that Bec may have been the place of origin of this style.[2] A Passionale from Canterbury in the British Museum (Arundel 91) may be cited as a type example. It contains a considerable number of initials by several hands but all are brilliant in handling and are characterized by that fresh colouring in red, pale green, yellow, and bright blue which serves to distinguish post-conquest work. The whole style is in fact more metallic and more decorative than was usual in Saxon times.

The most important series of manuscripts of this transitional period is now preserved at Durham, where there are a quantity of fine books which were either given to the cathedral by Bishop Carilef or were executed at his command. They are thus definitely dated, for Carilef became bishop in 1081 and died in 1096. He was in Normandy from 1088 to 1093, and may have brought some of the manuscripts from there with him or from some place such as Canterbury through which he passed on his way. Also he brought monks from Wearmouth and Jarrow to Durham, and

---

[1] It is now at Hildesheim. See A. Goldschmidt, *Der Albani Psalter in Hildesheim*, 1895.

[2] He examines the features that characterize the new art very thoroughly. See, 'The development of English illumination in the twelfth century', especially p. 32.

these monasteries had shortly before been repopulated from Evesham and Winchcombe.

Of the books that are associated with his name, the most important are a Commentary by St. Augustine on the Psalms, in
three volumes, and a Bible. Volume I of the Commentary is missing. Volume III was done, as a colophon indicates, between 1088
and 1093, during the bishop's exile; it is therefore probable that
it was written in Normandy. Volume II (B. II. 13) is closely
similar in style, and must have been done in the same workshop,
if not by the same hand, but there is no definite evidence as to
when or where it was produced. It would, however, seem likely
that it would have been completed before Volume III. It contains
a number of initials, one of which, an I on folio 102, takes the form
of a stylized portrait of Bishop Carilef with a figure representing
the painter, Robert Benjamin, kneeling at his feet (Pl. 86 a). The
folds of the costume show the influence of the characteristic Winchester manner, but the line is firmer and colder; the faces again
are heavier and show marked continental influence, as does the
colouring, where bright red, bright blue, and bright green are the
only shades, and where the pink and heavy flake-white so popular
in Saxon art are completely absent. The beasts' heads and the
acanthus leaves which form the basis of the composition of the
initials are in a more archaic style and clearly reveal their Saxon
heritage, but the hard metallic lines are new, and a little man
introduced into the letters C O on folio 68 has a distinctly Norman
visage (Pl. 86 b). The gryphons and other monsters again suggest
Romanesque rather than Saxon prototypes, and the general style
of the painting points to the continent rather than to England.
Perhaps the book was done at Bayeux or by a man who had come
from there; another possible location is Bec, which was important
as a scriptorium in the twelfth century.[1]

Carilef's Bible (A. II. 4) contains only initials, but they are fine
and elaborate and make use of figures almost as much as of dragons,
beasts, and acanthus scrolls. An L on folio 87 may be noted (Pl.
86 c). There are hints of the agitation of Winchester work in the
costumes, but the whole approach is different; it is decorative art,

[1] These early Norman manuscripts will be discussed in Volume III of this series.

not figural painting. The very fact that full-page scenes had given place to initials bears out this decorative approach. Shading and high lights have become purely formal pattern; the colouring, though richer than in the Commentary, is essentially decorative, and seeks neither naturalism nor modelling; the rather mystical outlook of Anglo-Saxon art, which bound it to that of the Byzantine world, has been left behind and clarity rather than imaginative interpretation is the hall-mark of the art. It is thus only in a few details of design that any Saxon influence is to be discerned; apart from these, the art is a new one, and the brilliant style of the Norman age seems already to be reaching maturity.

Some of the work in the famous Arundel Psalter (Arundel 60) in the British Museum is fairly close to that of the Carilef Bible, and a small Gospel book in the British Museum (Add. 11850) may also be compared; it has been assigned both to Durham and to the continent. If it is indeed continental, it serves as an example of the way in which the Winchester style spread overseas. In illumination, just as in sculpture, in fact Winchester ideas were assimilated by the French well before the time of the conquest. But as time went on the style changed and even before the turn of the century draperies had begun to cling tightly to the bodies rather than to flutter in the old Saxon manner.

A number of other Durham MSS. of Bishop Carilef's time contain initials, many of them of fine quality, and Mynors, in his publication of the Durham volumes, distinguishes as many as nine distinct types or classes.[1] Though not necessarily exclusive to Durham, they predominated there, and in the twelfth century the school must have become an important one.

Another feature which marks this early Norman age is the growth in popularity of a number of new types of books of secular content, such as the bestiaries and the herbals. These were produced in large numbers from the mid-eleventh century onwards and seem to have been more important here than ever they were on the continent; they probably followed Saxon prototypes fairly closely, and a few examples of the Saxon period still survive in various museums. Three copies of the Marvels of the East may be

[1] *Durham Cathedral Manuscripts*, 1939.

noted. The earliest is to be dated to about 1000, but its illustrations are poor and clumsy; it is in the British Museum (Cotton, Vitellius, A. XV).[1] The next in date, in the same museum (Cotton, Tiberius, B. V) is far finer and contains pictures of high quality. The third in the Bodleian (Bodley 614) is a twelfth-century copy of Cotton, Tiberius, B. V. The illustrations of Cotton, Tiberius, B. V. are very delightful; they consist of allegorical figures or fantastic animals which are mentioned in the text. The animals are often very oriental and are similar to those that appear in Islamic manuscripts of slightly earlier date. The colouring is vivid and curious. The river shown on folio 80v, of Tiberius, B. V, for example, is lapis blue, the ground behind it and the enormous ants that live there are pinkish-brick, the camels brownish-brick, and the rider's cloak the same blue as the river; details of the face and costume are in black ink (Pl. 87). The subject of this illustration is an entertaining one; beyond the river Gorgoneus lay a land where there lived ants as big as dogs who dug up gold during the day and brought it down to the valley at night. Thieves set out on camels to steal it, and when they crossed the river they left the young camels on their own side, taking the old male and female camels with them; having obtained the gold they turned for home; the female camels ran fast to join their young, the male ones dallied and were attacked and eaten by the ants.

Even more impressive is a large full-page illustration on folio 87v (Pl. 89), which depicts the magician Mambres at the mouth of hell; he holds his book of magic, with which his brother, after his death, attempted to summon up devils. The background here is emerald green, the rocks are pinkish-brick, the monsters greenish-grey, the devilish figure browny-purple, the cavern grey-purple, the figures of the damned greyish-white, while Mambres the wizard has lapis-blue hair and is clothed in a brick-red chiton and a pale grey-purple mantle; the detail of the costume is here much more in the Winchester style than in most of the other drawings, but the heavy, rather muddy colours are quite distinct from those of Saxon art on the one hand and from the Norman initials, as in

[1] All three are fully published with excellent plates by M. R. James, *The Marvels of the East* (1929).

the Carilef books at Durham, on the other. The effect that they produce is curious, and often delightful, even if it cannot be termed beautiful. Bound up in the same book, at the beginning, are twelve illustrations to the calendar tables, which are in composition and iconography identical almost line for line with those of the hymnal in the British Museum mentioned above (Cotton, Julius, A. VI). The reapers on folio 5 of the hymnal may be compared with those on folio 6 of Tiberius B. V (Pl. 85). In the latter the scenes are larger and are coloured in bright but rather heavy tones; the general result, though more striking, is less pleasing. In addition to the calendar illustrations there are also a series of zodiacal signs.

A number of medical books and herbals were also produced, many of which had numerous illustrations both in line and colour, of plants, but human and animal figures were included in a few of them; the majority were rather clumsy. Of a rather similar character is an incomplete copy of the works of Macrobius in the British Museum (Cotton, Vitellius, C. III); if it shows little elegance in drawing, it has great charm of colouring, its brilliant and oddly contrasting shades being peculiarly effective. It is to be dated to the first half of the eleventh century. The illustrations of plants and animals it contains are in a much broader and heavier manner than those of the religious books, and were probably by secular rather than monastic artists; in any case the training of the men who did such books must have been quite different from that of those who worked on the great benedictionals and missals. But two pages which are closer to the Winchester style do occur in the Macrobius; one (f. 11*v*) shows a tall figure transfixing a beast with a spear, while a smaller one presents a book to him; it is like the usual composition of Christ treading on the asp and basilisk. The other (f. 19) is a composition of animal figures, a centaur, Aesculapios and Plato, and must ultimately have been derived from a classical original (Pl. 88). Both are enclosed in foliated borders. Even if the colouring was added by the same hand that worked on the plants, the drawing is far finer and freer, and must have been done by an artist trained in the Winchester tradition.

VIII

MINOR ARTS

I. METAL-WORK

METAL-WORK is an all-embracing term, which includes all material from the roughest of spear-heads and swords to the most delicate of finger rings. But even so, two main typological groups may be distinguished in our period: an earlier, where weapons and objects of personal adornment were in preponderance, and a later, where ecclesiastical vessels of one sort or another were most usual. Objects of the former class that survive are not nearly as numerous as are those of pagan times, since with the adoption of Christianity they ceased to be included in the graves, and we have to depend on chance finds. Those of the latter are even fewer, for the treasuries to which they belonged were one and all despoiled if not by the Danes or immediately after the Norman conquest, anyhow at the time of the Reformation. At Ely, for example, it is recorded in the *Acta Sanctorum* that most of the metal treasures were melted down to satisfy the demands of William the Conqueror; the objects mentioned include crosses, shrines, chalices, patens, basins, buckets, fistulas, goblets, dishes, altars, and a figure of the Virgin and Child seated on a throne which was made by Abbot Elsin (*d.* 1016).[1]

This account not only serves to attest the wholesale nature of the destructions which were all too numerous, but also to indicate the tremendous wealth of the church. Its evidence is borne out by other documents. Archbishop Aldred, for example, had made a pulpitum or screen of bronze, gold, and silver to enclose the choir at Beverley; presumably while he was archbishop of York from 1061 to 1069. It was described as 'Opus Teutonicum',[2] and was perhaps similar in style to the doors made for Bishop Bernward of Hildesheim. King Æthelwulf took metal vessels with him as a

---

[1] *De S. Etheldreda Regina,* June, v, Paris–Rome (1867), 453.
[2] *Histories of the Church of York,* Rolls Series, ii. 353.

present when he went to Rome in 855, and Egbert also took metal-work to Rome at a later date. The Anglo-Saxons were indeed noted as goldsmiths on the continent, and the Liber Pontificalis bears witness to the fact that the popes ordered silver from them; there is particular mention of niello in the orders. Inventories of Waltham, Abingdon, Evesham, Peterborough, Winchester, and other monasteries record the wealth of metal treasures that were in their possession.

Before discussing this later work, which must be our main concern, the earlier period may be briefly considered, for one extensive hoard from this age has come down to us. It is that from Trewhiddle in Cornwall, which is of importance, first, on account of the very individual and characteristic style of the ornament on the objects which belong to it, and, secondly, because of the marked influence that this style exercised on the subsequent development of ornament, not only in metal, but in other arts as well. The hoard is, fortunately, accurately dated by reliable archaeological evidence to c. 875. The ornament of the objects is very distinctive, consisting of scrolls, ivy leaves, palmettes, or loose interlacings, done in light, thin lines. Distorted beasts set in small panels are sometimes also included. There is, of course, some resemblance to contemporary continental work, for the motives are mostly variants of the universal repertory of the time, but on the whole the style is a clear one and may be said to be essentially English. The Carolingian acanthus, moreover, does not appear as an ornamental motif on any of the Trewhiddle objects.[1] The forms of some of the objects are, however, less distinctive, and some of them follow foreign models closely. The most striking of them is a chalice now in the British Museum, which is of essentially Byzantine form (Fig. 14); one of the seventh century from Riha on the Orontes in the Royall Tyler collection may be compared.[2]

The Trewhiddle style seems to have dominated contemporary ornament all over southern England, and at the end of the ninth century ornament of this type began to spread from the south

[1] The Trewhiddle style will be discussed at greater length in the first volume of this series.
[2] F. Volbach, G. Salles, G. Duthuit, *Art Byzantin*, Pl. 53A.

towards the north. It is to be discerned in the decoration ot a number of objects produced between about 900 and 970, and though these are all of minor size and importance, it is probable that many of the more considerable objects which have perished were decorated in the same way. After about 970 a new type of ornament, derived from that of the manuscripts, began to supersede that of the Trewhiddle type.

But not all the finds of this period are so distinctively English. Scandinavian influence seems to have been exercised more strongly on the metalwork of the ninth and early tenth centuries than it was on sculpture in stone, and it remained important until the year 1000 or later, being especially marked with regard to the type and decoration of the weapons. As would be expected, the majority of the weapons that have come down to us have been found in those regions that were most involved in the fighting brought about by the Danish invasions, and they belong mainly to the period in which these invasions took place, that is, the ninth century. Many are obviously of Danish workmanship, others are Anglo-Saxon, but they often show Danish tastes in form and ornament. The most obvious of the Norse features, of course, is the nature of the decoration, for the familiar motifs of the Jellinge and Ringerike styles are usual. Some interesting pieces of metal thus show the latter style quite clearly, notably a copper-gilt plaque from the Thames at Hammersmith,[1] a bronze socket for a spear-head from York, now in the Pitt Rivers Museum at Farnham, and a bronze weather-vane from Winchester. The former is about 8 inches high and dates from the early eleventh century; its ornament is similar to that of the stones

FIG. 14. *Chalice from Trewhiddle,*
Cornwall, British Museum, c. 875

[1] British Museum, *Guide to the Anglo-Saxon Antiquities*, Fig. 114.

from St. Paul's churchyard (Pl. 23 *a*). The York socket is certainly an import and dates from about 1000.

In addition to the ornament, the form is also helpful in determining the origin, in any case of the weapons. The shape of the pommel thus distinguishes a particular type of sword of Danish origin; the most important example is one from Wallingford, now in the Ashmolean Museum. It is probably to be dated to the early tenth century. Its pommel-guards are adorned with thin silver plates, on which are figures of animals and foliage in reserve against a niello background, and such work seems to have been characteristically English, so that the sword as a whole is an hybrid. A fragment of a sword of similar type and date was dug up at Windsor, and hilts of the same Danish type are to be found in a number of collections, notably the British and the London Museums. A circular medallion in the Robinson collection, which bears ornament similar to that on the silver plates of the Wallingford sword is now thought to be a forgery. A particular type of stirrup with rectangular loop, sometimes inlaid with brass, is also to be associated with the Danish invaders in the ninth and tenth centuries. Examples are to be found in the British Museum, at Aylesbury, at Canterbury, and elsewhere.[1]

Hilts of a form similar to that of the Wallingford sword are to be seen in some of the illustrations to a copy of Ælfric's paraphrase of the Pentateuch in the British Museum (Cotton, Claudius, B. IV), which dates from the mid eleventh century. The other weapons illustrated—tall spears, large broadswords, and circular shields— are more definitely English. Some of the figures in the illuminations of the manuscript also wear chain-mail, and similar coats of mail are shown on the Bayeux tapestry; they are in the process of being removed from the bodies of the dead Saxons by ghoulish despoilers. The weapons used by the Saxons on the tapestry are different from those used by the Normans, whose tall, conical helmets with long nose-guards are quite distinctive (Pl. 94).

Jewellery, which was popular at the commencement of our

---

[1] The weapons and their ornament, even if of tenth-century date, are conservative in style; they will be dealt with in detail by Mr. Bruce-Mitford in the first volume of this History.

period, appears again to have been considerably influenced from Scandinavia. The most common form there was the circular brooch of silver or gold, with elaborate decoration, sometimes cast, sometimes engraved, and sometimes in filigree. Such brooches were exported to Britain and copied there, but the forms and designs often remained essentially Scandinavian. A brooch from Pitney in Somerset, now in the British Museum, and another from Wisbech in Cambridgeshire, thus bear decoration in the Urnes style, and motifs of the same type are to be found on book clasps at Peterborough, Lincoln, and Milton-next-Sittingbourne, as well as on three small cylinders of silver in the Guildhall Museum in London.[1] All these belong to Saxon times, but ornament of Urnes style is also to be seen on Bishop Ralph Flambard's crozier at Durham, which must date from about 1102. It has been regarded as an import, but Kendrick has shown that it is more probably of English workmanship. As he points out, it is, in its way, just as English as the Cross of Cong is Irish, though the decoration of both owes an outstanding debt to the Urnes style.[2]

A bronze terminal of Scandinavian appearance in the British Museum, dating from about 1000, may also be noted; a similar one from Nord-Trönberg is illustrated by Mahr and Raftery and described as the terminal of a drinking-horn.[3] On a smaller scale attention may be called to a number of tenth-century silver pins from the Londesborough collection, also in the British Museum. They show the survival of the old pagan spiral motif.

As opposed to these northern influences, that of the continent was also being exercised on metal-work in this country in the tenth and eleventh centuries, and both Germanic and Byzantine elements are to be distinguished. The great importance of Germany in this direction is borne out by the introduction of such terms as cullen, the medieval name for bronze, which was derived from the main centre of continental metal-working, Cologne. German influence is to be seen most clearly in the love of heavy bejewelling with semi-precious stones or pastes set in clasps or cloisons. These

[1] T. D. Kendrick, *Late Saxon and Viking Art*, 116 and Pl. LXXXII.
[2] Ibid. 117 and Pl. LXXXIII, no. 1.
[3] *Christian Art in Ancient Ireland*, vol. i, Pl. 32, no. 9.

gorgeous but rather barbaric settings were often used in Germany in association with work of Byzantine type, as on a late-tenth-century gold binding at Aachen, where an actual Byzantine ivory is framed by a number of scenes in repoussé work and this in turn by a border of cabochon of western type. Numerous other instances of the blend of the Byzantine and Germanic styles on the continent could be cited.[1]

This Byzanto-Germanic style undoubtedly exercised its influence on the development of ecclesiastical vessels, plaques, and so on, in England, and it can be studied in opposition to the Scandinavian influence which showed in the decoration of weapons and small objects of personal adornment. But it is unfortunately just in this type of work that the most serious losses have been experienced, and little remains. It may, however, be assumed that plaques of repoussé metal, bearing figures with their names beside their heads in the Byzantine manner were quite often made in England as well as on the continent. Cloisonné enamels of Byzantine style, or even sometimes Byzantine workmanship, were, we know, attached to metal grounds of English manufacture, and there was in much of the metal-work a close adherence to Byzantine iconographical and stylistic practices. The Byzantine influence is indicated by a love of clear-cut, low-relief figural work, as well as by the balance and reticence that are such invariable characteristics of the style. Of the examples that survive a silver bowl in the British Museum, from Halton Moor in Lancashire, which was found with coins of Canute (1016–35), is the most important (Pl. 90 c). It is probably English, though the animals in medallions that adorn it have a very Sasanian appearance, and the shape is also Sasanian; perhaps a Sasanian model was copied by English craftsmen, for Sasanian silver-work had certainly reached the west at an earlier date.

Another important example of ecclesiastical furniture of the later Saxon period is a portable altar in the Cluny Museum in Paris. It is an oblong slab of red porphyry framed in silver, which is engraved on both sides with figure-subjects of which the draperies

[1] A glance at the plates of any volume on Ottonian metal-work or enamels would prove the point. See, for example, the plates of H. Jantzen, *Ottonische Kunst.*

are gilded and the rest plain. On one side, at the top, is a very small crucifix between the ox of St. Luke and the eagle of St. John; at the bottom is the Agnus Dei between the angel of St. Matthew and the lion of St. Mark; on the sides are the Virgin and St. John above, the archangels Gabriel and Raphael below. On the

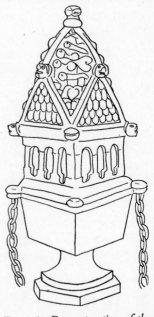

FIG. 15. *Censer cover from Pershore.*
After Romilly Allen

FIG. 16. *Reconstruction of the*
Pershore censer

reverse, at the top, is our Lord in a medallion, with an angel on either side and two saints accompanied by their names; at the bottom is the sacrifice of Abraham, in very spirited line like the drawings of the Utrecht Psalter, and at each end a saint. The altar was at one time regarded as German, but H. P. Mitchell pointed out the extremely Anglo-Saxon character of the figure-drawing and called attention especially to the similarity it shows to the figure work in the New Minster Register (B.M. Stowe 944), which is dated to between 1016 and 1020.[1] Rather earlier works, like the first Canterbury copy of the Utrecht Psalter, perhaps afford even closer parallels (see Pl. 66). The severer treatment of the figures

[1] 'Flotsam of later Anglo-Saxon art', *Burl. Mag.* xlii. 63.

on the altar is no greater than would be inevitable in metal engraving as opposed to pen drawing. There thus seems little doubt as to the Saxon origin of the altar; it is probably to be dated around the year 1000.

Such objects were doubtless at one time quite numerous, but the Cluny example now stands alone. Rather more common are

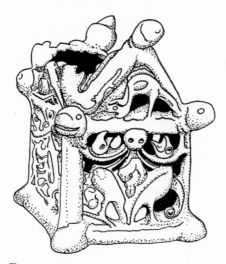

FIG. 17. *Bronze censer from the Thames.*
British Museum

examples of another class of ecclesiastical object, namely, censers and censer-covers of bronze. The lid of one of them was found at Pershore; it must date from the tenth or early eleventh century (Fig. 15). Only the top survives, but it is skilfully worked and of interesting design, being square, with a gabled roof shaped like the tower of Sompting church. The pattern in each pediment presumably represents roofing tiles. Above are lozenges with birds and foliage; below, on the horizontal band beneath the pediment is an inscription bearing the words 'GODRIC ME WVORHT'. It was first published by Romilly Allen and then by Sir Charles Peers.[1] A tentative restoration is given in Figure 16. A censer from the Thames, now in the British Museum, is closely akin, though perhaps rather later in date (Fig. 17). A third one from Canterbury,

[1] J. Romilly Allen, *Reliquary*, xii (1906), 50 ; C. R. Peers, *Proc. Soc. Ants.* xxi. 52–9.

also in the British Museum, is perhaps rather later still; Vallance has assigned it to the twelfth century, but Brønsted regards it as Saxon.[1] A date around 1075 is more probable. On all of them, acanthus motifs and inhabited scrolls similar to those on the Alcester Tau appear. A round censer of very similar type, and with the same simulation of tiles on its top, is preserved in the Glasgow Museum; it was dug up in Glasgow at the end of the last century. It is, however, hard to say whether it is eleventh or twelfth century.

Censers were extremely important objects in ecclesiastical usage, having considerable symbolic significance, and they were common on the continent at this time; the continental examples that have been found are, however, for the most part of round and not square form, and round ones are usually depicted in the manuscripts. In Britain the pinnacle type was probably the most usual, for it dominated all through the medieval period; examples from Ashbury in Berkshire, Whittlesea Mere, Ripple in Worcestershire, Dymchurch, Church Stretton, Garrock (Kincardine), Lyng near Elmham in Norfolk, and Alton Castle in Staffordshire may be noted, though they are later than the period with which we are dealing. The tops by which these censers were attached to their chains usually took the form of a lily; one such lily, which was probably made at Lyons, has been published by Nelson.[2]

Another interesting vessel of the period which has been published by Kendrick is presumably a cruet (Pl. 90 b).[3] It is closely akin in style to the Canterbury censer, and has therefore been assigned to much the same date, that is the mid-eleventh century. A number of strap-ends in the London Museum and elsewhere, which are very similar in style, are accurately dated on archaeological grounds to this period. The cruet is of bronze; its decoration is in relief, and consists of bands containing confronted pairs of birds in a foliated spray, except over the spout, where the bird appears in a different position. The spout is turned into a lion's head by engraving, and the handle takes on the form of a serpent.

---

[1] See A. B. Tonnochy, *Arch. Journ.* lxxxix (1932), 3; J. Brønsted, *Early English Ornament*, 265.   [2] *Acta Archaeologica*, v (1934), 182.

[3] *Arch. Journ.* xviii (1938), 377.

Kendrick regards the motif as southern English, brought probably from the Ottonian area; the border of Bede's life of St. Cuthbert at Corpus Christi College, Cambridge (No. 183), is closely akin, though the censer is probably later; the book is dated to between 935 and 939. Scrolls of this type survived for a long time; they are, for example, to be found at the end of the tenth century in the Aldhelm MS. at Lambeth; but the similarity of the cruet to the Cambridge book is close enough to suggest that it is to be assigned to the tenth rather than the eleventh century, as Kendrick holds.

Of actually dated pieces of metal-work one or two examples can be cited. One is a circular lead plaque from Bath bearing on the reverse a cross, indicated in outline, with an inscription on the vertical arms, and on the obverse another cross, more firmly designed, superposed on a smaller cross diagonally placed within a circle and also inscribed. The artistic value of the object is inconsiderable, but the historical and technical interests are great, for the crosses and inscriptions were cast, not engraved, and the inscription itself commemorates the death and burial of Queen Eadgyfu, third wife of Edward the Elder, in what is almost certainly the year 977. The cross was found on the site of a ninth-century church, built above the Roman baths at Bath. Closely similar crosses have also been found at Canterbury and at Bury St. Edmunds; the former bears the name of Abbot Wulfric's sister. Another dated object is a disk of bronze from Winchester known as the seal of Ælfric. It bears a short inscription and a bust, presumably of Ælfric himself. This man is probably to be identified with an Ælfric who commanded Æthelred's fleet in 992 and was killed in 1016, and the seal is therefore to be dated around the year 1000.[1]

Of the figural work, the only example that has survived is a small bronze with the Virgin and Child in the York Museum (Pl. 90 a). It is cast in low relief, and the matrix of the mould must have been akin in style to an ivory-carving, though the carving must have been of a very summary character. The agitated folds of the drapery show some resemblance to Winchester work, and on their evidence alone an eleventh-century date seems rather more

[1] Reginald Smith, V.C.H. Hampshire, i. 397.

likely than one in the twelfth, which has usually been assigned to
the bronze.

Of objects on a small scale, finger rings were no doubt the most
important, and quite a number have survived. The commonest
form seems to have been very simple, like a modern wedding ring;
a number of examples, some with inscriptions in Latin or runic

FIG. 18. *Finger ring from Berkeley Castle. After Baddeley*

characters, are preserved in the British Museum. Stylistically it is
not always easy to distinguish English from continental examples,
but the inscriptions help in this. A ring of Ælhstan, bishop of
Sherborne from 824 to 867, in the Victoria and Albert Museum,
thus bears an inscription ending with a runic n; this is a wellnigh
certain indication of English provenance. More elaborate forms of
rings existed. A four-lobed gold ring from Berkeley Castle, each
lobe being in the form of an animal's or perhaps a bat's head,
is probably fairly early (Fig. 18). It has been assigned to the reign
of Alfred by Baddeley.[1] Two rings in the British Museum, with
ornament in niello, may also be noted in passing, though both
date from before our period, for they serve to illustrate the
technique which was no doubt important subsequently. One bears
the name of Alfred's father Æthelwulf (836–58) and the other that

[1] 'Berkeley Castle', *Trans. Bris. and Glos. Arch. Soc.* xlviii (1926), 176 and Pl. i.

of his sister Æthelswith, queen of Mercia from 855 to 889. The Saxon Ð for th is used in the inscription.

Whether doors of bronze of the type that are preserved in numerous places on the continent from the tenth century onwards were ever produced in this country remains uncertain; no examples have in any case survived. There are, however, a few doors of wood, with iron strap-work or hinges, which have sometimes been assigned to the Saxon period. Most important are those at Staplehurst in Kent and at Stillingfleet in Yorkshire, though there are plainer ones at Eastwood in Essex, Haddiscoe in Norfolk, and Great Hormead in Hertfordshire. The style of the ornament is closely inspired by Viking art; at Stillingfleet a Viking ship, dragons' heads, and plaitwork attest this (Pl. 91 a), and the same motifs are present at Staplehurst (Pl. 91 b). The work may be compared to that at Ekeby in Uppland, which belongs to the mid-twelfth century. The question of the date of the English doors is debatable; the style is pre-Norman, but the buildings to which they belong are Norman. The ironwork of that at Stillingfleet, however, was obviously made for a larger opening, so that it was probably re-used, and the same may have been the case with some of the others. A date in that period of overlap, the second half of the eleventh century, seems most likely.[1] An ironwork grille at Winchester, which formerly surrounded the shrine of St. Swithin, has sometimes been dated to the end of the eleventh century, but it is more probably to be assigned to the twelfth as may some strap-hinges at St. Albans; in any case there is nothing Saxon about them, and they fall for consideration along with the fine ironwork of the twelfth century, examples of which are comparatively numerous.

Such are the few pieces of small-scale metal-work that have survived; a mere modicum of the riches that once existed, for in practically every abbey from the end of the tenth century onwards there seems to have been a great activity in metal-working, even abbots being famed for the work they did with their own hands. Dunstan was thus a noted metal-worker; Æthelwold is recorded to have made bells, lamps, crosses, a hanging coronal, a retable, and

[1] E. Yates, 'Notes on mediaeval church ironwork', *Journ. Brit. Arch. Ass.*, 3rd series, iv (1939), 175, gives good plates of all this metal-work.

other works; Brithnoth, a monk of Ely, was a carver and gold-smith; Leo of Ely was a silversmith; Ælfsig, abbot of Ely from 981 to about 1019, Ælfnoth of New Minster, Spearhoe, abbot of Abingdon (*c.* 1050), and Mannig, abbot of Evesham, were all famous goldsmiths. It is worthy of note that the records always refer to metal-working and not to ivory-carving or other similar arts in connexion with these ecclesiastical artists. All this, however, changed with the conquest. The Norman clerics had no tradition of craftsmanship, and seem to have regarded manual work as below their dignity. Very soon it became the custom to hire lay workers for all artistic execution except the illumination of manu-scripts. With regard to the minor arts this change was one of the most important marking the new régime, and if in later times abbots who were keen patrons were numerous enough, there appears to have been practically none who followed the old English custom of working with their own hands.

In addition to ecclesiastical work, objects of secular usage were also important; and the texts refer to them quite frequently. The extremities of pieces of furniture thus appear often to have been elaborate; candlesticks of silver gilt were usual; cups and other table vessels were as often as not of metal, or of wood or horn mounted in metal. But these have fared even less advantageously at the hand of time than the ecclesiastical metal-work, and two bronze disks from Saffron Waldon are practically the only examples that survive.

2. ENAMELS

Once again the picture is incomplete, and it is essential to remem-ber that very few examples still survive of what must once have been an extremely important art in England. In this art, unlike most of the others that we have been examining, the finest example that we know is early, namely, the superb Alfred jewel in the Ashmolean Museum at Oxford (Pl. 92 *a*); from later periods nothing so large or so spectacular has come down to us, and from the eleventh century we have nothing at all. The jewel is pear-shaped, just under $2\frac{1}{2}$ inches in height, and bears on the obverse a fine cloisonné enamel, showing a three-quarter length figure in green, with a red girdle, against a blue background. The flesh tints are pink, the eyes reddish-purple. The figure carries two gold sceptres or wands, one in each hand. Around the sides, in open-work lettering, are the words: AELFRED MEC HEHT GEWYRGAN, that is, 'Alfred had me made'. The reverse of the jewel is a gold plate, lightly engraved with a tree pattern. The narrow end is in the form of a boar's head in gold, covered with a delicate granulated design; into its mouth was originally inserted a support or stem. Various suggestions have been put forward as to the identity of the figure and the purpose of the jewel. It has thus been proposed that it formed part of a sceptre—used perhaps by Alfred himself—and that the figure represents either Alfred or one of his favourite saints. A pin-brooch from Clonmacnois is, however, of practically identical form, and it therefore seems more likely that it was a pin for ceremonial use.[1] The figure would thus more probably be a saint than that of Alfred. The iconography of the figure is close to that of Christ in the book of Kells (f. 202*v*), but the Byzantine affinities of the technique are so marked that some link with east Christendom seems likely, and by the latter years of the ninth century an unbearded Christ would hardly have been met with in any work that was linked with the Byzantine world. Further, iconographical prototypes in early Christian art, such as a silk medallion from Panopolis,[2] in the Kaiser Friedrich Museum, or a strip of textile from Akhmin, also in Berlin,[3] show not Christ but a figure which probably represents a saint or emperor. A silk like these might well have reached the west and been copied there. A very similar disposition, where two formal sprays are upheld, though the actual figure is distinct, occurs among the early Romanesque paintings at Tavant on the Loire.

In the case of the Alfred jewel, the technique of enamelling is extremely fine and the work very accomplished. It is true that

---

[1] Reproduced by J. Romilly Allen, *Celtic Art in Pagan and Christian times*, London (1904), fig., p. 221.

[2] J. Strzygowski, *Jahrbuch der königlichen-preussischen Kunstsammlungen*, xxiv (1903), 164. Reproduced in *The Alfred and Minster Lovell Jewels*, Ashmolean Museum, 1948, Pl. IV.

[3] W. F. Volbach and E. Kuehnel, *Late Antique, Coptic and Islamic Textiles of Egypt*, 1926, Pl. 74.

Saxon enamelling of the pagan period was very proficient also, but all the examples that are known had designs of a formal type, and figural work does not seem to have been produced. It is therefore tempting to suggest that the craftsman who made the jewel had learnt something of his art from a part of the world where fine figural work was done in the cloisonné technique, and the home of this technique in the tenth century was undoubtedly Byzantium. The Alfred jewel is clearly an English and not a Byzantine work, but it has something of the excellence and fluency of design which one would associate with the Byzantine capital. The whole feeling is distinct from that of the non-figural pagan enamels of England, the style of which is preserved in the Minster Lovell jewel in the same Museum (Pl. 92 b). The gold framework, on the other hand, shows the influence of Hibernian art, and the design is not unlike some of those that are to be found on crosses of the period; both were perhaps inspired by manuscript models.

In spite of these unsolved problems, namely, the identity of the figure, the use of the jewel, and the ultimate training of the crafts-man responsible for it, one thing is certain, namely, the outstanding quality of the work. The English elements in the jewel are clear, and it is obvious that it could not have stood alone. There is every reason to assign the Minster Lovell jewel to the same period. If not quite so fine, it is none the less of high quality and attests the fact that Alfred's reign must have been a time of true renaissance in art, and that it is to the vicissitudes of fortune rather than to any original paucity of examples that we must attribute the fact that we know so little about the work done at the end of the ninth and the beginning of the tenth century.

The next example of enamelling that has survived is the lovely Dowgate Hill brooch in the British Museum (Pl. 92 d). It is circular in form, with an enamel at the centre, surrounded by filigree work. The enamel is delicate and the fine subtle colours again attest a Byzan-tine prototype, but the pointed face and rather heavy drawing of the figure are northern; and there is every reason to suppose that the enamel was made in England. It may have come from the same workshop as the Alfred jewel and is to be assigned perhaps to around the year 900. Another enamel in the British Museum is, however, more probably an import from Italy or the Byzantine world, namely, the circular cloisonné panel, bearing a foliated cross at the centre, that adorns the Hamilton or Towneley brooch (Pl. 92 c). The cross is dark blue, with red centre and yellow extremities, on a translucent dark-green ground. The zone of applied scroll-work around it and the bosses on the outer extremity are western work, perhaps German; the eight small enamels around the rim are also probably foreign. The metal ground-work and the enamel are English, of tenth- or early-eleventh-century date.

A few examples of enamels with geometric patterns of the type common at an earlier date in Saxon graves are also to be assigned to our period and to this country, but none is very important. A circular brooch bearing a bird from Cambois near Bedlington in Northumberland, and now in the British Museum, and a very similar brooch at Winchester, which was found near Hyde, may be noted.[1]

A later group of enamels of a very distinct type has also been attributed to England by certain authorities. It consists of a number of reliquaries, decorated with enamels of very violent colour and crude design, and with large nails in rows along the sides and edges. The group, which was first recognized as a unity by von Falke, comprises eight reliquaries and one small fragment. All the examples date from the end of the eleventh or the first half of the twelfth century, but their style is close to that of ninth-century illuminations. Germany was originally proposed as the place of origin of the group; von Falke then suggested Denmark, England, and later Ireland. Norland regards Ireland as a possible but England as an unlikely home;[2] in this latter view he is certainly correct for whatever styles may be traced at the basis of English work, a native idiom invariably serves to distinguish the art of this country, and that idiom is absent in these enamels. On the whole Denmark seems the most probable home. At this date, though, the most important centres of enamelling were in Germany, on the Meuse and at Cologne, and in France at Limoges; the art associated with

---

[1] British Museum, *Guide to Anglo-Saxon Antiquities*, 101.
[2] 'An early group of enamelled reliquaries', *Acta Archaeologica*, iv (1933), 1 ff.

those places was truly Romanesque, and bore little resemblance to that of the reliquaries. Even before the twelfth century, France was on the way to becoming by far the most vigorous centre of production, while German work remained more conservative and more akin to the Byzantine. England seems to have fallen out as a centre of manufacture entirely. This was perhaps a result of the new policy adopted in the monasteries at the time of the conquest, when the handicrafts ceased to be as much practised by the monks as they had been in old Saxon times.

3. TEXTILES

In texts of the tenth and eleventh centuries the art of producing decorated textiles is frequently referred to as characteristically English, and in the twelfth century the finest textiles were on the continent automatically assigned to this country; soon after the title of 'Opus Anglicanum' became usual.[1] Indeed, textiles seem to have shared with metal-work what was unquestionably the highest place in contemporary esteem. The majority of them appear to have been embroideries. St. Dunstan designed stuffs for 'the pious Æthelbyra to embroider';[2] the daughters of Edward the Elder were noted by William of Malmesbury as practitioners of that art, as was Edith, queen of Edward the Confessor,[3] while Margaret, who married Malcolm Canmore, king of Scotland, tried to popularize the art in her new home.[4] William the Conqueror astonished the Normans when he visited Normandy by the richness of the robes he acquired in England, and his historian, William of Poitiers, also recorded the skill of the English women with the needle.[5] Whether textiles with woven patterns were also produced is uncertain, for the texts are not very specific, and the only examples that survive are embroideries, namely, the treasure from St. Cuthbert's shrine from Saxon, and the so-called Bayeux

---

[1] For a discussion of the exact implications of the term 'Opus Anglicanum' see A. G. I. Christie, *English Medieval Embroidery*, Oxford (1938), 2.

[2] 'De Sancto Dunstano', *Acta Sanctorum*, Paris, May, iv. 360.

[3] *Chronicles of the Kings of England*, ed. J. A. Giles, London (1847), 125 and 247.

[4] 'De Sancta Margarita Scotiae Regina', *Acta Sanctorum*, June, ii. 329.

[5] 'Willelmi Conquestoris gesta a Willelmo Pictavensis', Migne, *Patrol. Lat.* cxlix. 1267.

tapestry from Norman, times. The two are quite dissimilar in character, but both, in their different ways, are superb, and nothing could bear more irrefutable witness to the high quality of English materials than do these two isolated works. It is a major tragedy that nothing more has been conserved.

The St. Cuthbert textiles, which comprise fragments of a stole $2\frac{3}{8}$ inches wide and now about 6 feet long, of a maniple of the same width, and now 2 feet $8\frac{1}{4}$ inches long, and a few smaller pieces, were found together with some other textiles of near eastern origin when the tomb was opened in 1827.[1] They appear to have been introduced into the tomb by King Æthelstan in 934, when the shrine was at Chester-le-Street, for records of the time mention a stole, a maniple, a girdle, and two bracelets of gold tissue. The stole and maniple bear identical inscriptions at the ends, which read AELFFLAED FIERI PRECEPIT and PIO EPISCOPO FRIÐESTANO. The stuffs must thus have been made at the command of Ælflaed, and during the time that Frithestan was bishop. Ælflaed was the second wife of Edward the Elder, and died about 916; Frithestan was bishop of Winchester between 909 and 931. The textile must therefore have been completed between the commencement of Frithestan's bishopric in 909 and a time soon after Ælflaed's death in 916; this is a far more exact dating than is possible in the case of most works of art of the Anglo-Saxon age.

All the St. Cuthbert pieces are decorated in the same way, namely, with thickly embroidered figures of saints and prophets, with Christian symbols, with a border of acanthus scrolls and pairs of confronted animals. On the maniple the figures represent St. Sixtus and St. Gregory and the deacons Lawrence and Peter. On the stole there are thirteen saints and prophets; our illustration shows Daniel and Amos (Pl. 93). The figures stand upon conventionalized clouds, not unlike rocks, and their names are included in fine large letters on either side of the figures. The embroidery is extremely delicate, in threads of silk, around which metal has been wound. The ground is of silk, and the design was first traced on this in outline stitch.

At one time, when it was the fashion to believe that everything

[1] The best plates are those in Christie, op. cit., Pls. I, II, and III.

good came from the continent, it was questioned whether this textile was actually English. But since it was published by Professor Baldwin Brown and Mrs. Christie in 1913, the English origin has not been questioned. It is supported both on technical and stylistic grounds. The question of technique is complicated, and cannot be entered into here in detail;[1] of the stylistic factors the most important is probably the rather loose treatment of the acanthus motif in the border and background, which is far less severe than was usual on the continent. Both this acanthus and the treatment of some of the costumes seem to herald the light fluttering manner of the Winchester illuminations. These elements are an essential part of the design as drawn out, and not merely of the execution, and one may conclude that the designer was an Englishman as well as the craftsmen, or rather, the craftswomen, who executed the actual embroidery with the needle. A further English feature is the use of the letter Ð for th in the inscription; this letter was practically never used on the continent, but is one that was in normal use in England. In support of the English origin of the textile Baldwin Brown also called attention to the fact that the attitudes of blessing were those of western iconography; that the Dextera Dei was shown in a form identical with that on coins of Edward the Elder, and that St. Gregory, who was not popular in the Byzantine world, was included.

Since Baldwin Brown wrote, the Anglo-Saxon idiom has become more generally familiar, and no one would now wish to dispute the essentially English character of the work or to suggest that the textiles were continental products. But though the embroidery was certainly made by English craftswomen, working for the queen in some courtly centre, most probably Winchester, it must also be admitted that in many respects the iconography, the racial type of the figures, and a number of stylistic features are to be attributed to the influence of Byzantine art upon the Anglo-Saxon world. The colouring, the way in which high-lights are indicated, and details of the draperies are thus akin to what was characteristic of mid-Byzantine painting; the figures are Byzantine

---

[1] See G. Baldwin Brown and Mrs. A. Christie, 'St. Cuthbert's stole and maniple at Durham', *Burl. Mag.* xxiii (1913), 3 and 67 ff.

in appearance and stand in typically Byzantine attitudes, and, perhaps most important, the way in which their names are shown beside them, in fine large letters, is strikingly like that normal in the Byzantine world, but unusual elsewhere. Here, as in Byzantine art, the letters have a definite role to play in the composition of the picture, and do not seem to be included only for the purely practical purpose of indicating the name. As with so much of the stone sculpture, in fact, we have here a work which is unmistakably English, but which, on closer analysis, shows the influence, not of Carolingian or Ottonian, or even Italian, but of Byzantine elements.

A second maniple which was found in the tomb, but not on the body, is embroidered not with the figures but with elaborate acanthus scrolls; the leaves show a close resemblance to those in certain manuscripts of the Winchester school. It is of the same date as the other embroideries, as are a number of narrow strips of braid, some of which are attached to the embroidered pieces. These have stylized birds and leaf patterns woven in tablet weave and are also brocaded in gold. The patterns belong to the continental repertory, but the technique is, according to Mrs. Crowfoot, who has accorded an elaborate study to the braids, more probably related to the Norse world.[1]

No other important Saxon textiles have survived, but a few are mentioned in the texts, and it would seem that most of them were also embroideries. Such must have been the *auriphrisium* worked for the king and queen by Leviet.[2] In 1098 an English textile was much admired at the Council of Bari, and there is a record in Domesday that one Godric the Sheriff, who fell at Hastings, thought that an estate of land was not too high a fee to pay to a lady who taught his daughters embroidery in gold thread.[3] But that is all.

There is, however, one outstanding work that is to be assigned to the early Norman period, namely, the Bayeux tapestry (Pls. 94,

[1] See her article, 'The tablet-woven braids from the vestments of St. Cuthbert', *Antiquaries Journal*, xix (1939), 57. All the treasures from St. Cuthbert's tomb are about to be published together, in a sumptuous volume in which a number of experts have collaborated.

[2] *Domesday for Wiltshire*, ed. W. H. Jones, Bath (1865), 142.

[3] *V.C.H., Bucks.*, London (1905), i, 258.

95, and 96). In reality this is not a true tapestry, but a long strip of linen on which are embroidered as a panorama the events of Harold's life preceding the conquest as well as the story of the actual conquest itself and the progress of the Normans up to the death of Harold at Hastings. The story is told in a completely dispassionate, historical manner, favouring neither one side nor the other, yet it is amazingly vivid. The tapestry is in fact one of the most enchanting pieces of narrative art in existence, and the drawings which must have been made for the embroiderer to follow must have been even more expressive, for the degree of characterization even of the embroidered figures is often extremely high. On the margin above and below the scenes are also included a number of smaller figures, at times connected with the narrative, as when the lower margin is filled with corpses resulting from the battle of Hastings, at times of a decorative character. Some of these decorative motifs are purely English, e.g. the scenes of everyday life, such as a man with his plough and harrow, or the delightful illustrations of fables, like the fox and the crow; they are closely akin to contemporary miniatures in style and herald the miniature paintings of the Gothic spirit. Other motifs, though of foreign origin, are paralleled on other examples of English art; such are the oft repeated beasts, their tails twisted round their legs and over their backs. Ultimately of Scandinavian origin, they recall many an English sculpture of Saxon or early Norman times. Other motifs again are obvious imports, either direct from the Moslem east, or from Italy and the Byzantine world; such are the confronted animals or the pairs of fabulous gryphons and wyverns; there is little that is English about them, and we do not see them paralleled more than very occasionally on other monuments in this country.

The date and provenance of the work have been debated. The tall, beak-nosed Normans are striking portraits, and the inclusion of numerous small figures in each composition is a Norman rather than a Saxon characteristic. The style, even in the embroidery, is, however, much closer to that of English than to that of continental manuscripts, and this must have been even truer of the original drawings from which the embroideries were done, where the light flourishes typical of Saxon work but impossible to the needle were no doubt present. Further, the names, when not in Latin, are spelt in an English rather than in a continental way, and the English Ð for th is used; as noted above, this almost invariably constitutes a sure sign of English provenance. English embroidery was, moreover, famous in late Saxon times, so that the evidence of script, design, and technique alike point to this country. The prominence given to Bishop Odo, and the very fact that the tapestry comes from Bayeux, where Odo was bishop for nearly fifty years and where the reconstruction of the great cathedral was due almost entirely to his gifts, further suggests that the work was executed for him. A date between the Conqueror's death in 1088 and Odo's in 1092 has been proposed, since it has been argued that Odo would not have dared to give himself so much prominence while the Conqueror was living. But it has also been argued that the tapestry might well have been commissioned at the foundation of Bayeux cathedral in 1077, when Odo was at the height of his power, and this, on balance, seems the more likely.

Several other textiles which bore narratives of the same type are recorded in the texts. Thus one akin to but finer than the Bayeux tapestry was described by Baldric, abbot of Bourgueil, as hanging round the bed of Adela, daughter of the Conqueror, while another, which portrayed the deeds of Brithnoth, who fell at Maldon in 991, was worked by his widow Ælfleda and subsequently presented to Ely. But, like so many other treasures of the time, it no longer survives. We know of it from a text, by chance; how many similar works have perished unrecorded?

4. POTTERY

Practically nothing is known of Anglo-Saxon pottery of the Christian period and it has been assumed, on negative rather than on positive evidence, that the manufacture of the plain, thick, rather rough potteries of the pagan period continued until Norman times. This view is doubtless correct in so far as it goes, but recent finds suggest that these rough wares were not the only ones known, and fragments of very fine, hard-baked, white or pinkish wares, often covered with thin yellow or orange glaze, have recently been found at Thetford in Norfolk which are dated on sure archaeological grounds to between 870 and 905.[1] Similar glazed fragments have also been found at Stamford and in London, and these again appear to be of Saxon date. The rims of the Thetford fragments are of a form common in the Rhineland, and there is reason to believe that pots, and perhaps also potters, were imported from that region from the ninth century onwards. The glazes, however, are of a type not so far known from Germany, and suggest, rather, Byzantine prototypes; one group, indeed, where the glaze is thick and dark, and where a decoration of blobs has been added, is extremely close to a Byzantine group, usually classed as 'petal' ware.[2] The parallels are so close that it is tempting to suggest that the same thing happened here as we have suggested with regard to sculpture, namely, that some Byzantine craftsmen came to England and taught the local men their techniques; in no other way can we account for the completely new types of body and glazes.[3] These men may well have passed by way of the Rhineland, as did many of the carvers and sculptors, but the presence of rims of German type in the pottery found in England is more probably to be explained by the fact that they were already known to the local English potters when the Byzantine masters arrived, and were used with the new glazes and pastes by the local men.

We still know little of the history of Anglo-Saxon pottery, but discoveries in the last few years have been most interesting and encouraging, and there is reason to hope that future researches will produce more results of a concrete nature; pottery was in fact quite probably an important art of which we may well hope to learn a great deal more. It is, further, also possible that vessels of real artistic quality, like those of later medieval times, may also be unearthed, in addition to those of rough, common, pottery that we have known best up to now.

[1] I am most grateful to Group-Captain E. M. Knocker, who is in charge of the Thetford excavations, for showing me sherds and telling me of his discoveries.

[2] D. Talbot Rice, *Byzantine Glazed Pottery*, Oxford, 1930, Group A2.

[3] This conclusion was reached quite independently by T. C. Lethbridge, of the Archaeological Museum at Cambridge. See his 'Byzantine influence in late Saxon England', *Proc. Camb. Ant. Soc.* xliii (1950), 1.

IX

CONCLUSIONS

THE reader who is familiar with the story of later Saxon art will have noted that a number of conclusions have been drawn in the course of this book which either supplement, or are at variance with, those hitherto put forward. These affect both points of detail, such as the dating of particular monuments and points of wider significance, such as the position of Anglo-Saxon England in the development of early Romanesque art as a whole. These more general conclusions have in most cases already been noted in the text, but some of them may be elaborated or summarized here for the sake of greater convenience.

First, then, it is the writer's belief that a great deal of continental influence was exercised in the development of English art and culture from the time of Alfred onwards, and that very close contacts were maintained, not only with the Germanic area, but also with regions farther afield. And though Carolingian art at an early date, and Ottonian at a later, both played a very important role, the artistic influences that affected this country were ultimately not so much Germanic as Mediterranean. The characteristics that may be singled out as essentially Germanic in Carolingian and, more particularly, in Ottonian art—violent realism of treatment, a love of spirals or similar ornamental forms, a favouring of harsh, striking colours, a stressing of imperial dignity in disposition, and so on—are thus hardly to be seen in Anglo-Saxon England. Rather it is the elements that are ultimately to be traced to Byzantine art that played the most important role, even if they had already been assimilated in the German world before they came to this island. These elements are to be seen especially in stone sculpture, but other arts were affected as well to a greater or lesser degree; St. Cuthbert's stole is a striking case in point, for its whole iconography, colouring, and style are close to some Byzantine original, yet its spirit is clearly English.

This Byzantine influence was of long standing; it was important in the Northumbrian period and it was exercised on Mercian art, as, for instance, on the slabs at Breedon. But it was probably most marked in the last decade or so of the tenth century—a period, it may be noted, of great brilliance in the Byzantine world itself, and one at which relations with the west were close, as witness the marriage of Otto and Theophano in 972. After the last quarter of the tenth century Byzantine influence in English art became progressively less prominent as a result of the growing importance of Romanesque art in France. There was, however, a renewed, but quite distinct, wave of Byzantine influence in the early twelfth century, the effect of which is to be seen most clearly in manuscript-illuminations; it was perhaps also responsible for the very Byzantine character of the wall-painting of St. Paul in St. Anselm's chapel at Canterbury.[1] This second wave has long been recognized by scholars;[2] the earlier wave, or rather series of waves, which affected Anglo-Saxon art have hitherto hardly been considered, for writers have sought to explain the Mediterranean character of many of the monuments by looking back to the early art of Northumbria, where, of course, these elements were also clearly marked, though they originated independently. The existence of this second wave is, however, significant, for it helps to account for many of the similarities in style which make the works of the two ages at times so very alike.

A second important conclusion which I would wish to emphasize is that northern influence was much less important in later Anglo-Saxon art than many writers have supposed. A number of authorities who have studied Anglo-Saxon art, notably those of Danish, Swedish, and Norwegian nationality, have tended to look only for the northern elements and to neglect wellnigh entirely those appertaining to the Mediterranean world. Works of art

---

[1] Casson, noting this Byzantinism in the St. Paul, was tempted to regard it as a survival of Saxon art. This can hardly be admitted; it is rather the Byzantine influence at both periods that serves to account for the similarities. But see his article, 'Byzantium and Anglo-Saxon sculpture', *Burl. Mag.* lxi. 265 and lxii. 26.

[2] See O. Demus, *The Mosaics of Norman Sicily*, London (1949), 449. It is to the fore in some of the miniatures in Cotton, Nero, C. IV, in the British Museum; see F. Wormald, 'The development of English illumination in the twelfth century', Pl. XIX, B.

which are essentially English, but which, nevertheless, owe their character to a great extent to Viking influence, certainly do exist, and a number of them, like the Pitney brooch[1] or the stone from St. Paul's Churchyard in London (Pl. 23 *a*), are works of high quality. But on the whole, though Norse elements played an important role in the sculptured decoration of the crosses in the more northerly or more distant parts of the country, they were absent in the more polished and more accomplished carvings of the great centres, and hardly affected at all what is really the most glorious art of the period, namely, the full-page illuminations. It is in reality the works produced for the court and the monasteries—ivory book-covers, illuminated manuscripts, or sculptured slabs for internal use—that strike the true key-note of later Anglo-Saxon art and not the crosses of the north or the smaller pieces of ornamental metal.

Whatever the external influences may have been, and however important, it must, on the other hand, be stressed that the essential character of later Anglo-Saxon art was above anything else its Englishness. It was not merely an eclectic art, the outcome of a hotch-potch of casual influences from the past and from outside; it constituted rather a clearly defined and quite original style with a definite character of its own. The sculptures, the ivories, the textiles, and, above all, the manuscript-illustrations are quite easy to distinguish as English. They stand out, moreover, by virtue of their quality; it might even be said that nothing on the continent at the same time was quite the same and nothing, except perhaps in the Byzantine area, quite so good.

It would seem that the development of this distinctive style was remarkably continuous and that it went on uninterruptedly from the time of the renaissance in culture brought about by Alfred, until the middle of the eleventh century. It is the destruction of so large a percentage of the monuments throughout the succeeding centuries that makes the story incomplete rather than any original absence of monuments. The development of the style, set in motion by Alfred, was carried forward by the great ecclesiastical reformers and reached its climax early in the eleventh century. It seems to

[1] T. D. Kendrick, *Late Saxon and Viking Art*, Pl. LXXXII.

have suffered little check from the various invasions and conquests to which the country was subjected. The Danish invasion and the final Danish overlordship of Canute were thus in general but little reflected in art; a few essentially Norse monuments made their appearance even in the heart of Wessex, but the intrusive style was soon assimilated, and just as Canute was more an English than a Danish king, so the art of his age was more an English than a Danish art. Similarly, except in architecture, the Norman conquest brought about a far less violent or sudden break than has generally been supposed, and the change of style in art that eventually resulted, in the twelfth century, took a considerable time to mature. There was thus quite a long period of transition which was in itself fruitful and significant. And even when the new art had become established, old Anglo-Saxon ideas continued to find expression, and old Anglo-Saxon methods to be used, till they at times eventually outlived the Norman ones. The strength of the Saxon idiom was indeed considerable. Clapham has gone so far as to suggest that, had there been no Norman conquest, a distinct 'English Romanesque' architectural style of great quality might have resulted. Even if this opinion can hardly be accepted as it stands, in view of the fact that the best work in miniature painting was produced round about 1000, and not round about 1050, the excellence of Anglo-Saxon art cannot be disputed, while the wholesale destruction of Anglo-Saxon architecture can but be deplored.

Like most arts in which the individual has but a small part to play, the art of Anglo-Saxon England serves to throw quite a considerable light upon the general social complex of the age. The clearest picture is offered by the sculpture, for the manuscripts, though they are, aesthetically speaking, far finer, represent the work purely and solely of the monasteries, and of the other arts so little survives that it is impossible to draw any very general conclusions from them. But the sculptures do permit certain inferences. Thus the character of the large numbers of ninth- and tenth-century crosses in the north of England suggests that society in that region tended to look back to an age that had gone before; ideas were conservative, and there was little desire to see anything new.

In the south of England, on the other hand, and especially in most of the more prosperous centres which were in one way or another associated with the court, the nature of the art indicates that a more progressive and more experimental outlook ruled the day. This turn of mind was fostered by the great religious reformers of the tenth century. Indeed, at this time the church to a great extent supplanted the court as the principal centre of progressive thought, culture, and art. By about the year 1000 the monasteries had become the centres of much of what was best in the national make-up. This position they maintained for a long period, but with the Norman conquest and the introduction from abroad of a number of new abbots and bishops, it was as the centres of the dissemination of the new foreign ideas that their most outstanding role was played. During the three decades between the conquest and the beginning of the twelfth century it was in the country districts of Wessex that the native Saxon idiom survived as a clumsy but, nevertheless, sincere reflection of the more accomplished culture that had previously characterized the more important urban centres.

The picture of the age as presented by the arts is thus one of the gradual penetration of new ideas, sponsored first by the court and then by the church, till eventually a definite idiom in the new style was achieved round about the year 950. This idiom was then developed and disseminated as something fresh and vital, at all events until the end of the first half of the eleventh century. From that time onwards, however, the freshness tended to become less marked, and throughout the second half of the century the style survived as one of a declining, conservative culture. Yet even in the face of the brilliant new art of Normandy it left a great and fruitful legacy to the future.

So far as the continent is concerned, it must also be noted that the elements which affected the development of the arts did not all travel in one direction only, and if at the outset England drew from the continent, there was also, when once the later Anglo-Saxon idiom had been formulated, an important trend in the opposite direction. The effect that the miniatures of the Winchester school exercised on the development of early Romanesque ornament in France has been noted, and it is possible that the French sculptors of the later eleventh century also learnt something with regard to style and technique from what had been done in this country around the year 1000. Work of a distinctly Romanesque character was being produced in Wessex almost a century before Romanesque sculpture proper began to flourish in Burgundy and southern France.

As a result of some inexplicable law governing the transmutation of tastes, it is to the archaic style of Romanesque art that we, at the present moment of the world's history, tend to turn for delight and inspiration rather than to the competence of classic art or the sophistication of Gothic. For this reason, if for no other, later Anglo-Saxon art is of peculiar interest. Yet it was also an art of great power in itself, and without its legacy all that was done in subsequent centuries might well have been very different—perhaps also less glorious.

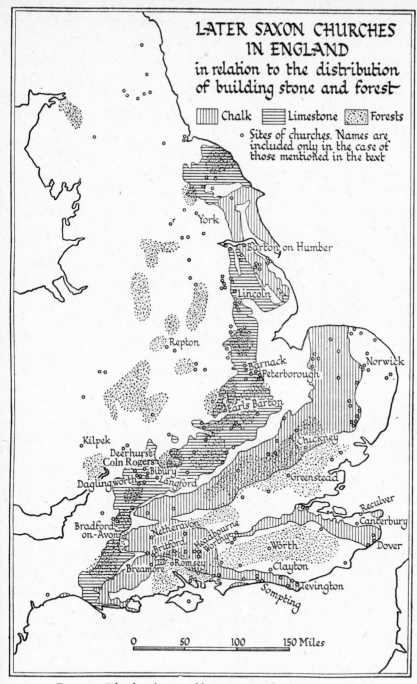

FIG. 19. *The distribution of later Saxon Churches in England*

BIBLIOGRAPHY

I. GENERAL

THOUGH the number of articles on various aspects of later Anglo-Saxon art is considerable, there is no single monograph devoted to the period with which we deal. A few very excellent books of a more or less general character which are mainly concerned with our period may, however, be noted for the reader's greater convenience. Of these the most important are Sir Alfred Clapham's two books, *English Romanesque Architecture*, Volume I 'Before' and Volume II 'After' the conquest. Sculpture is dealt with in addition to architecture, and there are excellent plates of both. The art of the earliest years of our period is discussed fully by Kendrick in his *Saxon Art to 900*. His second volume, *Late Saxon and Viking Art*, continues the story right down to the conquest. His approach, as the title suggests, is different from that of this book, and he accords much greater importance to the northern streams of art. Except for the chapter in that book on manuscripts, there is no up-to-date survey of that art as a whole; the excellent chapters in Herbert's *Illuminated Manuscripts* and Miller's *English Mediaeval Manuscripts* may, however, be noted, as may Homburger's *Die Anfänge der Malerschule von Winchester im X. Jahrhundert*. Much new material has become available since these books were written, notably that provided by Wormald in a number of specialized articles. Miss Longhurst's *English Ivories* is also of fundamental importance with regard to its subject, and for the history there is no better or more convenient book than Stenton's *Anglo-Saxon England*.

2. DETAILED BIBLIOGRAPHY

ALLEN, J. ROMILLY, *Celtic Art in Pagan and Christian Times*, London (1904).
—— *Christian Symbolism in Great Britain and Ireland*, London (1887).
—— 'Early Christian Art', *V.C.H. Norfolk*, ii (1906), 555.
—— 'Notes on the ornament of the early Christian monuments of Wiltshire', *Wilts. Archaeological and Natural History Magazine*, xxvii (1894), 50.
—— 'Pre-Norman cross shafts at Nunburnholme', *The Reliquary*, N.S. vii (1901), 98.

ALLEN, J. ROMILLY, 'The font at Alphington, Devon', *The Illustrated Archaeologist*, i (1894), 252.

—— 'The font at Dolton, Devonshire', *The Reliquary*, N.S. vii (1902), 243.

—— 'Sculptured Norman capitals at Southwell minster', *The Illustrated Archaeologist*, i (1894), 31.

—— 'The thurible of Godric', *The Reliquary*, xii (1906), 50.

ANDERSON, W., 'Nordische Bildkunst des ersten Jahrtausends', *Seminarium Kondakovianum*, ix (1937), 23.

ANDRÉ, J. LEWIS, 'Fonts in Sussex churches', *Sussex Archaeological Collections*, xliv (1901), 28.

ASHMOLEAN MUSEUM, *The Alfred and Minster Lovell Jewels* (1948).

ATKINS, SIR IVOR, 'An investigation of two Anglo-Saxon calendars', *Archaeol.* lxxviii (1928), 219.

AXON, W. E. A., 'The Angel stone in Manchester cathedral', *Jour. Brit. Arch. Ass.*, 2nd series, xi (1905), 169.

BADDELEY, H. ST. CLAIR, 'Berkeley Castle', *Transactions of the Bristol and Gloucester Archaeological Society*, xlviii (1926), 176.

BAKER, A., 'Lewes Priory and the early group of wall paintings in Sussex', *Walpole Society*, xxxi (1946).

BALTRUSAITIS, J., *La Stylistique ornementale dans la sculpture romane*, Paris (1931).

BARON, J., 'Sculptured stones at Codford St. Peter and heraldic stones at Warminster', *Wilts. Archaeological and Natural History Magazine*, xx (1882), 138.

BATTISCOMBE, C. F., 'The relics of St. Cuthbert', *Transactions of the Architectural and Archaeological Society of Durham and Northumberland*, viii (1937), 48.

BELL, CLIVE, *Twelfth-century paintings at Hardham and Clayton*, Lewes (1947).

BIRCH, W. DE GRAY, 'Liber Vitae; register and martyrology of New Minster and Hyde abbey, Winchester', *Hampshire Record Society* (1892).

—— 'On two Anglo-Saxon manuscripts in the British Museum', *Transactions of the Royal Society of Literature*, N.S. xi (1878), 463.

—— 'The ancient sculptures in the south aisle of the choir of Chichester cathedral', *Journ. Brit. Arch. Ass.* xlii (1886), 255.

—— *The Utrecht Psalter*, London (1876).

BISHOP, E., AND GASQUET, *The Bosworth Psalter*, London (1908).

BOND, F., *Fonts and Font Covers*, London (1908).

BONY, J., 'Tewkesbury et Pershore', *Bulletin Monumental*, xcvi (1937), 281 and 503.

BORENIUS, T., AND TRISTRAM, E., *English Mediaeval Painting*, Florence and Paris (1927).

BRÉHIER, L., *Le Style roman*, Paris (1941).

BRISTOL AND GLOUCESTERSHIRE ARCHAEOLOGICAL SOCIETY, 'Visits to various churches', *Transactions*, xli (1919), 188.

BRITISH MUSEUM, *A Guide to the Anglo-Saxon and Foreign Teutonic Antiquities*, London (1923).

—— *Catalogue of the Ancient Manuscripts in the British Museum*, Pt. II, Latin, London (1884).

—— *Reproductions from Illuminated Manuscripts* (1907).

BRØNSTED, J., *Early English Ornament*, London and Copenhagen (1924).

BROOKE, Z. N., *A History of Europe from 911 to 1198*, London (1938).

BROWN, G. BALDWIN, *The Arts in Early England*, London.

—— 'The Lechmere stone', *Arch. Journ.* xi (1931), 226.

—— AND CHRISTIE, Mrs. A., 'St. Cuthbert's stole and maniple at Durham', *Burl. Mag.* xxiii (1913), 3 ff. and 67 ff.

BROWNE, G. F., 'On pre-Norman sculptured stones of Derbyshire', *Derbyshire Archaeological Journal*, viii (1886), 164.

BUGGE, A., 'The origin, development, and decline of the Norwegian stave church', *Acta Archaeologica*, vi (1935).

CABROL, F., *L'Angleterre chrétienne avant les Normands*, Paris (1909).

CASSON, S., 'Byzantium and Anglo-Saxon sculpture', *Burl. Mag.* lxi. 265 and lxii. 26.

CHAFY, W. K. W., 'Rous Lench stones', *Proceedings of the Society of Antiquaries*, London, xvii (1897), 99.

CHAMBERS, R. W., *England before the Norman Conquest*, London, various editions.

CHESTER, G. T., 'Notice on sculptures of oriental design at Bredwardine and Moccas, Herefordshire', *Arch. Journ.* xlvii (1890), 140.

CHRISTIE, A. G. I., *English Mediaeval Embroidery*, Oxford (1938).

CHRISTIE, A. *See* BROWN, G. BALDWIN.

CLAPHAM, A. W., *English Romanesque Architecture.* I, *Before the Conquest*, Oxford (1930); II, *After the Conquest*, Oxford (1931).

—— 'Notes on the origin of Hiberno-Saxon art', *Antiquity*, viii (1934), 43.

—— *Romanesque Architecture in England*, The British Council (1950).

CLAPHAM, A. W. 'Some Disputed Examples of pre-Conquest Sculpture', *Antiquity*, xxv (1951).

—— 'The Benedictine abbey of Barking', *Transactions of the Essex Archaeological Society*, xii (1913), 86.

—— 'The carved stones at Breedon on the Hill', *Archaeol.* lxxvii (1927), 219.

—— 'The York Virgin and its date', *Arch. Jour.* cv (1948), 6.

—— 'Three carved stones in the collection of the Society of Antiquaries', *Antiquaries Journal*, xi (1931), 133.

—— AND PEERS, SIR C. R., 'St. Augustine's abbey church, Canterbury, before the Norman conquest', *Archaeol.* lxxvii (1927), 201.

COLLINGWOOD, W. J., 'A cross-base at Winchester', *Papers and Proc. of the Hampshire Field Club and Archaeol. Society*, ix. 219

—— 'Anglian and Anglo-Danish sculpture in the North Riding', *Yorkshire Archaeological Journal*, xix (1907), 267.

—— 'Anglian and Anglo-Danish sculpture at York', ibid. xx (1909), 149.

—— 'Anglian and Anglo-Danish sculpture in the East Riding, with additional material relating to the North Riding', ibid. xxi (1911), 254.

—— 'Anglian and Anglo-Danish sculpture in the West Riding', ibid. xxiii (1913), 129.

—— 'Anglo-Saxon sculptured stones', *V.C.H. York.* ii (1912), 109.

—— *Northumbrian Crosses of the pre-Norman Age*, London (1927).

—— 'Pre-Norman remains', *V.C.H. Cumberland*, i (1901), 253.

—— 'The Brailsford cross', *Derbyshire Archaeol. Journ.*, xlv (1923), 1.

—— 'The dispersion of the wheel cross', *Yorkshire Archaeological Journal*, xxviii (1926), 322 and xix (1907), 281.

COLLINS, A. H., 'The iconography of the Darenth font', *Archaeologia Cantiana*, lvi (1943), 6.

CONYBEARE, W. J., 'The carved capitals of Southwell minster', *Journ. Brit. Arch. Ass.*, N.S. xxxix (1934), 176.

COOPER, I. M., 'Westminster Hall', ibid. 3rd series, i (1937), 168.

COTTON, C., *The Saxon Cathedral at Canterbury and the Saxon Saints buried therein*, Manchester (1929).

COTTRILL, E., *Anglo-Saxon Leicestershire and Rutland*, Leicester City Museum and Art Gallery (1948).

—— 'Some pre-conquest stone carvings in Wessex', *Antiquaries Journal*, xv (1935), 144.

CRAWFORD, S. J., *Anglo-Saxon Influence on Western Christendom*, Oxford (1933).

CROWFOOT, GRACE M., 'The Tablet-woven Braids from the Vestments of St. Cuthbert', *Antiquaries Journal*, xix (1939), 57.

CUST, LIONEL, 'Kilpeck Church', *Walpole Society*, v (1917).

DALTON, O. M., 'An Anglo-Saxon ivory carving', *Proceedings of the Society of Antiquaries*, 2nd series, xxxii (1919), 45.

—— 'On a silver bowl and cover of the ninth or tenth century', *Archaeol.* lxi (1909), 357.

—— AND KING, H. H., 'A carved ivory fragment of the twelfth century discovered at St. Andrews', *Antiquaries Journal*, iii (1922), 1.

DAVIES, D. S., 'Pre-conquest carved stones in Lincolnshire', *Arch. Journ.* lxxxiii (1926), 6.

DAVIES, E. H., 'Notes on the origin of Maen Achwyfan, Whitford, near Holywell', *Journ. Brit. Arch. Ass.* xxxii (1926), 70.

DOBLE, G. H., *Pontificale Lanaletense (Bibliothèque de la Ville de Rouen, A. 27, Cat. 368)*, London, Henry Bradshaw Society, lxxiv (1937).

DOBSON, D. P., 'Anglo-Saxon buildings and sculpture in Gloucestershire, *Transactions of Bristol and Glos. Archaeol. Soc.*, lv (1933), 265.

DOREZ, L., *Les Manuscrits à peinture de la Bibliothèque de Lord Leicester*, Paris (1908).

DRUCE, G. C., 'The mediaeval bestiaries and their influence on ecclesiastical decorative art', *Journ. Brit. Arch. Ass.*, xxv (1919), 41 and xxvi (1920), 35.

ELLIS, J. W., 'The mediaeval fonts of the hundreds of West Derby and Wirral', *Transactions of the Hist. Soc. of Lancs. and Cheshire*, liii (1901), 59.

FIERVILLE, C., 'Les Préfaces du missal de Winchester, avec introduction et notes', *Recueil des publications de la Société havraise d'études diverse* (1880-1).

—— Note on the manuscript of the Winchester school (without title), in *Revue des Sociétés savantes*, 7ème série, vi, Paris (1882), 34.

FINNY, W. E. ST. LAWRENCE, 'The church of the Saxon coronation at Kingston', *Surrey Archaeological Collections*, xlviii (1943), 1.

—— 'The Saxon church at Kingston-upon-Thames', *Journ. Brit. Arch. Ass.* xxxii (1926), 253.

FLETCHER, E. G. M., AND JACKSON, E. D. C., 'Long and short quoins and pilaster strips in Saxon churches', *Journ. Brit. Arch. Ass.* ix (1944), 12 and xii (1949), 1.

FOERSTER, M., *The Exeter Book of old English Poetry*, London (1933).

FOERSTER, M., 'Zur Geschichte des Reliquienkultus in Altengland', *Sitzungsberichte der bayerischen Akademie der Wissenschaften, Phil.-Hist. Abt.*, Heft 8, München (1943).

FORBES-LEITH, W., *The Gospel Book of St. Margaret*, Edinburgh (1896).

FOWKE, F. R., *The Bayeux Tapestry*, London (1875) and later editions.

FOX, SIR C., 'Anglo-Saxon monumental sculpture in the Cambridge district', *Proceedings of the Cambridge Antiquarian Society*, xxiii (1920), 15.

—— 'Saxon grave slabs at Balsham, Cambridgeshire', ibid. xxxii (1932), 51.

FREEMAN, E. A., *History of the Norman Conquest*, Oxford (1865), and later editions.

FRYER, A. C., 'Gloucestershire fonts', *Transactions of the Bristol and Gloucester Archaeological Society*, xxxii (1909), 301.

GAGE, J., 'A dissertation on St. Æthelwold's Benedictional in the library of his grace the duke of Devonshire', *Archaeol.* xxiv (1832) 1.

—— 'The Anglo-Saxon ceremonial of the dedication of churches, illustrated from a Pontifical in the public library at Rouen', ibid. xxv (1834), 235.

GARDNER, A., *A Handbook of English Mediaeval Sculpture*, Cambridge (1935).

—— AND PRIOR, E. S. *See* PRIOR.

GARSTANG, J., 'Anglo-Saxon remains', *V.C.H. Lancaster*, i (1906), 257.

GASQUET, ABBOT, AND BISHOP, E. *See* BISHOP.

GATTY, A., *The Book of Sundials*, London (1900).

GAYTHORPE, H., 'A Norman tympanum with a runic inscription at Pennington near Ulverston', *Reliquary*, N.S. viii (1902), 200.

GILCHRIST, A. C., 'A mediaeval sculptured stone presented to Grasmere church in 1913', *Transactions of the Cumberland and Westmorland Antiquarian and Archaeological Society*, N.S. xxxv (1935), 73.

GILSON, J. P., *Description of the Saxon Manuscript of the Four Gospels*, York (1925).

GODDARD, E. H., 'Fragments of a Saxon cross shaft and silver ornament recently found in Wiltshire', *Reliquary*, v (1899), 129.

—— 'Notes on pre-Norman sculptured stones in Wiltshire', *Wilts. Archaeological Magazine*, xxvii (1893), 43.

—— 'On fragments of a Saxon cross shaft found at Minety and Saxon silver ornaments from Cricklade', ibid. xxx (1899), 230.

GOLDSCHMIDT, A., 'Der Angelsächsische Stil in der mittelalterlichen Malerei', *Festgabe für Felix Liebermann*, Halle (1921).

—— *Die Elfenbeinskulpturen*, Berlin (1914, seq.).

—— 'English influence on mediaeval art on the continent', in *Medieval Studies in Memory of A. Kingsley Porter*, ed. R. W. Koehler, Harvard (1939).

GOLLANCZ, SIR I., *The Caedmon Manuscript of Anglo-Saxon Biblical Poetry*, Oxford (1927).

GORDON, A., 'The old stone crosses of Somersetshire', *Reliquary*, ii (1896), 140.

GRAEVEN, H., *Frühchristliche und mittelalterliche Elfenbeinwerke in photographischer Nachbildung* (1898).

GREEN, A. R., 'Anglo-Saxon sundials', *Antiquaries Journal*, viii (1928), 489.

HAARSEN, M. B., 'Judith of Flanders', *Papers of the Bibliographical Society of America*, xxiv. 1.

HANDSCHEIN, J., 'The two Winchester Tropers (Corpus Christi College, Cambridge 473 and Bodleian 775)', *Journal of Theological Studies*, xxxvii (1936), 34 and 156.

HASKINS, C. H., 'A Canterbury monk at Constantinople, *c.* 1090', *E.H.R.* xcvii (1910), 293.

HENCKEN, H. O'NEIL, 'A gaming board of the Viking age', *Acta Archaeologica*, iv (1933), 85.

HENDERSON-HOWAT, A. M. D., *Royal Pearl: The Life and Times of Margaret Queen of Scotland*, London (1949).

HENRY, F., *Irish Art in the early Christian Period*, London (1940).

HERBERT, J. A., *Illuminated Manuscripts*, London (1911).

HERDMAN, W. A. *See* KERMODE.

HILL, A. DE BOULAY, 'A Saxon church at Breamore, Hants', *Arch. Journ.* lx (1898), 84.

—— 'Pre-Norman churches and sepulchral monuments of Nottinghamshire', ibid. lxxiii (1916), 195.

HODGES, C. C., 'The Anglo-Saxon remains', *V.C.H. Durham*, i (1905), 211.

HOLMES, R., 'An ancient sculpture at Cridling Park', *Yorkshire Archaeological Journal*, xi. 17.

HOMBURGER, O., *Die Anfänge der Malschule von Winchester im X. Jahrhundert*, Leipzig (1912). (Issued as vol. xiii of J. Ficker, *Studien über christliche Denkmäler*.)

HUDD, A. E., 'On the Saxon baptismal font in Deerhurst Priory church', *Transactions of the Bristol and Gloucester Archaeological Society*, xi (1886–7), 84.

HUGHES, H. H., 'The ancient churches of Anglesey', *Archaeologia Cambrensis*, lxxxv (1930), 239.

—— 'The carving of Maen Achwyfan', *Jour. Brit. Arch. Ass.* xxxii (1926), 59.

JACKSON, E. D. C. See FLETCHER, E. G. M.

JAMES, M. R., *Catalogue of Manuscripts at Corpus Christi College, Cambridge* (1911).

—— *Catalogue of Manuscripts at Pembroke College, Cambridge* (1905).

—— *Catalogue of Manuscripts at Trinity College, Cambridge* (1904).

—— *Marvels of the East*, Roxburghe Club (1929).

—— *On the Abbey of St. Edmund at Bury* (1895).

—— 'On fine art as applied to the illustration of the Bible in the ninth and following centuries', *Proceedings of the Cambridge Antiquarian Society*, vii (1888–91).

—— 'On two series of paintings formerly at Worcester Priory', ibid. N.S. iv (1895–1903), 110.

—— 'Sculptures at Lincoln cathedral', ibid. (1898–1903), 148.

—— *The Ancient Libraries of Canterbury and Dover* (1903).

JANTZEN, H., *Ottonische Kunst*, München (1948).

JOHNSTON, P. M., 'A pre-conquest grave slab at Bexhill', *Sussex Archaeological Collections*, xlviii. 153.

—— 'Poling and the Knights Hospitalers', ibid. lx (1919), 79.

—— 'Romanesque ornament in England; its sources and evolution', *Journ. Brit. Arch. Ass.*, N.S. xxx (1924), 91.

—— 'The parish church of All Saints, Kingston-upon-Thames', ibid. xxxii (1926), 229.

JUNG, J., 'Das Itinerar des Erzbischofs Sigeric von Canterbury und die Strasse von Rom über Siena nach Lucca', *Mitteilungen des Instituts für Oesterreichische Geschichtsforschung*, xxv (1904), 1.

KANTOROWICZ, E. H., 'The Quinity of Winchester', *Art Bulletin* (1947), 73.

KERMODE, P. M. C., *Catalogue of Manx Crosses*, London (1892).

—— *Manx Crosses*, London (1907).

—— AND HERDMAN, W. A., *Manx Antiquities*, London (1914).

KENDRICK, T. D., 'An Anglo-Saxon cruet', *Arch. Journ.* xviii (1938) 377.

KENDRICK, T. D., 'Late Saxon sculpture in northern England', *Journ. Brit. Arch. Ass.* vi (1941), 1.

—— *Saxon Art to 900*, London (1938).

—— *Late Saxon and Viking Art*, London (1949).

—— AND RALEGH RADFORD, C. A., 'Recent discoveries in All Hallows, Barking', *Arch. Journ.* xxiii (1943), 14.

KENT, E. A., 'On the Saxon windows in Heles church, Norfolk', *Journ. Brit. Arch. Ass.* xxxiii (1927), 187.

KEYSER, C. E., *Norman Tympana and Lintels*, London (1927).

—— 'Notes on a sculptured tympanum at Kingswinford church, Staffordshire, and other early representations in England of St. Michael the Archangel', *Arch. Journ.* lxii (1905), 139.

KING, H. H. *See* DALTON.

KIRK, J. R. *See* ASHMOLEAN MUSEUM.

KNOWLES, DOM D., *The Monastic Order in England*, Cambridge (1940).

KNOWLES, J., 'Symbolism in Norman sculpture at Quenington, Gloucestershire', *Arch. Journ.* lxiii (1905), 147.

KNOWLES, W. H., 'Deerhurst Priory church', *Archaeol.* lxxvii (1928), 141.

KOEHLER, W. R. W., Editor, *Medieval Studies in memory of A. Kingsley Porter*, Harvard (1939).

LAMPRECHT, *Initial Ornamentik des VIII. bis XIII. Jahrhunderts*, Leipzig (1882).

LANGDON, A. G., 'Early Christian monuments', *V.C.H. Cornwall*, i (1906), 407.

—— *Old Cornish Crosses*, Truro (1896).

LARKIN, F. C., 'The Kirkby fort', *Transactions of the Historical Society of Lancashire and Cheshire*, lxxii (1922), 44.

LEADHAM, A. D. H., 'Ancient sculptured stones in Boroughbridge church', *Reliquary*, vii (1893), 168.

LEGGE, W. HENEAGE, 'The villages and churches of the hundred of Willingdon in Sussex', ibid. N.S. vii (1901), 1 and 145.

LEICESTER CITY MUSEUM AND ART GALLERY, *Anglo-Saxon Leicestershire and Rutland* (1948).

LEROQUAIS, L'ABBÉ V., *Les Pontificaux manuscrits des Bibliothèques publiques de France*, Paris (1937), 3 vols.

LETHABY, W. R., 'The palace of Westminster in the eleventh and twelfth centuries', *Archaeol.*, 2nd series, x (1906), 131.

Lethbridge, T. C., 'Anglo-Saxon remains', *V.C.H. Isle of Ely*, i (1938), 305.

—— 'Byzantine influence in late Saxon England', *Proceedings of the Cambridge Antiquarian Society*, xliii (1950), 1.

Levison, W., *England and the Continent in the Eighth Century*, Oxford (1946).

Longhurst, M. H., *English Ivories*, London (1926).

Lopez, R. S., 'Le Problème des relations anglo-byzantines du septième au dixième siècle', *Byzantion*, xviii (1946–8), 139.

Lynam, C., 'Some pre-Norman crosses in Derbyshire', *Journ. Brit. Arch. Ass.* vi (1900), 305.

Macalister, R. A. S., 'The sculptured stones of Wales', in R. W. Koehler, *Medieval Studies in Memory of A. Kingsley Porter*.

Maclagan, Sir E., *The Bayeux Tapestry*, London (1945) (King Penguin).

Magoun, F. P., 'The Rome of two northern pilgrims', *Harvard Theological Review*, xxxiii (1940), 267.

Mahr, A., and Raftery, J., *Christian Art in Ancient Ireland*, Dublin, vol. i (1932), vol. ii (1941).

Millar, E., *English Illuminated Manuscripts from the Xth to the XIIIth Century*, Paris and Brussels (1925).

Mitchell, H. P., 'English or German?', *Burl. Mag.* xlvii (1925), 328.

—— 'Flotsam of later Anglo-Saxon art', ibid. xlii (1923), 63, 162, and 303, and xliii. 104.

Morgan, M. M., 'The abbey of Bec-Hellouin and its English priories', *Journ. Brit. Arch. Ass.*, 3rd series, v (1940), 33.

Mynors, R. A. B., *Durham Cathedral Manuscripts*, Oxford (1939).

Nash-Williams, V. E., *Early Christian Monuments of Wales*, Cardiff (1950).

—— 'Some early Welsh crosses and cross slabs', *Archaeologia Cambrensis*, xciv (1939), 1.

—— 'Some Welsh early Christian monuments', *Antiquaries Journal*, xix (1939), 147.

—— and Williams, I. See Williams.

Nelson, P., 'An ancient box-wood casket', *Archaeol.* lxxxvi (1936), 91.

—— 'A twelfth-century lily from a censer', *Acta Archaeol.* v (1934), 182.

Newall, R. S., 'Two recently discovered fragments of pre-Norman cross shafts in south Wilts.', *Wilts. Archaeological and Natural History Magazine*, xlviii (1937), 183.

NEW PALAEOGRAPHICAL SOCIETY, *Facsimiles of Ancient Manuscripts, etc.*, 1st series (1903–12), 2nd series (1913–30).

NIVER, C., 'The psalter in the British Museum, Harley 2904', in R. W. Koehler, *Medieval Studies in Memory of A. Kingsley Porter*.

NORLAND, P., 'An early group of enamelled reliquaries', *Acta Archaeologica*, iv (1933), 1.

OAKLEY, M. E. B., 'On some pre-Norman sculptured slabs at Daglingworth church', *Transactions of the Bristol and Gloucester Archaeological Society*, xvii (1892), 260.

OESS, G., *Der altenglische Arundel-Psalter*, Heidelberg (1910).

OMAN, SIR C., *A History of England before the Norman Conquest* (1937).

PALAEOGRAPHICAL SOCIETY, *Facsimiles of Manuscripts, etc.*, vols. i and ii (1873–83); 2nd series (1884–94). *See also* NEW PALAEOGRAPHICAL SOCIETY.

PANOFSKY, E., *Die deutsche Plastik des XI. bis XIII. Jahrhunderts*, München (1924).

PAPE, T., 'The round shafted, pre-Norman crosses of the north Staffordshire area', *Transactions of the North Stafford Field Club*, lxxx (1945–6).

PEERS, SIR C. R., 'A censer cover from Pershore', *Proceedings of the Society of Antiquaries*, xxi (1906–7), 52.

—— 'Reculver; its Saxon church and cross', *Archaeol.* lxxvii (1927), 241.

—— AND CLAPHAM, A. W., 'St. Augustine's abbey church, Canterbury, before the Norman conquest', *Archaeol.* lxxvii (1927), 201.

PHELPS, J. J., 'An ancient sculptured stone in Manchester cathedral', *Transactions of the Lancashire and Cheshire Antiquarian Society*, xxiii (1905), 172.

PLUMMER, C., *The Life and Times of Alfred the Great* (1902).

PORTER, A. KINGSLEY, *Lombardic Architecture*, New Haven (1915).

—— *Romanesque Sculpture of the Pilgrimage Roads*, Boston (1923).

—— *Spanish Romanesque Sculpture*, Florence (1928).

—— *Medieval Studies in Memory of*. *See* R. W. KOEHLER.

PRIEBSCH, R., *The Heliand Manuscript, Cotton Caligula A. VII in the British Museum*, London (1925).

PRIOR, E. S., 'English mediaeval figure sculpture', *Walpole Society*, vol. i (1912).

—— AND GARDNER, A., *An account of Mediaeval Figure Sculpture in England*, Cambridge (1912).

ROBINSON, J. ARMITAGE, *The Times of St. Dunstan*, Oxford (1923).

ROHDE, E. S., *The Old English Herbals*, London (1922).

ROOSVAL, J., 'Swedish and English fonts', *Burl. Mag.* xxxii (1918), 85.

ROUTH, T. E., AND CLARKE-MAXWELL, W. G., 'A corpus of pre-conquest carved stones of Derbyshire', *Derbyshire Archaeological Journal*, xciv (1937), 1.

SABBÉ, E., 'L'Importation des tissus orientaux en Europe occidentale au haut moyen âge', *Revue belge de Philologie et d'Histoire*, xiv (1935), 811–48 and 1261–88.

SALISBURY, *Eighteenth Annual Report of the Friends of Salisbury Cathedral* (1948).

SANDERS, W. B. *See* STOTHERD, R. H.

SAUNDERS, O. E., *English Illumination*, Florence and London (1928).

SAUVAGE, L'ABBÉ, 'Notes sur les manuscrits anglo-saxons et les manuscrits de Jumiège conservés à la bibliothèque de Rouen'.

SAXL, F., 'Lincoln cathedral: the eleventh-century design for the west front', *Arch. Journ.* ciii (1946), 105.

—— AND WITTKOWER, R., *British Art and the Mediterranean*, Oxford (1947).

SAYLES, G. O., *The Mediaeval Foundations of England*, London (1948).

SEAVER, E. I., 'Some examples of Viking figure representation in Scandinavia and the British Isles', in R. W. Koehler, *Medieval studies in Memory of A. Kingsley Porter*.

SCOTT, E., *A Guide to the Manuscripts, Authographs, etc. in the Department of Manuscripts in the British Museum* (1899).

SHETELIG, H., 'Specimens of the Urnes style in English art of the late eleventh century', *Arch. Journ.* xv (1935), 22.

—— *Viking Antiquities in Great Britain and Ireland*, Oslo (1940).

SMITH, G. LE BLANC, 'Derbyshire fonts', *Derbyshire Archaeological Journal*, xxv (1903), 217.

—— 'Some pre-Norman crosses of Staffordshire', *Reliquary*, xii (1906), 229.

SMITH, R. A., Articles on 'Anglo-Saxon remains' in the *V.C.H.* as follows:

Bedford, i (1904), 175	*Berkshire*, i (1906), 229
Buckingham, i (1905), 195	*Cornwall*, i (1906), 375
Devon, i (1906), 373	*Hampshire and I. of Wight*, i (1900),
Hertford, i (1902), 251	373
Huntingdon, i (1926), 271	*Kent*, i (1908), 339

SMITH, R. A., Articles in *V.C.H.* (*cont.*):

Leicester, i (1907), 221   London, i (1909), 147.
Northampton, i (1902), 223   Nottingham, i (1906), 193
Rutland, i (1908), 95.   Stafford, i (1908), 199
Suffolk, i (1911), 325   Surrey, i (1902), 255
Sussex, i (1905), 333   Warwick, i (1904), 251
Worcester, i (1901), 223.   York, ii (1912), 73

—— 'On sculptures of the Viking period from Bibury', *Proceedings of the Society of Antiquaries*, xxvi (1913–14), 60.

STENTON, F. M., *Anglo-Saxon England*, Oxford (1943).

—— 'The Danes in England', *Proceedings of the British Academy*, xiii (1927), 203.

STETTINER, R., *Die illustrierten Prudentius Handschriften* (1905).

STEVENSON, W., 'Bakewell and its sculptured cross', *Derbyshire Archaeological Journal*, xxxix (1917), 75.

—— 'Discovery of a Saxon inscribed and ornamented cross shaft at Rolleston, Notts.', *Reliquary*, N.S. iii (1897), 181.

STOTHERD, R. H., *Facsimiles of Anglo-Saxon Manuscripts*, London (1884).

THOMPSON, SIR E. MAUNDE, *English Illuminated Manuscripts*, London (1895).

TIKKANEN, J. J., *Die Psalterillustration im Mittelalter*, Helsingfors (1900).

TOLLHURST, J. B. L., 'An examination of two Anglo-Saxon manuscripts of the Winchester school, the Missal of Robert of Jumièges and the Benedictional of St. Æthelwold', *Archaeol.* lxxxiii (1933), 27.

TONNOCHY, A. B., 'A Romanesque censer cover in the British Museum', *Arch. Journ.* lxxxix (1932), 1.

—— 'Censers in the middle ages', *Journ. Brit. Arch. Ass.*, 3rd series, ii (1937), 47.

TROLLOPE, E., 'The Norman sculptures of Lincoln cathedral', *Arch. Jour.* xxv (1868), 1.

TUDOR, T. L., 'Pre-Norman cross shaft at Two Dales, Darley Dale', *Journal Derbyshire Archaeological and Natural History Society*, lvii (1936), 105.

—— 'Rowsley Cross', ibid. liv (1933), 7.

TURNER, SHARN, *History of the Anglo-Saxons*, London (1836).

VASILIEV, A. A., 'The Anglo-Saxon immigration to Byzantium', *Seminarium Kondakovianum*, ix, Prague (1937).

WALTERS ART GALLERY, *Illuminated Books of the Middle Ages and Renaissance*, Baltimore (1949).

WARNER, SIR G., *Gospels of Matilda, countess of Tuscany, 1055–1115*, Roxburghe Club (1917).

—— *Illuminated Manuscripts in the British Museum*, London (1903).

—— AND WILSON, H. A., *The Benedictional of St. Æthelwold*, London, Roxburghe Club (1910).

WARREN, F. E., *The Leofric Missal*, Oxford (1883).

WATKINS, A., *The Old Standing of Herefordshire*, Hereford (1930).

WESTWOOD, J. O., *Facsimiles of the Miniatures and Ornaments of Anglo-Saxon and Irish Manuscripts*, London (1868).

WHEELER, R. M., *London and the Saxons*, London (1935).

—— *London and the Vikings*, London (1927).

WICKHAM, W. A., 'The Anglian cross head at Aughton and other recent discoveries there', *Transactions of the Historical Society of Lancashire and Cheshire*, lxi (1914), 151.

WILLIAMS, I., AND NASH-WILLIAMS, V. E., 'Some Welsh pre-Norman stones', *Archaeologia Cambrensis*, xcii (1937), 1.

—— 'Some early Welsh crosses and cross slabs', ibid. xciv (1939), 1.

WILSON, H. A., *The Benedictional of Archbishop Robert*, London, Henry Bradshaw Society, xxiv (1903).

—— *The Missal of Robert of Jumièges*, London, Henry Bradshaw Society, xi (1896).

WORMALD, F., 'Decorative initials in English manuscripts from 900 to 1000', *Archaeol.* xci (1945), 107.

—— *English Kalendars before 1100*, London, Henry Bradshaw Society, lxxii (1933).

—— 'The development of English illumination in the twelfth century', *Journ. Brit. Arch. Ass.*, 3rd series, viii (1943), 31.

—— 'The English saints in the Litany in Arundel 60', *Analecta Bollandiana*, lxiv (1946), 72.

—— 'The survival of Anglo-Saxon illumination after the Norman conquest', *Proceedings of the British Academy*, vol. xxx (1944).

WORRINGER, W., 'Über den Einfluss der angel-sächsischen Buchmalerei auf die frühmittelalterliche Monumentalplastik des Kontinents', *Schriften der Königsberger gelehrten Gesellschaft* (1931).

YATES, E., 'Notes on mediaeval church ironwork', *Journ. Brit. Arch. Ass.*, 3rd series, iv (1939), 175.

INDEX

References in bold type are to the plates.

[1] MS. numbers in italic, page references in roman type.

1. EARL'S BARTON: TOWER. *c.* 980

2 *a*. BRADFORD-ON-AVON CHURCH. EARLY 10TH CENTURY
b. GREENSTEAD CHURCH. 10TH CENTURY

3. REPTON: THE CRYPT. _c._ 1000

4 *a*. DEERHURST CHURCH, LOOKING WEST. MID IOTH CENTURY
b. BARNACK CHURCH: WEST END. MID IOTH CENTURY

5 *a*. BREEDON: ARCHANGEL
b. BREEDON: VIRGIN

6. CODFORD ST. PETER, WILTSHIRE: STONE SLAB. LATE 9TH CENTURY

7 *a* and *b*. BRADFORD–ON–AVON: ANGELS. *c.* 950

8 *a*. WINTERBOURNE STEEPLETON: ANGEL. *c.* 910
b. DEERHURST: ANGEL. *c.* 910

9 *a*. STEPNEY: ST. DUNSTAN. CRUCIFIXION. *c*. 1020
b. RECULVER: FRAGMENT OF CROSS. PROBABLY 10TH CENTURY

10 *a*. JEVINGTON: CHRIST. *c.* 1050
b. STINSFORD: ANGEL. *c.* 1000

11 *a*. LANGFORD: CRUCIFIXION. 1020–1050
b. WORMINGTON: CRUCIFIXION. 1020–1050

12. BRISTOL CATHEDRAL: CHRIST. *c.* 1025

13. ROMSEY: THE ROOD. *c.* 1010

14. DAGLINGWORTH: *a*. CRUCIFIXION. *c*. 1050
b. ST. PETER. *c*. 1050

15 *a*. INGLESHAM: VIRGIN AND CHILD. *c.* 1060
     b. SOMPTING: SAINT. *c.* 1000

16 *a*. BREAMORE: THE ROOD. *c.* 1040
b. HEADBOURNE WORTHY: THE ROOD. *c.* 1030

17. LANGFORD: THE ROOD. *c.* 1020

18 *a*. DEERHURST: VIRGIN. *c*. 1000
b. ROMSEY: CRUCIFIXION. *c*. 1020

19 *a*. BARNACK: CHRIST. *c*. 1050
b. POITIERS, ST. RADEGONDE: CHRIST. 1083–9

20. CHICHESTER: THE RAISING OF LAZARUS. *c.* 1080

21. CHICHESTER: MARY AND MARTHA GREETING CHRIST. *c.* 1080

22. YORK: THE VIRGIN. PROBABLY EARLY 11TH CENTURY

23 *a*. LONDON: GUILDHALL MUSEUM: STONE FROM ST. PAUL'S CHURCHYARD. *c.* 1035
b. ROUS LENCH: SLAB. *c.* 1020

24 *a*. GOSFORTH: CROSS. LATE 9TH CENTURY
b. LEEDS, PARISH CHURCH: CROSS. 10TH CENTURY

25 *a*. WHALLEY: CROSS.   11TH CENTURY
   b. DARLEY DALE: CROSS.   10TH CENTURY

26 *a*. DINTON: TYMPANUM. EARLY 12TH CENTURY
b. SOMPTING: CAPITALS. EARLY 11TH CENTURY

27 *a*. KINGSWINFORD: TYMPANUM. THE ARCHANGEL MICHAEL.
EARLY 12TH CENTURY

b. MORETON VALLANCE: TYMPANUM. THE ARCHANGEL MICHAEL.
EARLY 12TH CENTURY

28 *a*. CHARNEY BASSETT: TYMPANUM. PROBABLY DAVID. EARLY 12TH CENTURY
b. SOUTHWELL: TYMPANUM. THE ARCHANGEL MICHAEL. *c*. 1030

29. DURHAM: CASTLE CHAPEL. *c.* 1070

30 *a*. DEERHURST: FONT. *c*. 910
b. MELBURY BUBB: CROSS SHAFT RE–USED
AS FONT. *c*. 900

31. IVORY CRUCIFIX. *c.* 950. BACKGROUND RHENISH

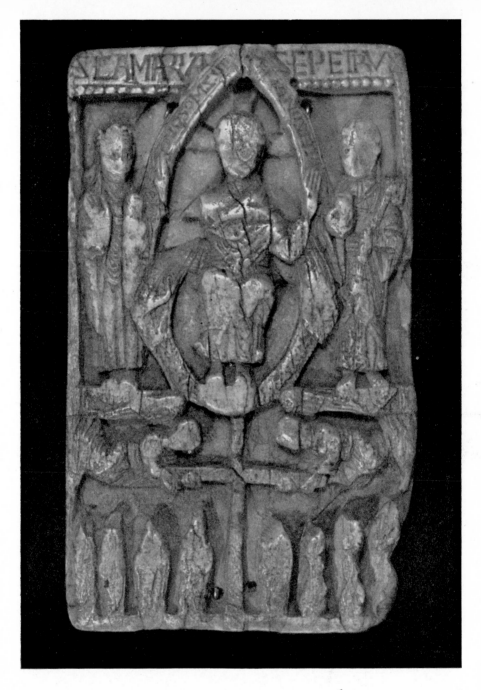

32. IVORY: CHRIST IN MAJESTY. *c.* 960

33. IVORY: TWO ANGELS. *c.* 970

34 *a*. IVORY PLAQUE: VIRGIN AND CHILD. *c*. 1000.
b. IVORY: VIRGIN AND CHILD. *c*. 1070

35 *a*. IVORY: THE BAPTISM. EARLY 11TH CENTURY
b. IVORY: VIRGIN AND CHILD. *c*. 1040

a

b

c

d

36 a. PECTORAL CROSS.   c. 1000
    b. PECTORAL CROSS. LATE 10TH CENTURY
    c. PECTORAL CROSS. c. 1000
    d. THE GODWIN SEAL. c. 1000

37. IVORY: THE NATIVITY. *c.* 950

38 *a*. BONE PLAQUE. THIRD QUARTER 11TH CENTURY
b. BOX-WOOD CASKET. EARLY 11TH CENTURY

39 *a* and *b*. IVORY: THE VIRGIN AND ST. JOHN. *c.* 1010

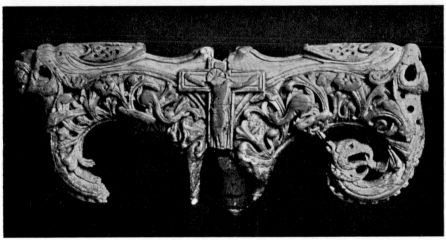

40. IVORY: THE ALCESTER TAU. EARLY 11TH CENTURY

41. IVORY CROZIER. *c.* 1060

a   b

c   d

42. INITIALS FROM 9TH-CENTURY MANUSCRIPTS

a. DE CURA PASTORALIS; *b*. AMALARIUS;
c. ARATOR; *d*. THE SHERBORNE PONTIFICAL

43. ST. DUNSTAN AT THE FEET OF CHRIST. *c.* 960

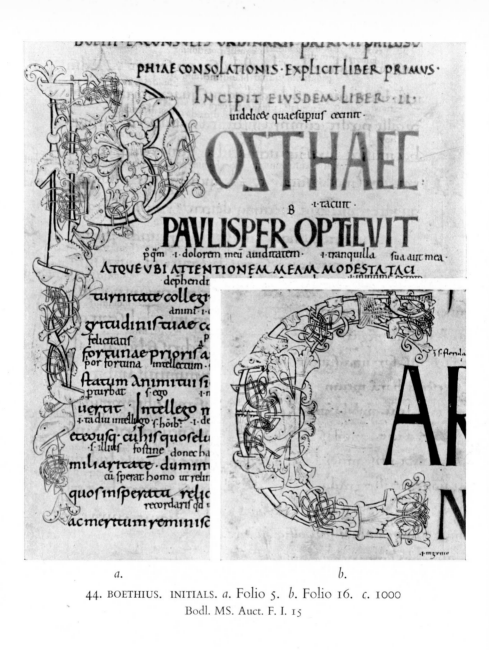

a.   b.

44. BOETHIUS. INITIALS. *a.* Folio 5.   *b.* Folio 16.   *c.* 1000

Bodl. MS. Auct. F. I. 15

b. BORDER FROM MS. LAON 63. 9TH CENTURY

45 a. EBBO GOSPELS. ST. JOHN. 816–35

46. KING EDGAR'S FOUNDATION CHARTER, WINCHESTER. A.D. 966. TITLE PAGE

47. FRONTISPIECE FROM BEDE'S LIFE OF ST. CUTHBERT. 935–939

48. THE BENEDICTIONAL OF ST. AETHELWOLD, 975–980:
THE PRESENTATION

49. THE BENEDICTIONAL OF ST. AETHELWOLD, 975–980:
THE ENTRY INTO JERUSALEM

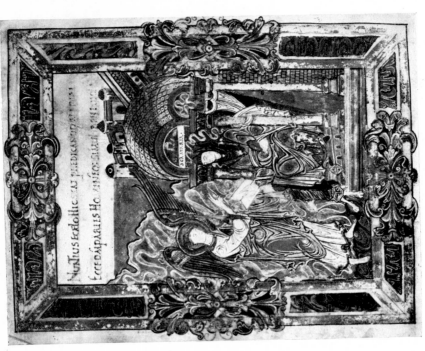

b. THE THREE MARYS AT THE SEPULCHRE

a. THE NATIVITY

51. THE BENEDICTIONAL OF ST. AETHELWOLD, 975–980

b. THE THREE MARYS AT THE SEPULCHRE

a. PENTECOST

52. THE BENEDICTIONAL OF ARCHBISHOP ROBERT. c. 980

53. THE SACRAMENTARY OF ROBERT OF JUMIÈGES. *c.* 1008

a. THE ADORATION

a. THE ASCENSION

b. THE THREE MARYS AT THE SEPULCHRE

55. THE SACRAMENTARY OF ROBERT OF JUMIÈGES. *c.* 1008

a. ST. JOHN

b. OPENING PAGE OF ST. JOHN'S GOSPEL

56. THE NEW MINSTER GOSPELS. EARLY 11TH CENTURY

57 *a*. PSALTER: INITIAL. *c.* 1025
MS. Arundel 155

b. THE BOSWORTH PSALTER: INITIAL. *c.* 990

58. GOSPELS: OPENING OF ST. MATTHEW'S GOSPEL. 1013–1020
MS. Roy. 1 D. IX

59. BOETHIUS: PERSONIFICATION OF PHILOSOPHY. *c.* 990
Trin. Coll., Cambridge, MS. O. 3. 7

a. ST. MATTHEW

b. THE OPENING OF ST. MATTHEW'S GOSPEL

60. GOSPELS. *c*. 1020. Trin. Coll., Cambridge, MS. B. 10. 4

b. HOMELIES: CHRIST IN MAJESTY. c. 1030
Trin. Coll., Cambridge, MS. B. 34

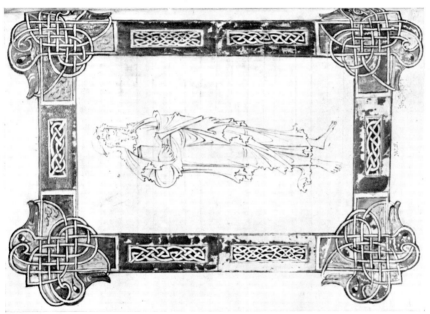

61 a. PSALTER: SAINT. c. 1050
C.C.C., Cambridge, MS. 411

62. GOSPELS: CHRIST IN MAJESTY. c. 1020
Trin. Coll., Cambridge, MS. B. 10. 4

63. GOSPELS: ST. LUKE. *c.* 1066
Pierpont Morgan, MS. 709

a. THE UTRECHT PSALTER. REIMS. *c.* 800

b. CANTERBURY. *c.* 1000

65. ILLUSTRATIONS TO PSALMS XV AND XVI

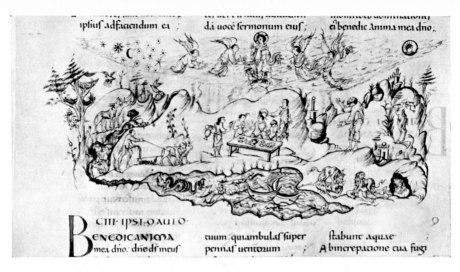

ipfiuf adfaciendum ea ·   d.i uoce fermonum eiuf ·   ei benedic Anima mea dno ·

CIIF IPSI OAUIO·
BENEDICANIOMA   tuum · quiambulaf fuper   ftabunt aquae
mea dno · dnedf meuf   pennaf uentozum   A bincrepatione tua fugi

Iudicare pupillo &humili ·
ut non apponat ultra mag
nificare fe homo fuper cer
ram

INFINEM   PSALOUS   DAVID · X ·
NONO CONFICO ·   iuftuf autem quid fecic ;   Plure fuper peccatoref la
quomodo dicitif anime   Dnf intemplo fco fuo · dnf   queof ignif · fulphur &fpf

66. CANTERBURY COPY OF THE UTRECHT PSALTER. *c.* 1000
a. PSALM CIV. *b.* PSALM XI

67 *a*. EASTER TABLES. *c*. 1065. MS. Cal. A. XV
b. TROPER: PENTECOST. *c*. 1040. MS. Cal. A. XIV

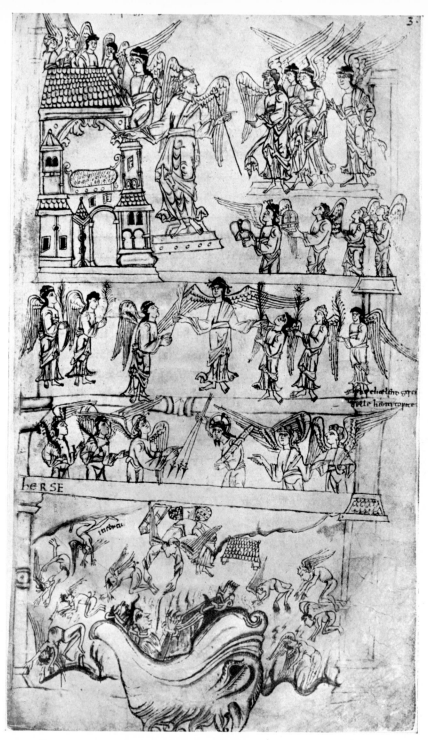

68. THE CAEDMON MANUSCRIPT: THE FALL OF THE REBEL ANGELS.

c. 1000

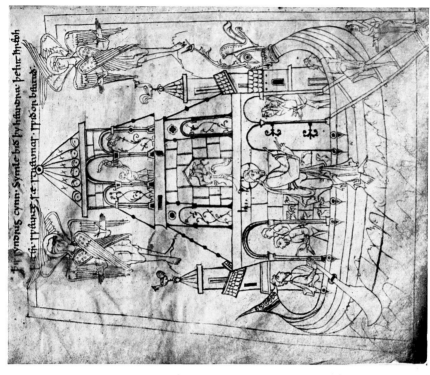

b. THE ARK

a. ADAM AND EVE CLOTHING THEMSELVES

69. THE CAEDMON MANUSCRIPT. *c.* 1000

b. GOSPELS: ANGEL: c. 1050
MS. Bodl. 155

70 a. PONTIFICAL: THE CONSECRATION OF A CHURCH. c. 1000
Rouen, MS. A. 27

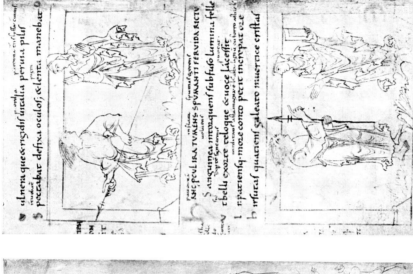

71 *a*. VATICAN PSALTER. *c.* 1040

b. PSYCHOMACHIA OF PRUDENTIUS. *c.* 1050

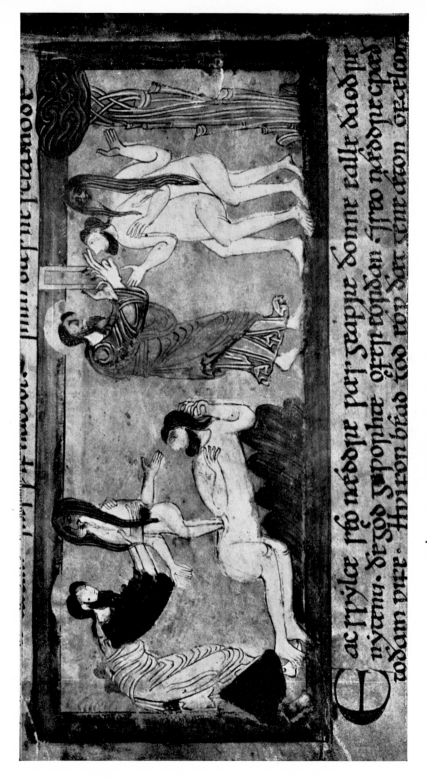

72. AELFRIC'S PARAPHRASE OF THE PENTATEUCH: SCENES FROM GENESIS. c. 1060

73 *a*. PSALTER: INITIAL. 974–986
MS. Harley 2904

b. GOSPELS: INITIAL. *c*. 1040
Wadham Coll. MS. A. 10. 22

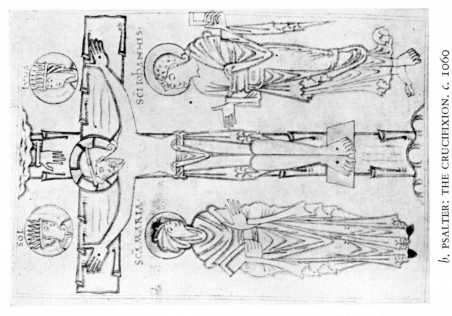

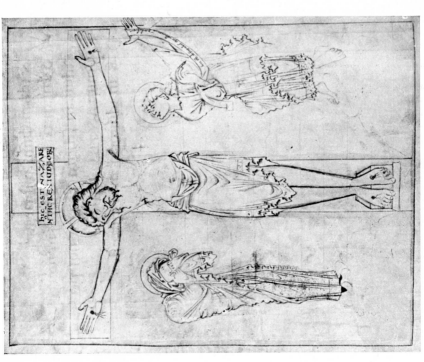

b. PSALTER: THE CRUCIFIXION. *c.* 1060
MS. Arundel 60

74 *a.* PSALTER: THE CRUCIFIXION. 974–986
MS. Harley 2904

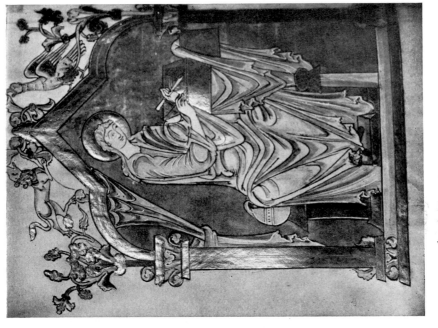

b. GOSPELS: ST. JOHN. c. 1050
Monte Cassino, MS. 437

75 a. PSALTER: CHRIST. c. 1020
Bodl. MS. Douce 296

b. QUEEN MARGARET'S PSALTER: ST. LUKE.
MID-11TH CENTURY

76 *a.* THE YORK GOSPELS: ST. MARK. LATE 10TH
CENTURY

b. GOSPELS: ST. JOHN. LATE 11TH CENTURY
B.M. MS. Add. 11850

77 a. THE HEREFORD GOSPELS: EVANGELIST.
SECOND QUARTER 11TH CENTURY

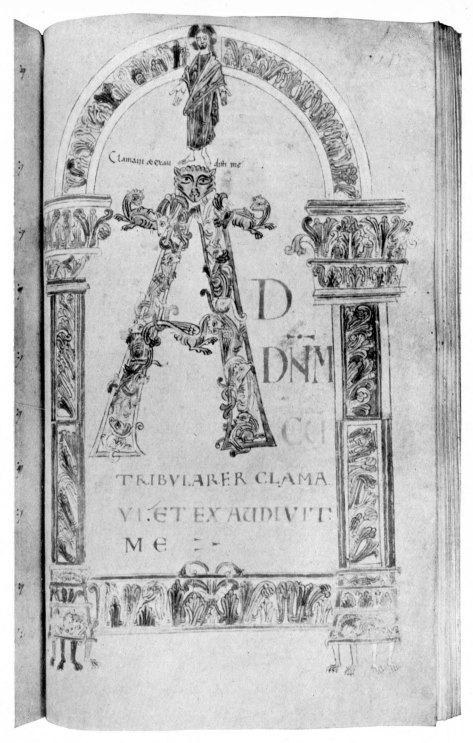

78. THE SALISBURY PSALTER: INITIAL. 992–995